MW01070338

MOBILE SUBJECTS

PERVERSE MODERNITIES

A Series Edited by Jack Halberstam and Lisa Lowe

MOBILE SUBJECTS

TRANSNATIONAL IMAGINARIES

OF GENDER REASSIGNMENT

AREN Z. AIZURA

DUKE UNIVERSITY PRESS   DURHAM AND LONDON   2018

© 2018 Duke University Press
All rights reserved
Printed in the United States of America
on acid-free paper ∞
Designed by Amy Buchanan
Typeset in Chaparral Pro by Westchester
Publishing Services

Library of Congress Cataloging-in-Publication Data
Names: Aizura, Aren Z., author.
Title: Mobile subjects : transnational imaginaries of
    gender reassignment / Aren Z. Aizura.
Description: Durham : Duke University Press, 2018. |
    Series: Perverse modernities
Identifiers: LCCN 2018014917 (print)
LCCN 2018016344 (ebook)
ISBN 9781478002642 (ebook)
ISBN 9781478001218 (hardcover : alk. paper)
ISBN 9781478001560 (pbk. : alk. paper)
Subjects: LCSH: Transgender people—Travel. |
    Sex change. | Medical tourism.
Classification: LCC HQ77.9 (ebook) | LCC HQ77.9 .A39
    2018 (print) | DDC 306.76/8—dc23
LC record available at https://lccn.loc.gov/2018014917

Cover art: Skowmon Hastanan, *Rubyscape*, 2003.
Digital collage, dimensions variable. Courtesy
of the artist.

TO ZOE BELLE,

whose frankness and wit stay with me

CONTENTS

ACKNOWLEDGMENTS

The list of people who have helped me in the labor of this book spans ten years and three continents. I am lucky and immensely grateful to be part of multiple political and intellectual communities across the width and length of the Pacific Ocean. Together we inhabit a gigantic, unruly conversation in which the aim is to incite each other to think differently than one thinks, and also to translate this thinking differently into political action of all kinds.

At the University of Melbourne, Fran Martin, Vera Mackie, Brett Farmer, and Audrey Yue oversaw my graduate work and were instrumental in how this project emerged. Brett suggested Thailand as a possible fieldwork site. Fran and Vera read countless drafts, challenged me to expand the terms and scope of my work, and gave me the resources to find the substance of the project on my own terms. Andrea Whittaker and Peter A. Jackson mentored me in Thai gender and sexuality studies. My fellow grad students at the University of Melbourne—Katsuhiko Suganuma, Bobby Benedicto, Mark Pendleton, Jonathan Williams, and Anja Kanngieser—were willing accomplices in writing and collaboration. Carolyn D'Cruz taught me how to teach and was constantly supportive and encouraging. Regrette Etcetera did theory with me like a drug. Angela Mitropoulos pushed me to write, to think, to read, and to be, especially at and for the most precarious times.

Many, many people embraced my entry into North American intellectual communities. Dean Spade, Chris Hanssmann, and Craig Willse wrote back and swapped mixtapes. Cyd Nova, Lex Young, Marion Finocchio, and others in the Bay Area made queer space for me. Susan Stryker has been a tireless and always supportive mentor, connector, collaborator, and intellectual game-changer; without her labor to bring transgender studies into being, my own work would not be possible. Jack Halberstam and David Valentine were generous outside readers of my dissertation and opened many opportunities for me. At Indiana University I survived US culture shock and learned the institutional ropes with the generous help of Mary Gray, Alex Doty, Melissa Stein, and Nick Clarkson, as well as the friendship of Hugh, LT, and others. At Rutgers University, Yolanda San-Miguel Martínez, Sarah Tobias, Kyla Schuller, Jasbir Puar, Louisa Schein, Carlos Decena, Mary Hawkesworth, Marlene Importico, and the faculty of the Women and Gender Studies Department made me feel a welcomed part of the intellectual community. At Arizona State University, Mary Fonow, Karen Leong, Heather Switzer, Wendy Cheng, Karen Kuo, Lisa Anderson, Ann Koblitz, and others were fantastic colleagues.

The Department of Gender, Women and Sexuality Studies at the University of Minnesota sustains and expands my intellectual and political horizons on a daily basis. Jigna Desai, Annie Hill, Richa Nagar, David Valentine, Susan Craddock, Naomi Scheman, Zenzele Isoke, Lorena Muñoz, Siri Suh, Tracey Deutsch, Catherine Squires, Kevin Murphy, Eden Torres, Kate Derickson, Sima Shakhsari, Lena Palacios, and Miranda Joseph are an inspiration in how to be politically engaged faculty and to create multiple undercommons within the university. Since arriving at UMN I've joined a writing group comprising, at different times, Annie Hill, Lorena Muñoz, Elliott Powell, Lena Palacios, Siri Suh, and Kari Smalkowski. Badass colleagues and interlocutors, they have offered extensive feedback on many parts of this book and are a joy to work with. I've also had transformative conversations with graduate students working in trans studies: Jacob Lau, Rye Gentleman, Lars Mackenzie, Nick-Brie Guarriello, Rachel Reinke, and a de la Maza Pérez Tamayo.

Numerous people have read chapter drafts, responded to hearing parts of this book, or been more informal interlocutors, particularly

Adi Kuntsman, Che Gossett, Silvia Posocco, Johanna Rothe, Gina Velasco, Jin Haritaworn, Eric A. Stanley, Sima Shakhsari, Afsaneh Najmabadi, Christoph Hanssmann, Kyla Wazana Tompkins, Mary Gray, William Leap, Elijah Edelman, Helen Leung, Penny Van Esterik, Toby Beauchamp, Tristan Josephson, Nael Bhanji, Eliza Steinbock, Eva Hayward, Amanda Swarr, Chandan Reddy, Heather Love, Ben Singer, Rachel Silvey, Rhacel Parrenãs, Grace Hong, Todd Reeser, and Nicole Constable. In Thailand and in relation to studies of gender and sexuality in Southeast Asia I am grateful to Prempreeda Pramoj Na Ayutthaya, Hua Boomyapisonparn, Nantiya Sukontapatipark, Dredge Kang, Nguyen Tan Hoang, Ara Wilson, Andrea Whittaker, Sam Winter, Penny Van Esterik, Timo Ojanen, Jillana Enteen, and Jai Arun Ravine. I also workshopped parts of this book at the following institutions: American University, University of Pennsylvania, Birkbeck College, the New School for Social Research, Rutgers University, the University of Pittsburgh, St. Cloud State University, Columbia University, the University of California–Los Angeles, the University of Wisconsin–Madison, Yale University, and Simon Fraser University. Thanks to those who listened, commented, and so generously engaged with me.

Outside the academy my involvement in the Trans Melbourne Gender Project (TMGP) and the Zoe Belle Gender Center anchored me to the realities of trans existence in Australia. Working with my collaborators and friends in TMGP and other organizations informed a praxis around trans health care and politics this project attempts to enact. Ash Pike, Tom Cho, Jak Lynch, Sally Goldner, Zoe Belle, Alyssha Fooks, Hunter McBride, Roz Ward, and numerous others were my accomplices in numerous trans health and community projects, all of whom influenced the scope and stakes of this book.

Family is a huge part of my capacity to be in the world and to write. Kit Aizura Ramstad brings me joy and asks the hard questions. Emmett Ramstad offered me abundant emotional support and intellectual assistance through writing, revising, and frequent bouts of procrastination and anxiety that the book would never be done. He read drafts, incited me to think bigger, and, throughout, gifted me his fierce, generous love and unwavering confidence. Vanessa Clarke and Owen Hankin offer assistance, love, and encouragement. In Minneapolis, Josie Winship, Marc Lamm, Eric Ramstad, Otto Ramstad, Olive Bieringa, and Uma Ramstad welcomed me into the family and care for us on a daily basis. In the tradition of honoring care, I'm also grateful to Britt

Malec, Ashton Kulesa, Lindalee Soderstrom, and the staff at Seward Child Care Center, whose childcare labor made the revision of this book possible.

I thank the people who participated in interviews and fieldwork for giving their time and energy and their willingness to talk to me. Without their assistance, this project, in all its ambitious scope, would not have been possible. They kept me anchored to the complexity and materiality of the mobilities I attempted to theorize.

This book would not have been possible without significant institutional support. During doctoral research the University of Melbourne awarded me an Australian Postgraduate Award and travel funding for fieldwork in Thailand in 2006 under the Travel for Research in Postgraduate Study and the PhD Fieldwork funds. The Thai Queer Resources Network employed me as a research assistant in 2007–8, enabling me to return to Thailand for a second fieldtrip. As a postdoctoral fellow at Indiana University–Bloomington and as a Mellon Postdoctoral Fellow at Rutgers University, I had the opportunity to rethink and revise the project.

Finally, I am indebted to many individuals' editorial expertise. Throughout the long process of shepherding this book to publication Ken Wissoker has been a supportive and attentive editor. Cathy Hannabach edited the entire manuscript, prepared the reference list, and indexed the book, with assistance from Summer MacDonald. Jade Brooks and Olivia Polk were fantastic editorial assistants; Christi Stanforth was a helpful and encouraging production editor. I'm also grateful to Skowmon Hastanan for the cover artwork and to Amy Ruth Buchanan for her inspired book design. Finally, I thank the anonymous readers who offered their generative, generous insights during manuscript revision.

An earlier version in a different form of chapter 1, "The Persistence of Trans Travel Narratives," appeared in Trystan Cotten (ed.), *Transgender Migrations: The Bodies, Borders, and Politics of Transition* (New York: Routledge, 2011). An earlier version in a different form of chapter 5, "The Romance of the Amazing Scalpel: 'Race,' Labour and Affect in Thai Gender Reassignment Clinics," appeared in Peter A. Jackson (ed.), *Queer Bangkok* (Hong Kong: Hong Kong University Press, 2011).

PROVINCIALIZING TRANS

The following text sits on the front page of *TS Roadmap*, a US-based self-help website:

> Welcome! Transsexual transition is simply a journey. Just like a trip, you decide on
>
> - your destination
> - the time you'll need to get there
> - the money you'll spend
>
> This road map is a travel guide to set priorities and choose your route.
>
> It's about making informed purchasing decisions and setting realistic, achievable transition goals.
>
> First time visitors should start here.[1]

Created by the trans advocate and celebrity Andrea James, *TS Roadmap* is a beacon of transgender self-help online. The website offers free advice, information, and resources for trans women who are "on the road" to gender transition.

Gender transition, affirmation, or reassignment—the process of modifying social identity and/or physical embodiment to confirm a gender identity different from the gender assigned at birth—is often articulated in English-language trans culture as a "journey." *TS Roadmap*'s pedagogy of transsexuality tends to valorize passing as a man or woman. Its target audience appears to be mainly trans women. The table of contents below the text quoted above illustrates what James's imaginary of gender reassignment looks like: a section called "Getting Started" lists "Customizing your transition timetable" before sections on finding information, "Real World" issues (such as legal and workplace transition), and information about physical transition and appearance, such as hormones, surgery, clothing, and reproductive options. Historically, *TS Roadmap* has sustained a large community of people who identify as trans and who are looking for guidance about transition. "We need to map a course of the transitions of those brave people who came before us, to guide those who will come after," James's welcoming text advises. This journey narrative frames gender reassignment as a move from one gender or another—and sometimes as a move from liminal space to returning "home" in the desired sexed embodiment.

Trans studies scholarship has recently explored how trans narratives are governed by temporalities: Kadji Amin shows how medical, autobiographical, and popular accounts of transsexuality legitimate trans experience through what Elizabeth Freeman calls "chrononormativity," the temporal form that organizes embodiment into hegemonic temporal patterns.[2] Laura Horak identifies "hormone time" as the linear and teleological timeframe through which trans subjects anticipate progress toward "harmony between the felt and perceived body."[3] Meanwhile, Trish Salah outlines the stakes of accounting for trans chrononormativity: not only temporal frames that regulate the time of the individual subject, but also temporalities attached to gender systems imbricated in colonial modernity and capitalism, which can act to enable or terminate different forms of trans and gender nonconforming life.[4]

As crucial as this work on temporality has been to challenging trans normativity, such a focus on temporality risks losing sight of the spatial and geographical figures that animate understandings of transition and gender reassignment. Eli Clare points out that we think of trans as "a suspension bridge between negatives."[5] This figure of the bridge is spatial: it emplaces male and female as separate, originary territories and depicts the trans subject as one who moves between these territories in order to transform gender. In this way, gendered personhood itself is made possible by mobility. Yet as Salah shows in relation to time, that seemingly isolated figure of the bridge or border between genders also relates to how trans functions within transnational geopolitics.

In this book I contend that tropes of transnational geographical travel are central to the cultural and political intelligibility of gender reassignment. What I call "gender reassignment" in this book goes by many names: *transition, gender confirmation* or *affirmation*, and others. I scrutinize transnational imaginaries of gender reassignment that emerge in trans cultural productions—autobiographies, documentaries, online journals, and graphic novels—and also in persistent cultural understandings about transsexuality and transgender. Popular ideas about gender reassignment reflect the assumption that transness is the same for most people (we often assume that trans people desire hormones or surgery, for example). Yet these accounts are also socially, geographically, and historically specific: they occur in narratives that tend to understand gender itself as binary to begin with, and from within the cultural landscape of European and North American colonialism. Representations of transnational mobility, in particular, appear in English-language trans historical narratives, autobiographies, novels, and films as metaphors for gender transformation.

If we accept that accounts of transness as movement across borders both dominate the landscape of trans culture and emerge from specific cultural locations, we must take seriously how travel and mobility themselves are concepts freighted with the history of global and transnational travel and its representation: colonial and imperial exploration and settlement and migration by sea, land, and air. We must also investigate how travel and migration have opened up capacities for particular subjects but closed down possibilities for others. Imaginaries of transness as movement carry the freighted meanings of transnational mobility with them, colonial and imperialist imaginaries as well as stories about how geographical mobility maps onto social mobility, self-transformation, and possibilities for reinvention. I argue that transsexuality, the normative Euro-American category of trans subjectivity, becomes intelligible as a modern concept through its staging as a journey through "elsewhere" spaces: spaces in which it is necessary, momentarily, to inhabit a gendered indeterminacy that is intolerable under the law of heteronormative binary gender but also necessary for narrating the seeming impossibility of gendered transformation.

Displacing gendered indeterminacy to an "elsewhere" makes the impossible possible. This is a normative imaginary of gender reassignment. This imaginary of gender transition proceeding spatially is by no means the only available imaginary to narrate transness or transition, yet it shapes the expectations and experiences of actual gender nonconforming people who find themselves traveling—as well as revealing how specific that narrative is to a Euro-American geocultural mapping of the world. A tension lies at the heart of gender reassignment imaginaries: if a physical journey is necessary to confirm one's gender identity and to gain autonomy, that journey is always already imbricated within and facilitated by formations of political economy and post- and neocolonialisms.

The Necessity of Trans Mobility

The ideas for this book germinated during my own and others' struggles to access body modifications in my hometown of Melbourne, Australia. It began in 2003, when I visited a psychiatrist to request a diagnosis of gender dysphoria, which would allow me to obtain chest reconstruction surgery. Like most trans visits to a psychiatrist, previous accounts of similar appointments shaped my response to the space before I arrived. The primary care provider who referred me to the clinic gave me a brochure, which cautioned that the clinic treated only people diagnosed as "true transsexuals." Others could not be helped. The psychiatrist's waiting room had retro green carpet and dark wood furnishings and a secretary was typing on a manual typewriter: these details cemented a feeling of going back in time. The psychiatrist, Dr. K., was in her seventies. She peered at my referral letter and asked why I had begun taking hormones under the care of a gay doctor. "The gay community is not very *supportive* of transsexuals," she said. "They don't care much, you see." She smiled regretfully, as if telling me this for my own good. She asked me predictable questions about my sexual history and what kind of toys I'd played with as a child. I had, in fact, climbed trees and ridden a BMX bike, but these answers seemed to disappoint her. All very well, dear, but had I played with *trains*? And why was I teaching something as bizarre as gender studies? She offered no diagnosis then, but told me to return in three months. As I was leaving her office, she waved her arm and commanded me to "write something for her." What should I write? "About how all this," with another wave of the arm, "makes you feel."

I was a white person in my late twenties, educated and articulate. I felt that these privileges protected me, and thus I did write about how the appointment made me feel—on a public blog. I critiqued the indignities of the medical-industrial complex and the narrative of transsexuality I was unwilling to provide. At the next appointment Dr. K. told me she thought I really was a transsexual ("It's genetic, you know!"). However, a "concerned person" had sent her a link to my blog post. She said I shouldn't write publicly about what happened in appointments with her. Given my bad behavior, she would not give me a diagnosis. I had disobeyed her unwritten rules and must be punished. I was also a legal liability: What if, in my angry recalcitrance, I decided to "reverse" my sex change and sue her? This was paranoid but rationally so: two previous patients were suing the clinic after retransitioning to their birth-assigned genders; the lawsuits were financed by evangelical Christian groups.[6] At that time no other health professionals in the state would diagnose gender dysphoria or refer patients to surgeons.

As evidenced by this experience, access to surgical and hormonal gender reassignment in Australia is overwhelmingly medicalized. Euro-American medicine understands transsexuality as a psychiatric condition called gender dysphoria (previously gender identity disorder), listed in the *Diagnostic and Statistical Manual of Mental Disorders* (*DSM*) and the World Health Organization's International Classification of Diseases. This medicalization framework categorizes gender nonconforming behavior as a psychiatric disorder that professionals must diagnose. Access to body modifications—surgery or hormone therapy, among other forms—is usually contingent on diagnosis but also on the patient's meeting a number of eligibility requirements. However, specific health systems produce very peculiar interpretations of these protocols. In the United States transgender health emerged within universities and teaching hospitals, which were medicalized, but also within community and nonprofit health clinics (often focused on HIV or LGBT health) that pioneered harm reduction and informed consent approaches to transgender health. Private surgeons offered gender reassignment surgery (GRS) and were known to exercise individual discretion in regard to protocols.[7] In Australian trans communities it was well known that North Americans could generally access hormones and surgery, as long as they could afford it. Australian medical practitioners tend to follow these protocols in a more conservative fashion. Although individual clinicians in Australia might prescribe hormones on the basis of informed-consent or harm reduction models, access to GRS is generally restricted to those who obtain a diagnosis of gender dysphoria.[8] The clinic where I encountered Dr. K., Monash Gender Dysphoria Clinic, is the only clinic in Australia that both diagnoses gender dysphoria and has surgeons on staff.[9] With few exceptions, doctors across Australia refer patients there for a diagnosis of gender dysphoria so they can then access GRS.[10] In general that also means obtaining surgical procedures from the surgeon employed by the clinic. The few surgeons who perform gender reassignment procedures privately require a diagnosis of gender dysphoria and letters from qualified psychiatrists or psychologists, so their patients often seek a diagnosis from the Monash Clinic.[11]

The Monash Clinic flyer given to me in 2003 reads thus: "If a patient is considered on our assessment to be a true transsexual who might benefit from reassignment surgery, then a minimum period of two years living full time in the chosen gender role with regular supervision by clinic members occurs."[12] This language of true transsexualism reflects the diagnostic criteria Dr. Harry Benjamin developed in the mid-1960s; Benjamin thought that people requesting hormones, GRS, and social recognition as a different gender could be divided into "true" and "nonsurgical" transsexuals.[13] "True," or primary, transsexuals were those whose case histories demonstrated a strong cross-gender identification from a very early age, the ability to pass as a member of the desired gender identity, a complete disidentification with homosexuality, and the desire to engage in heterosexual relationships posttransition.[14] This limited the approval of surgical candidates to those who could pass as respectable and upstanding members of society.[15] Beginning in 1979 the Harry Benjamin International Gender Dysphoria Association (HBIGDA) published and revised a document, "Standards of Care for Gender Identity Disorders," which medical practitioners adopted by international consensus. (Trans activists regarded this protocol as conservative.) At the time I saw Dr. K., even practitioners within HBIGDA regarded the precepts of "true transsexuality" as outdated.[16]

I did not consider myself a "true transsexual," however, or a transsexual at all. The term *transsexual* was invented by medical professionals to describe a binary system wherein "transition" involves a straightforward move from male to female or vice versa, requiring surgery and hormones. I rejected the fixity of binary gender scaffolding this ideology and instead identified more with *transgender*. I wasn't interested in totally rejecting femininity, and I certainly wasn't invested in being a masculine *man*. What could I do? I talked to trans people in the United States online and fantasized unrealistically about flying there for top surgery. But how could I save the $17,000 needed for plane tickets, accommodation, and the cost of surgery? At the time I was living on welfare; it was impossible. And as I already knew, experiences like mine were common. As the convener of a trans and genderqueer support group in Melbourne between 2002 and 2007, I heard many similar stories. The people who called our support line and attended meetings often had difficulty finding trans-literate doctors to begin with, but at least primary care was state-funded and easily accessible. When they tried to access surgery, they hit a wall. Dr. K. was rumored to recruit her patients to spy on others she deemed insubordinate. In fact I discovered later that another trans man patient had sent her the link to my blog. This entrenched bitter divisions within the Melbourne trans community. Some trans people seemed to echo or internalize the gender dysphoria clinic's logic of true transsexuality. One support group worked with the clinic to unofficially sort trans women who fit the true transsexuality model from those who didn't. Patients who did not fit the criteria were penalized or ejected from the support group. Some tried and failed to get diagnoses; others carefully navigated the clinic's guidelines and Dr. K.'s temper to "win" the coveted gender dysphoria diagnosis. Other trans people in the community expressed desires for body modifications of various kinds but feared they would be rejected out of hand.

Many Australian trans women I knew hoped to avoid the gatekeeper model of the Monash Clinic by obtaining GRS in Thailand or in the United States. Thai surgeons had created a niche market providing GRS to non-Thai visitors within the larger Thai medical tourism industry. In the United States GRS was privately available based on surgeons' discretion. As I began graduate research, I interviewed trans women from many countries who were accessing GRS in Thailand. I became the researcher, a position of relative empowerment and ostensible objectivity, detached from the scene of trauma. Some of these women bypassed Dr. K. by traveling to Thailand. While many had found supportive primary care, their appointments with Dr. K. often sounded far worse than mine. Dr. K. stalled one trans woman's request for surgery for two years because she wore jeans rather than skirts to appointments. "Women only wear skirts," she said. Another patient said she had been stalled for four years because she told Dr. K. she wanted to undergo surgery in Thailand.

As these stories illustrate, individual negotiations with health care providers take place against a backdrop of discontinuities between local or national medicojuridical regulation of gender reassignment (sometimes within the same nation-state, but equally often among nations). Many trans and gender nonconforming people are experts at cobbling together adequate health care and treatment from disparate locations or gravitate toward living in particular locations based on the availability of health care and gender reassignment technologies. Historically, GRS has often been a matter of transnational travel, contingent on the locations in which surgeons practice and the fact that relatively few surgeons specialize in such a field. Particular locations—Bangkok, Thailand; Casablanca, Morocco; and Trinidad, Colorado—have become known as centers of GRS. This relates to and often coincides with the practice of lesbian and gay migration to queer-friendly urban centers, but trans and gender nonconforming trajectories of flight from and gravitation toward certain places are based on different configurations of health care, legal recognition, population density, and all kinds of other indices of livability and survivability.[17] As I continued research it became clear that traveling to access health care and a wide range of social "goods" was central to a twentieth-century model of Euro-American transgender life, and that model is shifting in the twenty-first century along new geographical trajectories aligned with the globalization of health care, gender nonconforming subjectivities, and other trends. Tracking these historical and geographical shifts became a crucial part of the project.

These historical shifts have occurred within a larger history of colonial discourse that understands the West as the center of everything and the originator of new identities, cultures, and ideas, including transsexual and transgender identities. The imaginaries of gender reassignment I write about in this book also reflect colonial discourses that pit the modernity of medically facilitated transsexuality against the alleged premodernity of the non-West. I use the term *provincializing* to point to the origin stories of transgender mobility and to question the narrative equating gender transition with geographical mobility.[18]

Such a narrative draws from modern European liberalism to frame the transsexual subject as autonomous, self-inventing, and enabled by the division of the world into a domestic or national *here* and an unfamiliar or unimportant *there*. Provincializing allows me to trace the circuits of value that reproduce that claim to inevitability and to critique the arrogation of the outside of Europe to the status of modernity's other. This also involves rejecting the concept of the non-West as a homogeneous site with similar dynamics and histories of imperialism.[19] Thus I draw attention to how transgender studies has foregrounded the experiences of diverse gender nonconforming bodies and subjectivities within the Global North. However, the Euro-American specificity of the category "trans" too often remains invisible. Provincializing incites transgender studies to interrogate the universalist assumptions that underpin it as an emergent discipline.

In 2006 I returned to Dr. K. If I apologized for my past behavior, I thought, perhaps she would give me a diagnosis and I could finally get the flat chest I wanted. At this new appointment Dr. K. proposed I write good reports about the clinic on social media and become an ambassador for her. In return she would write me a referral letter to the surgeon of my choice. I agreed. She wrote the letter. I wrote something very vague on the local trans listserv explaining that Dr. K. had approved me for top surgery and that she wasn't as bad as I previously thought. I had surgery the following February. I never returned to the clinic, and they never contacted me again. Dr. K. died in 2011. On a local trans message board people shared memories of her and details of her memorial. Although some people remembered her as an inspiration, the last post was titled "Ding, dong, the witch is dead," referencing the Wicked Witch of the West in *The Wizard of Oz*. This scathing farewell captures how cruel and arbitrary some of Dr. K.'s patients found her care, the clinic, and the pathologization of transsexuality. As should be evident in my recounting of this story, transgender resistance to medical authority manifests in myriad forms. It can be individual and collective, or both, directed toward individual care providers and the institutions they work in; it can be direct and indirect, including strategies aimed at legal recognition, creative and informal tactics, or affects such as humor and irony.

Yet work in critical trans politics reminds us that medicalization is only one of the issues trans people face. Demands for the depathologization of trans and gender nonconforming identities founder when they uphold the entrenched inequality of private or income-based health care provision. Disability studies also teaches us that depathologizing gender dysphoria is meaningless without engaging the classification of all mental disorders as a form of biomedical regulation.[20] As transgender visibility grows globally, trans people face rising levels of violence. This violence especially targets trans women of color, leading many to argue that poverty, racialized violence, and police criminalization of and brutality toward trans women of color are issues just as important as, if not more important than resisting medical authority. It's a principle of this book that colonial and racial violence set the scene for knowledge production about transgender subjects. In a similar way transgender political demands for legal and social recognition risk naming transgender as an identity that exists independently of race, class, ability, or geographical location and heralding white, middle-class transgender subjects as the only subjects of transgender political movements. This identity-based movement, which Dean Spade calls "liberal trans politics," often demands legal and social recognition that consolidates the institutions that create injustice rather than deep social transformations. Until recently many transgender theorists of rights and recognition had viewed them as necessary evils, to be approached cautiously yet ultimately embraced.[21] Spade's work reveals the stark insufficiency of trans campaigns for hate crimes laws, antidiscrimination legislation, and military inclusion, while offering an account of what he names a critical and intersectional trans politics, one that sees prison abolition, wealth redistribution, and organizing against border securitization as central to trans political gains.[22] In that spirit, this book pushes at the individualized strategies of negotiating inadequate health care by sidestepping or fleeing it, while asking how this negotiation affects people who are unable to harness geographical and economic mobility to sidestep or flee injustice.

Defining Transgender and Gender Reassignment

In this book I focus on cultural texts and ethnographic research featuring trans women because of their hypervisibility in the historically specific narratives I'm tracing. In the current context of North American trans culture, trans women are still most visible in popular culture as objects of representation or critique; trans men and trans masculine people tend to occupy positions of researcher or professional expert. I see this not as an indication of the invisibility of trans men, as some have argued, but of the hypervisibility of trans women and trans femininity. Often this hypervisibility is actively transmisogynist, evidenced by a mainstream cultural preoccupation with trans women's performance of womanhood that extends from pop culture to porn.[23] I have no desire to reproduce that transmisogyny here. However, precisely because trans women are so visible, their narratives tend to carry a cultural weight that transforms both trans culture itself and dominant cultural attitudes toward transness.

Speaking about trans and gender nonconforming practices and identities also involves careful deployment of terminology. The political struggles around terminology even within English-speaking gender nonconforming cultures and communities are complex. Even for a researcher who identifies as transgender those debates often defy one's ability to condense them into a neat précis. Historically it has been common for researchers writing about this topic to universalize very specific terms across a wide gamut of experiences. In contrast, when I use *transsexual* or *transgender*, I deploy those terms to describe culturally and geographically specific lexicons. For instance, *transgender* was first used in the 1960s by Virginia Prince to speak of a nonoperative trans person, and later emerged in the early 1990s as a political rallying cry and umbrella term for many gender nonconforming practices and cultures.[24] Precisely as the term was becoming representative of a political movement, many trans and gender nonconforming individuals disidentified with transgender, particularly outside of the mostly white, intellectual-activist class milieu where the term had become popular.[25] Even as *transgender* travels outside of that milieu, this genealogy reminds us to remain cognizant of its potential to erase other lexicons of gender nonconforming life. *Transsexual*, meanwhile, emerged within sexology and psychiatry as a term to describe individuals who wished to alter their bodies surgically and hormonally. This term carries with it the weight and violence of pathologizing medicalization. For that reason I caution readers to remain alert to the political significations attached to such terms.

There is no politically neutral category to describe the practices and identities that have been called *gender crossing, trans*, and *gender diverse*. *Trans* and *gender nonconforming* have recently become shorthand within North American academia and social services to describe a diverse gamut of experiences, identities, practices, beliefs, and subjectivities that are unintelligible within a logic that understands gender (or sex) exclusively as something naturally evident at birth, based on genitalia. The term *gender nonconforming* attempts to ameliorate the Eurocentrism of *trans*: as I interrogate the cultural and genealogical specificity of transgender's geographical imaginary, I can hardly deploy *trans* elsewhere as a blanket descriptor. However, I do use *trans* as an adjective to speak about English-speaking communities who might recognize in *trans* a category they inhabit. Thus *trans people* refers to gender nonconforming subjects in these particular contexts without specificity. *Trans woman* and *trans feminine* refer to what has been described elsewhere as *male-to-female* or MTF; *trans man* and *trans masculine* refer to what has been described elsewhere as *female-to-male* or FTM. I am also aware that many trans and gender nonconforming people do not identify with these terms. In other words, many gender diverse communities actively disidentify with the logic of passing wholly from one gender to another, just as they disidentify with the term *transition* to describe body modification processes in pursuit of presenting as a different gender. However, the pursuit of finding the precisely correct labels with which to identify gender nonconforming populations will always fail. Thus one has to make do with the insufficiency of language, even as one remembers the violence of that insufficiency.

In its focus on gender reassignment, *Mobile Subjects* spends a lot of time analyzing gender reassignment technologies, in particular surgeries. I take gender reassignment seriously as an object of transnational materialist analysis; this is crucial to a political vision of making trans health care provision accessible and equitable. Some trans studies scholars refer to "gender affirming health care" or "trans health care" to avoid reproducing a public preoccupation with surgical procedures.[26] Although this is important, the medical obsession with genital transformation as the "truth" and logical endpoint of gender transition means that surgery attracts particular forms of attention, circulation, and importance. In this book I refer to *gender* reassignment surgeries and somatechnologies rather than *sex* reassignment. Using sex as a self-evident category reaffirms gender normative preoccupations with the body (especially genitalia) as providing some proof of sex or gender.[27] However, the term *reassignment* is itself vexing. In recent years some have begun using *gender affirmation* or *gender confirmation* as a way to signal that trans body modification brings the body in line with an individual's true gender identity. Although these terms' cultural ascendance reflects an increased acceptance that body modification is necessary to trans mental health, I question whether the language of affirmation/confirmation invests in the idea that everyone has a "true" gender identity that has always been, and that surgery merely reflects that inner, lifelong identity. Hormonal and surgical body modifications should be available without the need to affirm a primary gender identity. Thus I have retained *gender reassignment* as a term while acknowledging its inadequacy to describe the complexity of the embodied, psychic, and social practices to which it refers.

It is equally important to define what counts as gender reassignment somatechnologies. By understanding trans and gender nonconforming body modifications as somatechnics or somatechnologies, I emphasize how such body modification practices lie at the interface of embodiment, technology, and bodily practice.[28] Often genital surgery stands in as representative of "gender reassignment surgery." However, materially this is not the case. In the few statistical studies that exist, only 17.4 percent of people identifying as trans men or trans women reported having genital surgery in a 2011 US survey.[29] In this book GRS includes a range of procedures that work on multiple areas of the body, for instance, facial feminization surgery, including tracheal shave, facelifts, brow lift, and forehead contouring; hairline work and hair regrowth; and bilateral mastectomy and breast reduction or augmentation. Some of these procedures are understood as aesthetic or cosmetic surgery in different contexts (and sometimes in the context of GRS itself). GRS may also include a range of genital modifications and reconstructions, including procedures aimed at constructing neogenitalia such as vaginoplasty, metoidioplasty, and phalloplasty, as well as procedures that remove or transform reproductive organs and genitals, including orchiectomy, vaginectomy, hysterectomy, and oophorectomy.

Conceiving of gender reassignment somatechnologies in this way requires rethinking assumptions about the affordability and accessibility of various procedures. Precisely because of this, rethinking it involves exploring how GRS alternately behaves as a commodity, a right, and a service. Literature on transnational medical travel, health economies, and biomedicalization is enormously useful here to contextualize the transnational economies of GRS and how it signifies differently in different contexts.[30] In terms of actors this involves looking at the people who demand particular procedures and somehow produce the necessary money to pay for them; those with the technical skills to perform particular procedures (surgeons, but also people in paramedical professions and sometimes peers); and those who make up the web of care, both medical and nonmedical, that surrounds surgical procedures requiring recovery time, including nurses, psychiatrists, care workers, clinic administration workers, financial officers, and travel agents.[31]

Questions of economic access to health care also throw into relief GRS as a comparatively privileged resource. To access GRS in the first place means being able to access economic resources in the form of private savings, debt, or (rarely) health insurance benefits that will pay for transgender-related claims. (Increasingly US health insurance companies are honoring transgender-related claims, which is transforming the availability of US trans health care.) At every scale—transnational, regional, national, and local—trans and gender nonconforming people struggle to access affordable basic health care, including trans-literate general health checkups, reliable access to hormone therapy, and sexual health care such as sexual health testing and HIV prevention and treatment. Trans health care is complicated by the gatekeeping model, which also presents a barrier to health, despite feminist, queer, and community health activists' attempts to train, provide, and reproduce sustainable and accessible trans-literate health care. Predictably these barriers to adequate health care fall disproportionately on trans and gender nonconforming people of color and on trans and gender nonconforming people living in poverty.[32] From the perspective of a trans health philosophy aimed at reducing inequality and dismantling those barriers, research on GRS might seem to include in its frame only elite trans people. However, surgical procedures are desired and practiced by a diversity of populations. As feminist studies of biomedicalization show us, studying the classed and racial stratifications within gender reassignment can complicate this narrative and provide a better overview of how to make all trans health care, including the most expensive procedures, accessible.

Following as Method

The sites I examine in this book constitute an archive documenting traces of past narratives, assumptions, and power relations that are still circulating within the contemporary moment. The archive is not static or enduring, as historical archives are sometimes assumed to be.[33] Reading an early draft of this book, Heather Love called my practice "following the actors." Following the actors could be read as archaeological labors of tracing, discovering footprints, or as an act of tuning in or listening.[34] Thus my research design has been to follow the actors, both human and nonhuman, across the lumpy space of this archive, where disparate discourses fold into each other in contingent and messy ways. I trace the intersections between geographical mobility and trans and gender nonconforming life across a dozen categories of texts and their discursive frameworks, including literary texts, films, autobiographies, historical documents, photographs, online journals, corporate employment policy, trans employer/employee handbooks, and others. I am most concerned with narratives that circulate about trans mobilities within trans and gender nonconforming cultural productions. Self-made accounts form an archive of trans cultural production that has existed between the cracks of the sexological, medical, legal, and academic discourses that produce trans and gender nonconforming bodies and practices as the objects of a rational scientific-juridical gaze. Alongside these discursive formations I have adapted ethnographic methods from anthropology and cultural studies: interviews, field observation, autoethnography, and the obsessive collection of anecdotes from friends, relatives, fellow researchers, and random strangers about trans mobility. These research methodologies are unrepentantly and ambitiously interdisciplinary. I undertook extensive fieldwork in Thailand and Australia between 2006 and 2009, interviewing not only trans people who underwent gender reassignment surgeries in Thailand but also surgeons, nurses, clinic managers, and workers in Thai gender reassignment clinics.

Following also has other meanings: to trace the thread of an idea across the archive of imaginaries of gender reassignment also indexes the transnational scope of this book, which harnesses the sometimes unwieldy category of the transnational to juxtapose multiple local scenes, routes, and individual practices. The rich tradition of critical ethnography guides me in finding strategies to document the inchoate but extraordinarily complex practices of trans people who travel overseas to obtain GRS. This project traces what might usefully be framed as looking at what James Clifford has called "traveling cultures"—in the sense of transnational cultural movement and cultures that are concerned with modes and economies of travel.[35] Nonetheless, situating this project as an investigation of culture is still insufficient. Ethnographic methods that move beyond fetishizing culture, such as multisited ethnography, have been extremely useful. For George Marcus, multisited ethnography allows a researcher to juxtapose locations of material and cultural production that have not been thought in relationship to each other, "creating empirically argued new envisionings of social landscapes."[36] Multisited ethnography is not defined by multiple field sites but by the process of creating what Kaushik Sunder Rajan calls a "conceptual topology" that asks different analytical questions of the world, necessarily involving different methodologies, sources, and narrative strategies.[37] Moreover multisited ethnography does not begin and end at a cross-cultural analysis that assumes comparison between regions, nations, or communities as the central hermeneutic. Particularly in relation to anthropologies of sexuality and gender, focusing on cross-cultural analysis means that translation of sex/gender/sexuality systems attains a rhetorical importance that supersedes other modes of analysis.[38] Even if that translation involves tracing the historical shifts of such systems, the very historicity invoked means making an assumption of past stability. For example, to trace transnational GRS markets is irreducible to a discussion of identity categories or sexual practices, although GRS markets exist in the forms they do precisely because of contradictions and inconsistencies among sex, gender, and sexuality systems.

The term *following* also indexes feminist science and technology studies and anthropologies of medicine and technology that map the disparate contexts of (concepts') transnational materialization, as Adele Clarke writes, "to understand [their] networks and broader situation or arena of action."[39] Closer to home I draw influence from David Valentine's work in *Imagining Transgender*, in which he constructs an ethnography not of a geographically bounded community but of the term *transgender* across a number of different cultural scenes. Readers might assume that *following* also means a labor of translation: translating trans and gender nonconforming practices, vernaculars (language and also knowledge) to make them intelligible for uninformed readers. However, to frame this labor as translation risks objectifying the people I am writing about, the practices and acts recounted, and separates them as objects from the flows of data, institutional forms of life, knowledges, and coercions they need to negotiate to survive or thrive. In effect this is what every institutionalizing tendency does: to separate out individuals and their "choice" to remain in states that are antithetical to optimism. Moreover I reject the terms of a conversation in which I, as author and expert, translate and mediate the acts of my interlocutors for a remote audience. Appropriately for a book about mobility, *following* also presumes that the target is always in motion. To follow is thus not simply to be a reader but to engage in a reciprocal flow of words, affects, and transformative shifts, to abandon proprietary language and accede to languages one might not be able to comprehend in advance.

Theoretical Genealogies

Mobility is a key term I use in this book to pivot between analysis of spatial or geographic and social or economic spheres. *Mobility* has multiple meanings: it can signal geographical movement as well as movement between different spaces within a given architecture (a city, nation, or region). Yet *mobility* also traditionally signifies transcending the limits of class identity or background. Both meanings rely on and mutually support the other: the politics of individual mobility within contemporary liberalism dictate that movement does not signify the mere traversal of space. Individuals are exhorted to move "up the social ladder" by relocating themselves spatially: migration from the slums to the suburbs, from the third world to the first world. However, the markers of upward mobility are not limited to geographical relocation: upward mobility also involves assimilation and normalization through a range of disciplinary and biopolitical practices that encourage individuals to transform their inner and outer selves. Both forms of mobility are supposed to confer something important: identity, self-transformation, and reinvention.[40] A consideration of this double meaning opens the way to understanding mobility's central relationship to the workings of capital.

Mobility as an object of scholarship has emerged relatively recently within the social sciences, following the preoccupation of anthropology, literary studies, and cultural studies with global hybridity and traveling cultures.[41] In this book I maintain an alertness to how the circulation of *mobility* as a term is subject to divisions of ethnicity, class, geography, language, gender, and sexuality, as are its different significations in such widely disparate terms as *travel, migration, displacement,* and *tourism*. Caren Kaplan observes that within the circulation of travel tropes, "immigrants, refugees, exiles, nomads, and the homeless also move in and out of these discourses as metaphors, tropes and symbols but rarely as historically recognized producers of critical discourses themselves."[42] The imaginaries of gender reassignment I examine are often specific to gender nonconforming life, but they echo and reproduce particular discursive structures in mapping desires onto geography. Mapping itself began as a colonial project related to the exploration and annexation of land for Europeans to settle. Geographical imaginaries, as Mary Louise Pratt observes, are (almost) always seen through imperial eyes. The historical production of travel narratives has therefore involved both constructing *place* in the imagination and embedding its narrators in particular subjective locations. If maps are shaped by their conditions of existence, they also shape the minds of those who read them.[43] Imaginaries of gender reassignment emerge within the configuration of transnational queer and transgendered cultural practices based on the consumption of particular services, technologies, and experiences. Queer of color critiques of tourism also enable me to critique transgender medical travel. As Jasbir Puar cautions, queer tourism discourses privilege white, middle-class, and affluent queer tourist practices while relegating the specter of the (nonwhite) other to the status of the desired object.[44]

Mobile Subjects also situates itself within a transgender studies that is both critical and transnational. Much of it was written prior to the consolidation of transgender studies as a field and in conversation with scholarship that was just coming into being. One of the most important efforts was Jack Halberstam's queering of geography and temporality through asking how transgender itself functions in relation to time and space.[45] Spatial metaphors abounded in 1990s-era queer and transgender theorizing, yet remained figural fabric to account for skirmishes between gender identities. For instance, the "butch-FTM border wars" mapped lesbian and trans conflicts onto the popular idea of the borderlands.[46] In one of the earliest engagements of trans theory with transnational geography, Jay Prosser draws attention to how geographical mobility has always been associated with transsexuality in a popular lexicon and in autobiography in particular. Showing how exoticism and orientalism in these mainly white, European trans autobiographers' descriptions of Casablanca relate to a sense of gendering through place.[47] While Prosser considers this exoticism problematic, he contends that the process it represents integrates the subject's sense of her gendered or psychic "self" with her sexed or corporeal "other" and thus is necessary to the transsexual subject's identificatory stability. This book builds on Prosser's insight but turns it toward interrogating the racializing aspects of liberal transgender culture writ large. More recent work has pointed out how analogies that equate gender with national belonging persist in cultural understandings of transgender, but without dwelling on the historical origins or consequences of this.[48]

A more wide-ranging exploration of transgender mobility and migration has appeared since, denaturalizing the transgender subject and asking in what spaces trans subjects of all kinds circulate differently. Trystan Cotten theorizes transgender migrations as "movements of desire, agency, and generativity without unitary subjects or foundations. They are heterotopic, multidimensional mobilities whose viral flows and circuits resist teleology, linearity, and tidy, discrete borders."[49]

No matter how we understand the potential of trans movement, however, we need to contextualize it within the historical and socioeconomic conditions of the world right now. This means a substantive responsiveness to both political economy and racialization, which manifests in an analysis of neoliberal capital (or, as some would have it, late capitalism or post-Fordism). As I show in this book, the historical conditions of neoliberalism are central to the imaginaries by which trans people plot their own access to health care, survival, and the good life, as well as central to how many trans subjects are unable to access something that looks like the good life at all. Neoliberalism is generally defined as a set of policies aimed at different social institutions that increase the gap between rich and poor and increase securitization to consolidate wealth among an ever-decreasing minority of owners and managers.[50] I argue that transgender and gender nonconforming subjectivities do not exist independently of historical formations of capital and labor but are shaped by and in response to them. In doing so I draw on a tradition of historical materialism.[51] Further, I theorize sexual and gendered subjectivities as deeply imbricated with what Marx calls the "real subsumption of labor." Real subsumption names how capitalism appropriates labor not only in its formal setting (i.e., the factory floor, during working hours) but also through social practices and everyday life outside the workplace or the social factory.[52] Queer and trans embodiment and identity might be read as part of the production process of this social factory, formed by, resisting, always already reappropriated back into but simultaneously always exceeding capitalism's cycles of value extraction. In this way we see how technologies intended to make life livable for transgender people are also commodities that function within historically specific transnational markets, and how transgender subjectivities (like all gendered subjectivities) also rely on forms of intimate or affective labor that validate and affirm transgender embodiment.[53] This becomes particularly important in chapter 5, when I examine how practices of care in gender reassignment clinics perform gendering and racializing functions.

To locate transgender theory as a site of critique of capital requires historical materialism to bend to the social formations that expose naturalized gender normativity as a myth. Simultaneously queer of color critique begs attention to the racializing contortions through which liberal tenets of freedom include and incorporate white or upwardly mobile and aspirational queer and transgender people, while further cementing a foundational state violence that criminalizes and renders monstrous those who cannot aspire to the social capital of whiteness. This methodology calls to account the silences of Marxian materialist analysis and poststructuralism on queer and trans people of color through reading them against woman of color feminism and subaltern queer theory. For Roderick Ferguson this means dispensing with the liberal ideology that "race, class, gender, and sexuality are discrete formations, apparently insulated from one another." Further, queer of color critique models a form of historical materialism that acknowledges the co-constitution of gender, race, sexuality, and political economy by accounting for how capitalism itself engenders "emergent social formations" that destabilize and exceed racialized heteronorms.[54]

I also heed Gayatri Spivak's warning that theorizing immaterial labor without attending to racialized and gendered international divisions of labor may result in "a mere political avant-gardism."[55] Transgender and gender nonconforming life in the Global North is enabled by asymmetrical transnational divisions of labor and histories of racialization and primitive accumulation—histories of settler colonialism, imperialism, slavery, and colonial occupation—and struggles to decolonize land, nations, and thought. This becomes starkly evident when we look at trans and gender nonconforming subjects who are racialized as nonwhite and whose embodiments are mediated by their locations in biopolitical categorizations of disposable or surplus life or of devalued and low or unwaged labor, as I do in chapters 3, 4, and 5.

At this historical moment transgender subjects are being positioned internationally as the newest recipients of civil rights. In the United

States this has played out via trans rights claims echoing a nationalist exceptionalism particularly directed at transgender military inclusion. Transgender exceptionalism tracks a logic through which the US nation fantasizes its superiority and tolerance toward transgender life, against other nations and cultures deemed to be intolerant, barbaric, and transphobic or homophobic.[56] This work owes significant debts to trans of color scholarship showing how trans of color bodies are placed in an impossible dilemma within nationalist trans rhetoric. Chandan Reddy posits that the freedom demanded by mainstream queer and transgender politics conceals a foundational racial violence that reaffirms the US state's commitment to violence against those named "irrational" or racially deviant.[57] And as Jin Haritaworn and Riley Snorton observe, when campaigns against transphobic violence identify migrants and racialized others as the uncivilized or intolerant subjects who are responsible for violence and must be reeducated or further criminalized along with efforts to securitize and gentrify communities of color, trans people of color and trans immigrants are also subject to the same efforts to securitize, gentrify, and criminalize.[58] Meanwhile the "utterly unremarkable and uneventful exploitation to which poor, racialized people and sex workers are regularly subjected" goes unnoticed.[59]

Transposing the different local, regional, and state forms through which racializing discourses erupt in different locations forms a key part of the theoretical agenda for this book. Merely speaking of neoliberalism or racialization as if they are the same object transnationally elides how institutional discourses circulate transnationally, transform according to the contingencies of time and space, and emerge looking different. This is equally true of the term *transgender* itself. Much of this book is concerned with how migrating and mobile gender nonconforming subjects take up or are taken up by these shifting terminologies. The global universalization of sexual and gender categories such as *gay* and *transgender* within rights discourses acts as a method of modulating distinctions between civilized subjects who can be included in the Western liberal citizenship and those deemed barbaric or not worthy of saving.[60] Inevitably trans migrating subjects attain a spectacular value as examples of Global North states' tolerance but remain caught in the same structures of poverty, violence, and criminalization that affect other racialized populations.

In assembling a transnational methodology I draw on transnational queer studies, in particular Gayatri Gopinath's contention that discourses of sexuality are "inextricable from prior and continuing histories of colonialism, nationalism, racism, and immigration."[61] Inderpal Grewal and Caren Kaplan's methodology of transnational gender and sexuality studies invites us to map different medical traditions and conceptions of the body in relation to the historical effects of globalization, colonial and postcolonial formations, and the contemporary asymmetries of transnational capital.[62] Along with showing how queer subjects and objects of analysis may subtend acknowledgment of colonial and racial power, transnational queer studies has also interrogated the racial and transnational divides that structure globalized lesbian and gay modernity and the contemporary formal and political recognition of queerness. However, this line of critique founders on a simplistic understanding of the transnational spread of LGBT as relentlessly imperialist and homogenizing of indigenous and local sexual cultures. Twenty years ago Dennis Altman wrote nostalgically that globalization in the form of an expansion of American capitalism was transforming diverse sexed and gendered subjects in the non-West into "gay" subjects.[63] As critiques at the time pointed out, this analysis misses the complex hybridizations and interactions of local, regional, and global queer cultures evident when we understand the globe as more than a division between West and non-West, as well as the diasporic and decolonial formations of queer culture that emerge in immigrant communities within the Global North itself.[64] Like Chakrabarty's provincializing technique, queer transnational scholarship has actively worked to complicate the monolithic concepts of modernity that condition such assumptions, posing modernity as both fantasy and differentiated according to region.[65] This attempt to track both the fantasy and material-historical iterations of modernity while sitting with the complexities of sexuality, gender, race, colonization, and capital encapsulates my approach in *Mobile Subjects* and offers a model for the kind of transgender scholarship this book imagines into being.

Chapter Outline

This book is in two parts. Part I addresses grammars of movement: historical representations of gender travel and representations in autobiographies and documentary film. I consider how travel relates to historical representations of trans and gender nonconforming life, from the earliest representations of transsexuality to autobiographical texts from the 1960s to the 1990s and documentary films produced in the early 2000s. Part II considers what I call "material patterns of movement." These chapters examine trans and gender nonconforming mobilities by asking how gender nonconforming subjects themselves articulate mobility in their everyday lives, particularly in relation to GRS. I investigate how trans and gender nonconforming people use mobility to skillfully negotiate the inconsistencies between transnational, national, and local health care formations to access GRS in Thailand.

Chapter 1 examines the emergence of the transsexual in the 1950s as a personage representing the capacity of the modern or capitalist subject for mobility and transformation. Reading an archive of the first publicly known American transsexual, Christine Jorgensen, I argue that, although the emergence of transsexuality as a nameable category allowed gender nonconforming subjects some self-determination, it was also made possible by the emergence of an emphasis on the modern citizen as part of an international class: upwardly mobile, geographically nomadic, and engaged in a utopian project of technological mastery over the human body and the world. Transsexuality's twinning with modernity defines it not only temporally but spatially by what it is not: neither the premodern gendered indeterminacies assumed to be the terrain of the non-West nor the hybrid, monstrous indeterminacy of postmodernity.

In chapters 2 and 3 I focus on representations of gender travel in transsexual autobiographies and documentary film, particularly the symbolic topography of Western transsexuality and its imbrication in orientalist and colonialist narratives. Chapter 3 examines transsexual autobiography as a powerful template for the subjectivation of transsexuality within a travel narrative. Reading two autobiographies in depth, Jan Morris's *Conundrum* and Deirdre McCloskey's *Crossing*, I argue that each deploys the metaphor of travel in a different way. Morris frames the non-West as the imagined space in which gendered transformations occur, marking it as a space that supplements her femininity through its exoticism. McCloskey appropriates a racialized understanding of the migrant to account for the ways in which gendered transformation seems to be a traversal of space.

Chapter 3 also reads documentary films that present transgender and gender nonconforming subjects engaged in transnational and rural-to-urban migrations, arguing that a central narrative governs trans and gender nonconforming representation in this genre: the metronormative migration plot. The metronormative migration plot dictates that migrating from rural spaces to urban ones, or migrating transnationally, can offer the possibility of self-fulfillment and the freedom to be who you are: by moving, trans people can find bearable and worthwhile lives in which their gender identity or sexuality (or both) is accepted, even celebrated. Posing questions about the specificity of geocultural location, this chapter examines representations of trans and gender nonconforming travel in which the dominant narrative of a journey elsewhere, followed by a return home, finds limited or no traction.

Part II turns to the contemporary intersection between geographical travel, medicolegal constructions of transsexuality, and the role of states and capital in the commodification of trans subjects as patients and consumers. In these chapters I use ethnography to follow the actors—patients, care workers, surgeons, and so on. Rather than beginning with an analysis of large-scale institutions, following foregrounds how individual trans and gender nonconforming people (including myself) use mobility to negotiate the contradictory, multiple regulatory assemblages that make up the transnational medical, legal, and administrative systems through which we access body modification technologies, health care, and juridical recognition or misrecognition. Where the first part of the book offers a historical and representational context for how mobility inflects the formation of trans subjectivity and critiques its geographical and racial specificity, in the second part I interrogate trans and gender nonconforming mobilities by asking how gender nonconforming subjects articulate their own understandings of mobility in an everyday sense.

In chapter 4 I explore the material obstacles to obtaining decent trans health care by an autoethnographic and ethnographic examination of the differences between Australian welfare-state provision of gender reassignment surgeries and Thailand's growing GRS industry. Just as Casablanca became a center for GRS in the 1960s, so Thailand has become such a center in the later twentieth and early twenty-first centuries. In this chapter I theorize Thailand as a GRS destination in which an entrepreneurial consumer framework of learning about and obtaining surgical procedures appears empowering in contrast with the gatekeeper model of obtaining GRS. Individual trans and gender nonconforming people negotiate the contradiction between the gatekeeper model, in which they are interpellated as a subject of psychiatry who is dependent on medical authority to approve them for soma-technological body modifications, and a biomedical entrepreneurial consumer framework, in which they are interpellated as consumers of body modification as a commodity. By denaturalizing the figure of the transsexual-as-patient that dominates understandings of transgender health care in the Global North, I map a transnational perspective on gender reassignment and complicate assumptions about medical authority in transgender scholarship on health care and medicine.

In chapter 5 I make a detailed ethnographic account of gender reassignment clinics in Thailand frequented by non-Thais as a form of medical travel. A confluence of factors—including the late 1990s Asian economic crisis, cultural and social attitudes toward gender nonconforming people in Thailand, and minimal medical litigation in Thailand (meaning an increased ability to take risks in generating new surgical techniques)—means that Thai surgeons are among the most in demand in the world for GRS procedures. While it might make sense to assume that this would result in an increased interconnection between Thai and non-Thai gender nonconforming subjects, this is not necessarily so. Most transgender medical travelers to Thailand appear to develop significant relationships with (mainly female) Thai domestic and care-giving clinical workers. These include nurses, carers, and interpreters who are regarded as performing exquisite Thai femininity, often a femininity to aspire to or model. The stereotypical magic of Thailand creates a fantasy subject position of transsexuality as endlessly mobile, able to manage vast amounts of money in the search for the perfect female (or male) body, locatable only in a foreign space that generates femininity through its specificity as non-Western. Thai clinics mobilize the same fantasy to market the exclusivity and cachet, that is, the higher symbolic value of the Thai gender reassignment tourist care package.

PART I

CHAPTER ONE

THE PERSISTENCE OF

TRANS TRAVEL NARRATIVES

Mining Ground Zero

When *transgender* emerged as an umbrella term attached to claims for rights and justice in the United States in the early 1990s, history was the vehicle used to animate those claims. Trans organizers involved in Transgender Nation and Transexual Menace wanted to make history through political organizing. These were the heady days of the 1993 protest at the American Psychological Association national convention, protesting the inclusion of gender identity disorder as a mental disorder in the DSM; the 1995 courthouse vigil for Brandon Teena in Falls City, Nebraska; and the emergence of Camp Trans, an annual protest of the trans-exclusive Michigan Womyn's Music Festival.[1] Activists recognized that social change depended on the material production of written history. Gordene Mackenzie's book *Transgender Nation*, Leslie Feinberg's *Transgender Warriors*, Lou Sullivan's *From Female to Male: The Life of Jack Bee Garland*, and Jason Cromwell's *Transmen and FTMs* all took up this call. These historical narratives indexed a strong desire for ancestors. Addressed to trans readers, such historical accounts offer a sense of filiation and connection with a past experienced as lost, a past that must be reparatively reconstructed to regain both a sense of trans community and individual wholeness. For the non-transgender world, these historical accounts annex legibility and recognition for trans political claims by proving that trans and gender nonconforming people have always existed.

The figures inhabiting this lost past were legion. In the 1996 book *Transgender Warriors*, Feinberg relates spending an afternoon in 1974 at the New York City Museum of the American Indian looking at gender nonconforming clay figures of unspecified origin. The lesson, Feinberg writes, was that "trans people have not always been hated."[2] From this anecdote Feinberg constructs an alternative history of gender in the United States that critiques gender normativity as a weapon of European colonization. In a more primordialist move, hir book frames Native gender nonconforming traditions as a "gift" to Feinberg—and by extension hir transgender readers.[3] For Feinberg, this gift is a lost history that extends into the present to include the book's readers. It is a history of the transgender warriors who show us how to fight for survival in a hostile world, relieving the isolation of understanding trans people as rare and abnormal.

Transgender Warriors betrays a genealogical order, however, with its own cultural, geographical, and historical investments. The first chapter begins with an autobiographical account of Feinberg's childhood. As Feinberg relates, there were no trans or gender nonconforming people in Feinberg's hometown, no one to offer advice or to be a model. But the young Feinberg knew of at least one public figure who was as "similarly 'different'" as Feinberg hirself: Christine Jorgensen. Feinberg was three years old in 1953, the year Jorgensen returned from Copenhagen to the United States after having undergone "sex change" surgery there. Jokes abounded in Feinberg's family about Jorgensen's gender. Somehow, Feinberg writes, ze understood enough about Jorgensen to ask a babysitter whether Jorgensen was a man or a woman. "She isn't anything," the babysitter replied, "She's a freak." The timing of this discovery makes Jorgensen *the* transgender warrior for Feinberg. Jorgensen's story is proof of trans people's capacity to rise to triumph, despite the world's scorn: "Just as her dignity and courage set a proud example for the thousands of transsexual men and women who followed her path, she inspired me—and who knows how many other transgendered children. . . . Christine Jorgensen's struggle beamed a message to me that I wasn't alone. She proved that even a period of right-wing reaction could not coerce each individual into conformity."[4]

Dignity, courage, individual triumph: to Feinberg, Jorgensen's story has an epic quality.

Jorgensen also represents the ground zero of transgender history for historian Susan Stryker. In "Christine Jorgensen's Atom Bomb" (1999), Stryker plays punningly on Jorgensen's appearance in the atomic age: "Through Jorgensen, the spectacle of transsexuality mushroomed into public consciousness during the early days of the Cold War with all the force of a blistering hot wind roaring across the Trinity Test Site. Transsexuality was nothing short of an atomic blast to the gender system."[5] Like a time capsule, the myth of Christine Jorgensen packs dense layers of historical meaning into a tight, singular reference point for North American transsexual emergence—which is often unintentionally universalized as all transsexual history. It's not a new observation that Jorgensen has the status of the originary transsexual in transgender history. But origin myths emerge as much from the historiographic desires of those who write history as from the individuals who populate historical records or the epochal shifts that sever us from them. Queer historians have already turned from the business of generating reliable epistemological accounts to exploring the consequences of writing affective histories, mining, as Heather Love writes, the "identifications, the desires, the longings, and the love" that structure encounters with the queer past.[6] Until recently debates about trans and gender nonconforming history have centered on reclaiming as transgender those historical figures whose cross-gender practices had been written into lesbian or gay history.[7] As Love observes, however, to make methodological and knowledge production debates explicit means acknowledging our investments in particular visions of the queer or transgender past.[8] In particular we might ask about the kind of temporal marker that the ground zero of Jorgensen represents. *Ground zero* refers not only to Jorgensen's appearance on the world stage, or her celebrity, but the event of her public return to the United States from Denmark. If the famous joke punned that Jorgensen "went abroad and came back a broad," the departure and return is just as important to her story as the event of gender transformation. Jorgensen's historical significance shows us how gender reassignment is structured by particular temporal and spatial logics. In this chapter I argue that the transsexual narrative of departure and return assumes an ideal trans subject who can mesh with the demands of liberal individualism by reinventing herself in toto. By provincializing this narrative—showing its grounding in specific geographical and historical locations—I question both the departure and return narrative and its primacy in transgender historiography. To place this story at the center of transgender history privileges whiteness and the imperative of social mobility, as well as an imperialist division of the world into a national *here* and a colonial *elsewhere*.

Many scholars have understood gender reassignment as governed by medicine and law; the "standard transsexual narrative" issues from the late twentieth-century sexological and psychiatric governmentality of transsexuality.[9] This standard transsexual narrative has also, however, tended to structure popular biographical and autobiographical accounts addressed to a general readership. Jay Prosser observes that the act of writing autobiography constitutes the transsexual as a recognizable subject.[10] The imaginary of transsexuality in its most public form must also make intelligible *how* transsexuality happens: its temporal rhythm, its pace, its chronology, and its narrative structure. *Transition* is the colloquial term in English that indexes the event of gender transformation, with all its attendant processes. Transition might include changing social and administrative gender markers (pronouns, name) as well as modifying one's physical body with hormones, surgery, or other techniques. No transsexual narrative is complete without an account of transition; transition, or as Prosser puts it, "how I got here," is a textual motor that both accounts for the transsexual subject's history and propels a coherent story in which the beginning is narrated retroactively to provide a causal link to the "end."[11]

In "Exceptional Locations: Transsexual Travelogues," Prosser calls attention to the enormous archive of transsexual autobiographies that utilize a metaphor of journeying to create a consistent account of "how I got here." Of necessity this chapter works the same material as "Exceptional Locations," so a short reading of it is useful. Working with a pre-2000 canon, Prosser lists book titles to make the point, including *A Girl's Journey to Manhood*, *April Ashley's Odyssey*, and *Journal of a Sex Change: Passage through Trinidad*.[12] Numerous other autobiographers reference some kind of transformative journey at the point of transition, such as Jan Morris in *Conundrum*. More recently the film *Transmerica* builds its story around a road trip that predictably ends in the protagonist's gender reassignment surgery. Prosser's prognosis is that the "desire to perceive a progressive pattern" precipitates these transsexual autobiographers' choice of a travel metaphor: "The life/narrative is a journey because there is a need to depart from somewhere (to get away from a specific body/place) and to arrive somewhere else (a place more habitable)."[13] This nearly psychoanalytic, resolutely literary reading leads to an analytical predicament for Prosser. Since he reads the tendency for these autobiographers to resort to a journey metaphor as a psychic necessity, he forecloses the opportunity to conceptually separate the narrative itself from the individual psychological contingencies of *being* transsexual. The effects of this predicament are twofold. On the one hand, Prosser ontologizes transsexuality as a singular interior condition that requires a journey motif to explain itself. On the other, the only referent that can explain this interior condition is autobiography itself, which brings us back to the texts—as if they transparently relate the truth of transsexual experience. Prosser can't escape the language of traveling or journeying in this passage; following a close reading of two transsexual autobiographies, he suggests that the relation between geographic movement and gender transition is so close that "physical travel reads as a sublimation of the quest for a gendered home."[14] For Prosser, it seems, transforming one's body really is crossing a gendered border. As Gayle Salamon observes, this desire for an "uncomplicated literalism" returns us to discourse rather than delivering us to a correspondence between the material and the narrative.[15] Prosser also neglects to consider the narratives of trans people whose experience of gender identity or life trajectory evokes immobility, continuity, or remaining at home (whatever home might mean). While in *Second Skins* he considers Feinberg's *Stone Butch Blues* as an exception to the one-way journey narrative, Prosser manages to present a scenario in which all trans narrators are preoccupied with travel or are travelers. This not only reifies mobility as the defining narrative form for trans subjectivity but also elides how the subject position of "traveler" is itself racially and colonially marked.

Appropriately for the trajectory of this chapter, when Prosser does arrive at a materialist moment it concerns Christine Jorgensen. "From the moment it enters the popular lexicon and becomes a cultural phenomenon, transsexuality begins with a trip abroad and a return home: George Jorgensen's trip to Copenhagen and her return to the U.S. as Christine."[16] This of course is because at the historical juncture in the 1950s and 1960s when Jorgensen, Jan Morris, and other early public trans women were writing, it was impossible to find a surgeon in the UK, Europe, or the United States who would perform GRS; trans people desiring surgery in the Global North had to travel. As Morris did, many trans women traveled to Casablanca, Morocco, to visit Dr. Georges Burou. This impels Prosser into a reading of the orientalist overtones of Morris's memoir *Conundrum*. Leaving aside this important text for the moment (and offering a teaser for the reading of *Conundrum* in chapter 3), it's important to question how Prosser moves on so swiftly from this materialist account rather than dwelling on the moment at which transsexuality enters the popular lexicon. What would happen if we did that work? What different accounts might we arrive at by deconstructing the travel metaphor's historical, geographical, and racially specific logics rather than understanding the travel metaphor as impelled by individual autobiographers? If we can productively dislodge transsexual travel metaphors from autobiography and instead read them as logics through which gender reassignment becomes an intelligible narrative in a range of public national contexts, who emerges as the ideal subject of that narrative? To explore these questions, I first deconstruct the contemporary idea of the transition vacation: the myth that trans people must take a short vacation before returning to their daily life, having changed their gender presentation. The idea of taking a vacation or being invisible at the moment of crossing contains the threat of gender indeterminacy and the possibility that gender may be performative and socially constructed.

I then trace a genealogy of what was specific about the origin moment of transsexual travel narratives. I engage with the place of Jorgensen in the transgender historical archive: how her story is remembered by later transsexual autobiographers and transgender historians. Transgender archivists negotiate a host of contradictions embedded in this emerging subjectivity—contradictions, I argue, that they use Jorgensen's narrative to reconcile.[17]

Transsexuality repackages elements of modern identity itself, including desires for self-transformation and what Foucault calls the "attitude of modernity," laboring to make oneself in one's own ideal image, and the notion that medical science can radically transform a body. Jorgensen's story, and the departure and return narrative that grew from her example, institutes conflicting and contradictory tropes echoing the great themes of American modernity. These tropes index self-invention, beating unbeatable odds, and the triumph of the individual and of capitalist liberal individualism. I argue that the dominant trans travel narrative's emphasis on geographical mobility also necessitates social mobility. Further, I argue that respectability and social mobility map onto transsexuality as attributes of the "ideal" transsexual subject. I suggest that transsexual autobiographers' and historians' preoccupation with travel comes about not only because many of the first publicly documented gender reassignment cases involved international voyages but because of the specific geographic, cultural, political, and economic site in which transsexuality itself emerged: the era of American liberal individualism. It is precisely because Jorgensen's story can be narrated through a framework of liberal individualism that the travel narrative gains its literary or ideological force. I argue that as it emerged in the late twentieth century as a progress narrative, transsexuality is metaphorized not only as a journey through gendered space but as a kind of social mobility, premised on success and heroic acts of self-transformation. Geographic mobility in this context cannot be thought without its role in fantasies of *social* mobility and capitalist consumption. The availability of the idea that people could work on their body and reinvent themselves completely—consume self-transformation—was contingent upon a host of social and historical changes, not least the material conditions of the United States in the late nineteenth and early twentieth centuries.

In the final part of the chapter I provincialize the terms of this narrative of transsexual travel enabling social mobility. *Provincializing*, a term I draw from Dipesh Chakrabarty, allows us to question the process through which transgender studies has come to narrate trans history and to look outside the narrow confines of the North American origin story, for spatial and geographical logics govern temporal narratives. I consider how transgender historical accounts of Jorgensen as ground zero might be read differently outside of an epochalism marking Jorgensen (and transsexuality) as a herald of the postmodern condition. Moreover if we think about US transgender history from the perspective of settler colonialism, how might that unsettle the narrative of transition, surgical body modification, and sublime gendered embodiment that has come to define transsexual embodiment?

Containing Indeterminacy

A genealogy of gender reassignment travel narratives begins, in my account, with a seemingly counterintuitive critical move toward deconstruction: a deconstruction of how the narrative of a journey out for gender reassignment and return home shores up, or destabilizes, gender normativity. To illustrate this fully I critically interrogate the context in which the journey-out-and-return-home narrative of gender reassignment is articulated. These early twenty-first-century accounts draw on earlier trans narratives and the mythology of Jorgensen and others like her to formulate a professionalized narrative of gender transition.

One domain in which this narrative clearly becomes recognizable is the workplace and public life. Public announcements and media coverage of transitioning employees often narrate transition as the declared intention that one will go on holiday and return presenting as a different gender. The cause of the vacation is taken to be self-evident, yet it is consistently noted. A 2007 *Forbes* article about a transitioning journalist declares, "L.A. Times sportswriter named Mike Penner told his readers that he would take a vacation and return as a woman, Christine Daniels."[18] Another article in the gay and lesbian lifestyle magazine *The Advocate* echoes this formulation almost verbatim: "Sarah Blanchette was a computer programmer for Saint Anselm College in Manchester, N.H. In March 2004 she informed her superiors that she would return from a two-week vacation presenting herself as female. St. Anselm College then fired her."[19] While discrimination against transgender people is the article's primary concern, the vacation and return appears here as an incidental aside, which nonetheless serves to render transition intelligible for readers.

Similarly advice pamphlets for employees and employers about workplace transition often note the necessity of trans employees taking a leave of absence for medical reasons (i.e., surgery); others make enigmatic references to trans employees preferring to take a short vacation and assume new pronouns and public gender presentation upon their return. A University College London policy document written for transgender employees outlines the following: "Good practice is for the Trans person to take a short holiday before the day of transition (the day s/he will come to work dressed in the clothes of their preferred gender)."[20] *Gender Reassignment: A Guide for Employers*, published by the British government's Women and Equality Unit, offers similar wisdom: "At the point of change of gender, it is common for transsexual people to take a short time off work and return in their new name and gender role. This is often used as an opportunity to brief others."[21]

Janis Walworth, writing for the trans employment resource website Gender Sanity, offers the same advice to employers:

> How much time off does he anticipate needing and when? Some transsexual people want to have some surgical procedures done before they start working in their new role. They may have such procedures several weeks or months before or immediately before assuming their new role. Depending on the procedure, they may need to take off a few days to a few weeks. In addition, the transsexual employee may want to take off a little time between roles to adjust his appearance and take care of paperwork. He may be planning to schedule additional surgeries after he has been working in his new role for several months or a year or more.[22]

Another article on Walworth's site observes that transitioning workers "prefer to coordinate their transition with a vacation period to give themselves and their co-workers time to adjust."[23] Time off between roles is assumed to benefit the trans person; it also gives coworkers time to adjust in the absence of the transsexual employee. However, the fantasy narrative of "time to adjust" does not make explicit what must be adjusted to or what difficulty the absence of the trans person will ease.[24] The adjustment necessary for the hypothetical trans employee and her coworkers to feel comfortable with each other rests on the assumption that everyone will benefit from the trans person's temporary absence from the workplace and from everyday workplace sociality.

What logics govern this narrative? More important, what is foreclosed by the fantasy narrative of gender reassignment involving a journey out and a return home? The possibility of changing sex, or changing gender, opens up a space that threatens a biologically determinist separation of male and female, a space I call "gender indeterminacy." The there-and-backness of the narrative renders transsexuality intelligible within a gender binary by containing gender indeterminacy. This argument should be familiar to readers of queer and feminist theory: Judith Butler argues in *Gender Trouble* that gender nonconforming acts reveal the failure of heteronormativity (while shoring it up at the same time). Marjorie Garber argues that gender variance indicates an "epistemological crux that destabilizes comfortable binarity, and displaces the resulting discomfort onto a figure that already inhabits, indeed incarnates, the margin."[25] Queer feminist theory's characterization of drag and other modes of gender nonconformity as either fundamentally subversive or normalizing has been met with justifiable criticism. Yet the formulation I advance here relies on a reading of gender as performative, as an "enabling violation" that is destined always to fail precisely because it is never complete.[26] Gender indeterminacy does not necessarily refer to transsexuality, or any particular gender nonconforming identity category. With this term *gender indeterminacy*, I'm indexing two related possibilities: first, that somatic or psychic identifications beyond male/masculine and female/feminine exist; second, that it is impossible to exhaustively determine a correlation between biological sex and gender identity. Gender indeterminacy includes the surplus of gendered acts, practices, affects, and feelings that take place in relation to the heterosexual matrix.[27] To willfully misquote the Marxian adage, gender indeterminacy is the *specter haunting gender*: the terrifying possibility that any given being's gender identity might not equate to a stable, static equivalence between male and masculine or female and feminine. This possibility endures even as the logic of gender normativity dictates that such a thing is impossible.

Transsexuality, then, is an assemblage constituted both by medicalizing discourses that regulate the material procedures of gender reassignment and the constellation of cultural understandings that circulate about how gender reassignment may proceed or what transsexuals are like. This assemblage reterritorializes gender indeterminacy through the application of gender norms and regulates who may access gender reassignment technologies or social recognition as a trans subject. Thus the ideology that gender is biological (i.e., determined from birth by the shape of one's genitals) provisionally and inconsistently gives way to a new idea. Individuals may "change sex"; indeed, this process may be a socially permissible act. But they may be recognized as doing so only if they conform to particular heteronormative constraints about somatic gender. These constraints may be discursively contested, but gender persists as binary and normative.

The diagnostic logic of gender identity disorder offers a cogent illustration of this. In Dean Spade's words, the diagnostic criteria produce a "fiction of natural gender, in which normal, non-transsexual people grow up with minimal to no gender trouble or exploration."[28] Gender is not as stable as diagnostic instruments fantasize it to be. One could read these possibilities—that no one embodies gender norms in a fixed manner, or that gender is not stable—as what I am calling gender inde-terminacy. The specter haunting gender is that no one really embodies normative masculinity or femininity. To be socially legible, transsexu-ality as a discourse must contain and domesticate that indeterminacy. Transsexuality comes to be socially and culturally tolerable in a limited sense only if it conceals the possibility that gender is not binary and if it presents transsexuality as a one-way trip from man to woman or woman to man. In particular, transsexuality is more tolerable if there is some temporal gap between the subject's visible embodiment of one gender and another: the "little time between roles to adjust his appear-ance" suggested by the employer advice columns.

The Limits of the Vacation Narrative

The journey-out-and-return-home narrative displaces the gender inde-terminacy that haunts all gender to a spatially contained location: the "elsewhere," or the liminal event when and where the transgender in-dividual is imagined to cross from one gender to the other. The border between genders is figured as liminal and impossible space. When the employment policy documents I cite above recommend that transition-ing individuals absent themselves temporarily from the workplace "to give themselves and their coworkers time to adjust," they formalize the displacement of gender indeterminacy simultaneously to a contained moment and to a space outside the workplace. Within this idealized narrative the transsexual person changes pronouns and appearance in the private sphere (or outside the nation-state altogether) and returns to the workplace and public space transformed. Rather than benefit-ing the transsexual employee, the advised transition vacation seems to benefit others in the workplace, assumed to be non-transsexual, for whom the transsexual person's temporary absence may provide some marker that clearly distinguishes between the past and the future, the old and the new, of the transsexual person's gender. In this way transi-tion vacations relieve the confusion that gender indeterminacy is as-sumed to pose for non-transgender people and the workplace itself as a bureaucratic system.

It should already be clear that gender reassignment in an individ-ual, material sense may not follow this idealized temporal template. In actuality the template has very little or no relevance for many gen-der nonconforming subjects. Conservative studies estimate that less than 20 percent of trans and gender nonconforming people seek genital reassignment surgeries, perhaps because of the prohibitive cost or perhaps because they are not desired.[29] Some of the workplace policy documents I consider above negotiate this contradiction between the commonsense expectation that transition ought to happen all at once, in a conveniently marked fashion, and the far more complex reality, while others neglect complexity in the interests of rendering transsexuality bureaucratically manageable. In all of the manuals I mentioned, however, gender nonconforming people are permitted to access the medicalized legitimacy of transsexuality only if they do not reveal that gender is socially constructed or performative.

The narratives accounting for a geographical absence, a journey out and return home, are particular in that they all occur in English-language publications and focus on white, middle-class subjects who occupy what they might understand as the geographical center of the world. Even setting aside the rather structuralist, Butler-inflected analysis I made earlier, the particular advice to take a transition vacation places us firmly in a corporatized framework of neoliberal racialized citizenship. By neoliberal racialized citizenship I refer to new governmentalities that protect those who are "valuable to capital" while devaluing those who are not.[30] By incorporating the difference of transness, the neoliberal workplace finds value in a class of workers it might have previously rejected. Additionally we need to remain alert to the racial and colonial overtones of "elsewhere" in this fantasy of an ideal gender transition. The journey-out-and-return-home narrative picks up on older narrative forms that necessitate an Odyssean journey for the hero to take his place in the social field.[31] The distinction between home and elsewhere maps onto a range of oppositions that refer us to the history of the nation-state, citizenship, and European colonialism and imperialism: familiar/strange, home/away, center/periphery, West/East, civilization/barbarism, rootedness/traversal, and (the most key opposition here) domestic/foreign. In the context of the Euro-American orientalist colonial imaginary, as Edward Said instructs us, the "civilization" of domestic national space can only be fantasized as singular or homogeneous through its differentiation from the uncivilized world. Of course clearly distinguishing between the domestic and the foreign is useful only in the context of nationalism: the desire to expel the other and institute a national imagined community of the same.[32] This is precisely why preoccupations with home sentimentalize belonging, obscuring the radical differences that subsist within the nation.[33] In workplace transition guides the workplace stands in for home, but it also incorporates the trans subject into the matrix of capitalist productivity on behalf of the nation as a national subject, no longer excluded.

Such distinctions are operationalized to render difference intelligible. De Certeau's reading of the fourteenth-century French explorer Jean de Léry's accounts of exploring North America is instructive here. By deconstructing de Léry's ethnographic description, de Certeau examines traditional ethnography's implicit differentiation between writing—the act performed by the ethnographer, which has the capacity to expand, conquer, represent, and render intelligible—and the "unselfconscious" speech or acts performed by the other, which is what ethnography translates and renders intelligible. For de Certeau the traditional narrative structure of ethnographic writing also distinguishes between "here" and "there," via a trope of journeying out and returning: "The literary operation that [enables ethnography] has a condition of possibility in a structural difference between an area 'over here' and another 'over there.' . . . The separation (between 'over here' and 'over there') first appears as an oceanic division: it is the Atlantic, a rift between the Old and the New World." Such a structural difference between here and there, Europe and the New World, effects a textual and spatial operation of return that is central to the narrative's teleology: "The narrative as a whole belabors the division that is located everywhere in order to show that the other returns to the same."[34] This return domesticates otherness, transforming it from the alleged unintelligibility of speech and practices (what is studied by the ethnographer) into translatable writing (what is produced by the ethnographer). In the process it buttresses the identity of both the ethnographer and the West, the Old World. While it would be reductive to generalize this difference between old and new worlds in de Certeau's critique of ethnography to the transnational gender reassignment imaginaries under consideration in this chapter, a similar narrative logic still takes place. Staging gender transition as a return home retains the distinction between *home* and *elsewhere*. Even if the transsexual subject undergoes an embodied transformation in a location that is not home, the specific location of that elsewhere is not important. The elsewhere, in this transsexual imaginary, is a place to be offstage, a place from which to return transformed. Importantly, it is also separate from the private space of the home.

A gender reassignment imaginary that positions transition as taking place outside of the public sphere, returning the subject to a gender normative national or public space, also assumes the whiteness of the trans or gender nonconforming subject. What happens to subjects whose racial, ethnic, or class differences make them undesirable as candidates for incorporation? As I and others have argued, the publicly intelligible form transsexuality takes as "coming home to the right body" requires transsexual bodies to behave as proper citizens: ideally white and generative of national and racial capital through the reproduction of racially specific norms of economic, social, and cultural citizenship.[35] If one cannot reproduce such norms, one runs the risk of being ejected as recalcitrant or undeserving. Gender nonconforming people of color are often subjected to an even more insidious form of domestication in trans political spaces and trans-friendly workplaces as the token brown person or cultural diversity representative. Brown and black bodies, however, betray the radical difference at the heart of the fantasy of home or nation. As Nael Bhanji points out, racialized bodies jeopardize the "fictive unity of belonging precisely because of [their] disorienting presence."[36] Constituted always already as threats, these bodies may never be able to access the seamless integration promised by the transition vacation. What if the transsexual subject never returns home? What if they can never leave in the first place? What if they never access a full-time job in which vacation leave is an option? To adequately respond to these questions, we need to return to historical analysis and to Christine Jorgensen.

Mobility's Promise

"To follow the complex course of a descent is to maintain passing events in their proper dispersion," Foucault writes in "Nietzsche, Genealogy, History."[37] For Foucault, genealogy reexamines a narrative of continuity, locating its "minute deviations" and historical accidents. Keeping this methodological axiom in mind, I now reconsider historical accounts of Jorgensen's journey abroad, to ask how it becomes enshrined as the model for the journey-out-and-return-home narrative, animating what later would become known as transsexuality. This involves rethinking Jorgensen's place in readings of transsexuality's emergence, to which I turn after a brief historical overview.

In February 1953 a beautiful blonde bombshell stepped off an airplane in New York City. Wrapped in a sumptuous fur coat and surrounded by paparazzi, this beautiful woman was none other than Christine Jorgensen, America's first transsexual celebrity. In the late 1940s Jorgensen had unsuccessfully sought out US doctors who would perform GRS on her. In 1950 she sailed to Denmark on vacation, resolving to obtain GRS in Europe. Serendipitously a doctor in Copenhagen, Christian Hamburger, agreed to arrange her treatment. Jorgensen returned home to New York three years later to a flurry of media excitement over her prodigal transformation.

In the 1930s and 1940s the science of endocrinology was developing on both sides of the Atlantic. Endocrinologists had isolated estrogen and testosterone by the 1920s, although it wasn't until the late 1940s that pharmaceutical companies began to produce synthetic formulations of what were then called "sex hormones."[38] At this moment a theory of human bisexuality had become popular in medical circles. Theories of human bisexuality circulating at the time proposed that both hormones and gonads determined biological sex (rather than just gonads) and that male and female bodies both secreted estrogen (the "female" hormone) and testosterone (the "male" hormone). Consequently "sex change" no longer demanded as fantastical a leap of the imagination as it had previously.[39] North American surgeons had performed castrations and early experiments with gender reassignment surgeries on those characterized as inverts since the 1880s; Earl Lind, a "self-proclaimed invert, androgyne, homosexual, and fairy," obtained a castration from a doctor in 1902.[40] At around the same time European sexologists such as Magnus Hirschfeld were developing diagnostic criteria for individuals who, differentiated from homosexuals and those who merely wanted to wear the attire of the "other sex," desired to *be* the "other sex." Hirschfeld referred to this condition as *Transsexualismus*.[41] In the 1930s and 1940s, on both sides of the Atlantic, the popular press ran various accounts of individuals who went through "sex reversals." In Europe at least three athletes gained notoriety for having transitioned from female to male, the subjects of a quasi-scientific pamphlet titled *Women Who Become Men*.[42] No one quite agreed on what condition caused these "sex reversals" or whether they were evidence of a psychological or biological condition. Neither was it widely known what precise surgical and endocrine technologies doctors were using to assist such individuals. A public discourse naming the condition transsexualism and debating the efficacy of surgical and hormonal reassignment did not emerge in the United States until the 1950s. To sum up, medical debates about surgical and hormonal gender reassignment did not catapult "sex change" into the public eye. Christine Jorgensen did.

More detailed accounts of Jorgensen's life already exist, so here I'll briefly offer some essential details.[43] Jorgensen was born in New York and worked in many industries, including filmmaking and photography. She joined the US Army during World War II before beginning to research sex change as a possibility in the late 1940s. Returning to New York from where she'd been living in Los Angeles, Jorgensen enrolled in a human biochemistry course to learn the basics of endocrinology; after careful research she obtained estradiol from a pharmacist and began hormone-replacement therapy. Gender reassignment surgery was little talked about in the United States at the time, although early versions had been practiced in Europe for decades. Determined to access surgeries no American doctor would approve, Jorgensen sailed to Denmark in 1950 to seek out doctors who would treat her. In Copenhagen she discovered the doctor who would "make history," Christian Hamburger. She persuaded him to use her as a "human guinea pig" for a gender reassignment program that included electrolysis, hormone therapy, "resocialization," and, finally, genital surgery.[44]

What instigated the media blitz that erupted late in 1952, culminating in Jorgensen's very public return to New York in 1953, is somewhat open to debate. In her autobiography Jorgensen recounts that a family friend read letters between Jorgensen and her parents and leaked the story to the press. Since Jorgensen's death, close friends have revealed that Jorgensen herself decided to leak her story; the resourceful Jorgensen may have seen an opportunity to sell her story for some much-needed cash, and perhaps to generate career opportunities. Alternatively she might have reasoned that she better leak the story before anyone else did.[45] Plagued by telegrams from reporters, Jorgensen negotiated a deal with *American Weekly* magazine to pay for her return trip from Denmark in exchange for an exclusive story. She arrived at Idlewild Airport in New York on February 13, 1953, where a sea of journalists, fans, and the curious witnessed her first press conference. Describing the storm of notoriety that accompanied the newspaper headlines about her arrival, Jorgensen reports "descending into a new and alien world."[46] Soon after, *American Weekly* published Jorgensen's own account of her transformation in a five-part series, accompanied by numerous photos establishing her now very feminine embodiment.[47]

It is doubtful that Jorgensen could have foreseen the explosion of publicity around the case or the consequences of being constantly in the public eye. Nevertheless the events of 1953 turned her into a legend and role model for others. "The media coverage of Christine Jorgensen's story and her autobiography of 1967 produced a narrative model for many [transsexuals]," understates Prosser, so much so that the phrase "a trip to Denmark" became shorthand for having GRS.[48] This has created something of an echo chamber in transsexual memoirs and histories. All accounts seem to lead inexorably to Jorgensen: from Leslie Feinberg's story of hearing about Jorgensen as a child to Mario Martino's recounting his father repeating the pun "Imagine going abroad and coming back a broad!"[49] Joanne Meyerowitz's history of transsexuality in the United States details numerous others who recognized themselves in Jorgensen's story.[50] Like Feinberg, numerous other transgender writers cite Jorgensen as the first transsexual person they knew of as children. The story circulated transnationally.[51] In 1970 it was made into a B-grade film, *The Christine Jorgensen Story*, the tagline for which was "Christine Jorgensen: the first man to become a woman." Documents, newsreel footage, and photographs of Jorgensen are archived online, and Susan Stryker and other historians have written extensively on Jorgensen's film and photography career.[52] To add to this abundance of material, a new biography of Jorgensen by Richard Docter appeared in 2008.[53]

Of course Jorgensen was not the first person to confirm her female gender identity. Even though Hamburger had never treated a transsexual woman before, stories about European surgeons performing GRS abounded. Jorgensen went to Denmark on the trail of such stories. Meyerowitz's accounts of "sex reversals" indicate that even as Jorgensen was traveling back to New York from her transformative sojourn in Denmark, other gender nonconforming people in Europe, the United Kingdom, and Denmark itself were also undergoing hormone treatment, electrolysis, resocialization, and gender reassignment surgeries. However, their stories are not enshrined in mythology quite like Jorgensen's.[54] Jorgensen's story resonated with the media and has continued to be regarded within trans history as especially significant because the facts—the journey overseas, Jorgensen's own transformation on a number of levels—could easily be accommodated within a template defining transsexuality as the new form of self-transformation. Those narratives are specific to the geographical and cultural context Jorgensen inhabited—and, of course, her temporary absence from that context.

Jorgensen caught the public's attention, Meyerowitz observes, because she was white, conventionally feminine, and embodied the public desire for stories about individual success and social mobility, making good in the face of obstacles through self-transformation. Jorgensen's story "offered the public an unusual twist on a tried-and-true tale of individual striving, success, and upward mobility . . . a mythic version of American individualism."[55] Her autobiography emphasizes her sense of connection to the great American dream of overcoming hardship through reinvention. She narrates how, living in Los Angeles in the 1940s, she sought out hormonal and surgical treatment for her feeling that she was a really a woman, and tells the story of a visit to the Hollywood Athletics Club, where she encounters an army colonel who tells her the story of losing his fortune in the 1906 San Francisco earthquake. Despite the destruction of his house and business, the undaunted colonel made his way to Hollywood and took up life in the movie business. Jorgensen reflects on the significance of this story for her own life at the time:

> "Why should I accept defeat any more than the Colonel did?" I thought. . . . He didn't settle down in the ashes and moan about it, he sought a solution. It slowly registered in my mind as an object-lesson. . . . In my own case, I knew my tragedies were emotional and physical, and though I had earnestly tried to understand these conditions, I had never done anything positive about them. . . . I had never sought a cure.[56]

It is equally significant that Jorgensen identifies the key moment in her transformation not, as some might expect, as her Copenhagen surgery but the moment when she arrives back in New York and must begin a new life as a social and extroverted person. Prior to transition, she had been "shy and introverted"; her return as Christine is attended by a "difficult social adjustment" in which she learns "a new ability to meet people and to be accepted by them in return."[57] This could be attributed, we might imagine, as much to the necessity of lubricating the wheels of the publicity machine as to Jorgensen's newfound confidence as a woman. The *American Weekly* articles, published just after Jorgensen arrived back in New York, riff on this same spirit of self-transformation. Jorgensen remarks that she was so poor in Copenhagen that she taught herself to sew to make her own clothes, and yet in photographs taken during and after her time in Copenhagen, she is always presented as glamorous and ladylike, clad in tailored, expensive-looking gowns and accessories.[58] If the public was going to regard her sympathetically as an example of the classic American Dream, it was important that she appear to have conquered poverty single-handedly, with the help of a trusty sewing machine. That we now know Jorgensen decided to enter public life by leaking her story to the press only enhances the image of her resourcefulness. However, she desired public recognition, and public recognition may have demanded that the transformation she accomplished be not only from male to female but from undistinguished to glamorous, retiring to outgoing. More important, Jorgensen's transformation is also narrated as a transformation from a drifting, rather undirected male existence to success as a female, a life with direction and meaning produced through conscious self-work.[59]

This emphasis on direction and meaning, conquering hardship through individual triumph, resonates with the great narratives of American modernity, not just during the postwar period but throughout the history of US democracy. In the eighteenth century Alexis de Tocqueville pointed to the alleged lack of a class system in the United States as intrinsic to the idea of progress, as well as "the idea of the indefinite perfectibility of man": [as] the classes of society draw together, as manners, customs, and laws vary, because of the tumultuous intercourse of men . . . [a person] infers that man is endowed with an indefinite faculty for improvement."[60] Under the terms of liberal democracy, infinite perfectibility becomes not only a capacity of the individual but a responsibility: if each individual is free, then each individual is responsible for regarding himself as a set of capacities to be improved. This attitude of self-transformation resonates with the modern attitude Foucault evokes in "What Is Enlightenment?," which he parses Baudelaire's *fin de siècle* manifesto on dandyism. "To be modern," writes Foucault, "is to take oneself as object of a complex and difficult elaboration: what Baudelaire, in the vocabulary of his day, calls *dandysme*. . . . Modern man, for Baudelaire, is not the man who goes off to discover himself, his secrets and his hidden truth; he is the man who tries to invent himself. This modernity does not 'liberate man in his own being'; it compels him to face the task of producing himself."[61] In the early to mid-twentieth-century United States, similar attitudes toward self-discovery and infinite perfectibility intersected. Both discourses took the body as the vehicle for transformation, with the popular emergence of cosmetic surgery as a route to increased success through aesthetic improvement.[62] Alongside aesthetic surgeries, gender reassignment surgeries developed as well, enabling the corporeal transformation that would later become understood as transsexuality.

It's helpful to reflect here on the context in which these self-transformation discourses were circulating. Jorgensen, Meyerowitz points out, refused to comply with being labeled freakish or perverse, despite being represented as such. "She insisted on her place in the mainstream," writes Meyerowitz, and maintained public appeal as a ladylike, respectable specimen of "sex change" even as many popular accounts of her life stressed deviance.[63] Jorgensen was not alone: many early public transsexual people emphasized that they desired to occupy the mainstream of society rather than its fringes. Dan Irving points to a trans woman quoted in Harry Benjamin's 1966 book *The Transsexual Phenomenon* who said, "We prefer the normalcy's [*sic*] of life and want to be accepted in circles of normal society, enjoying the same pursuits and pleasures without calling attention to the fact that we are 'queers' trying to invade the world of normal people."[64] Drawing attention to precisely the same transformation in Jorgensen's living conditions, from poor, shy man to successful woman, Irving reads Jorgensen as parsing her self-image through the "productive potential" of her condition.[65] The urgency of social recognition, Irving argues, often forces transsexual people to frame their recognition demands in terms that emphasize their earning potential and to behave as exemplary productive citizens. Irving sees this as part of capitalist alienation, in which minorities are forced to premise identity claims on their capacity for "productive citizenship."

The need for transsexual subjects to echo dominant discourses of assimilatory desires to be "normal" and to be productive members of society contributes much to my argument that transsexuality discursively invokes self-transformation while emphasizing the productive capacities of the individual. However, the twentieth- and twenty-first-century US call to engage in self-transformation assumes that one has the cultural and racial capital to become socially mobile in the first place. While Foucault glosses over the class implications of Baudelaire's writing on the dandy, it seems clear from the passage I quoted earlier that to "invent oneself" one has to be bourgeois, wealthy, ideally white, and have the free time and economic resources to devote oneself to self-transformation. As I noted above, this is a gendered invocation that applies to men but also, in a different way, to wealthy, middle-class women.

This is one reason the travel narrative is so central to the founding moment of transsexual culture and recognition. Jorgensen's travel narrative contains the temporal moment of gender indeterminacy within a spatialized elsewhere. As this had already taken place, her ability to be accommodated within the narrative of American social recognition and legitimacy, premised on individual triumph over the odds, increased. Mobility requires more than social resources, however. The American myth of universal social mobility rests on the assumption that American society is classless. Thus theorizing geographical mobility is impossible without thinking about political economy, citizenship, and liberal democracy, and, specifically, how social mobility discourses inflect all three. For Mark Simpson, mobility is a primary symptom of "entangled ideologies of national identity and progress" that "bind together two traits supposedly intrinsic to 'the American': the need to move (freedom as geographical expansiveness) and the need to rise (freedom as social mobility)." Simpson argues that the myth equating individual movement with the subject's freedom under US democracy institutes a "fantasy of classlessness," concealing and sustaining class and racial difference.[66]

Transsexual peoples' travel within that fantasy of classlessness marks a mode of cultural distinction. Jorgensen's story works as a template for that fantasy: that transsexuals must gather the resources to get to Denmark (or Casablanca, or wherever a surgeon is available) to return triumphantly, having privately accomplished the feat of self-transformation. This also determines the temporal structure of Jorgensen's and others' stories. The journey-out-and-return narrative can be told only retrospectively, after recognition has already been won. A blow-by-blow serial account of Jorgensen in the process of transition would not have generated nearly as much public interest.

The Jorgensen story also demonstrates that the journey-out-and-return narrative can double as a narrative of social mobility. The contrast between Jorgensen's passage to Denmark on a ship because she could not afford to fly and all-expenses-paid return trip institutes a fantasy of recognition premised on the transsexual subject's capacity for a particular mode of self-transformation, not only from male to female or from female to male but from outsider to insider. It also encodes the perfection of femininity as a route to wealth and fame, obscuring the gender wage gap and the feminization of poverty.[67] The origin story of the transsexual is all about autonomy, self-will, self-transformation through heroic acts of will, hardship, and heroic publicness—heroic attempts to gain public recognition. That myth informs a larger progress narrative about the twentieth-century transformation of public recognition for gender nonconforming people. This is the myth that Jorgensen made it all possible because she was a public heroine. In fact numerous discontinuities and contingencies set her story apart; for example, instead of being an unwilling victim of a malicious leak to the press, she approached the media herself, seeing the opportunity for a major scoop in her transition and the possibility of a triumphant return from Denmark as a star. Indeed these discontinuities threaten to destabilize the fantasy of spontaneous recognition via self-transformation (which Jorgensen labored to put into effect). Perceptions of "cheating" or being *too* resourceful might result in minoritized American Dream subjects' acquiring the notoriety of the charlatan, a privilege which rich white men may inhabit with abandon, but minoritized subjects cannot risk.

Against Trans Epochalism

To read the Christine Jorgensen story genealogically—that is, to see Jorgensen's place as the first public American trans woman not as a foregone conclusion but as contingent—affords us an opportunity to place her and the narrative of trans people as the ultimate self-transformers in a broader historical and geographical context. From the perspective of transnational transgender theorizing, the North American moment in which Jorgensen gained public recognition begins to look rather provincial. What stands out is the transnationality of her transformation and her canny negotiation of different medical and social codes in Denmark and the United States. This negotiation is a recurrent theme of the transnational gender reassignment imaginaries I write about later in this book. In a similar way transgender studies is beginning to look outside the frame of the national and particularly outside the context of the United States.

The concept of provincializing is productive here, a concept I take from Dipesh Chakrabarty's *Provincializing Europe*. For Chakrabarty, to provincialize Europe is to reject the just-so story that capitalism, democracy, nationalism, and the other central tenets of modernity developed in Europe and then spread to the Global South. Given that colonized territories in Asia, Africa, Oceania, and North and South America provided labor, land, and materials to produce the commodities that fueled the Enlightenment (sugar, tin, coffee, gold), as well as offered useful testing-grounds for modern governmentalities, we need to rewrite the history of modernity both in and as emanating from the colonies. Provincializing also refigures historiography without historicism. According to this postcolonial critique of historicism, historicism rationalizes a Eurocentric idea of history that posits modernity as global over time, that is, originating in one place (Europe) and only later emerging elsewhere. More important, Chakrabarty rejects historicism as "the idea that to understand anything it has to be seen as both a unity and in its historical development." I agree with Chakrabarty that history is an instrument deployed in the service of political ends, and "given and privileged narratives of citizenship" are always policed through institutional violences.[68] This includes the institutional violence visited upon colonial and subaltern gender nonconforming populations in the United States and elsewhere, for whom medicalized transsexuality is considered the only legitimate option, and the symbolic violence of displacing gender indeterminacy to an exoticized "elsewhere"—where, as the following chapters show, colonial relations of orientalism are alive and well inside and outside of trans cultural productions and community spaces.

Chakrabarty directs us to pay attention to the geographical specificity (as well as the historical moment) into which a discourse erupts. Here we begin to understand the precise difference between the North American emergence of transsexuality in the 1940s and the earlier instances of gender reassignment taking place in Europe. As Meyerowitz observes, the European cases of the 1920s and 1930s, preceding Jorgensen's trip to Denmark by twenty or thirty years, were marked by mass-media coverage. This includes the case of Zdenek Koubkov, a Czechoslovakian athlete who was assigned female at birth and competed in the 1932 Olympics as a woman before reassigning his gender as male: "In his early twenties (or in one account, even earlier) 'a great light dawned,' and [Koubkov] realized he was a man. He consulted a doctor who confirmed his masculinity, and unspecified operations, 'the flick of a surgeon's scalpel,' followed." Koubkov was known outside Europe; indeed he visited New York and performed on Broadway, and, as Meyerowitz further observes, the American press covered his case quite extensively.[69] One might ask why Koubkov isn't known as the first transsexual. But he was not traveling from home to elsewhere in the North American imagination, so his was not a story that fit the American narrative of liberal self-transformation closely enough to push it into the realm of mythology. Neither did it take place at a time when future generations of North American transgender activists would recall it. That Jorgensen's story did contain such amenable elements is a historical accident and demonstrates the contingency of the historical narrative of transsexuality's progress across the twentieth century and the importance of geographical location in the emergence of transsexuality as an intelligible object worthy of cultural, scientific, or popular attention.

In understanding Jorgensen's case to be the moment in which transsexuality comes into being, we may also forget that, in fact, Jorgensen did not think of herself as a transsexual; indeed the term was only just coming into widespread use by David O. Cauldwell, Harry Benjamin, and Benjamin's colleagues. Jorgensen did not define her condition with a label. Despite this, many journalists described her as a pseudo-hermaphrodite, a person who exhibited the characteristics of a "true" hermaphrodite but whose ambiguous sex characteristics could not be located on her body.[70] From the beginning Jorgensen's narrative indexed public recognition and acceptance. In its capacity to overcome the contradiction that gender reassignment presented by spatially concealing the destabilizing moment at which man became woman, the story of Jorgensen's Denmark trip installs recognition at home as the highest investment in transsexual existence. Geographical travel enables recognition *in particular spaces*—in the space of the modern nation—from the beginning.

To provincialize transsexuality also means reconsidering the logic by which temporal narratives have governed accounts of transsexual and transgender history itself. When Susan Stryker poses transsexuality as the signifier of a global transition from modernity to postmodernity, she frames the story of twentieth-century US gender variance as a template for a broader progress narrative about the wonders and perils of technological advancement. As I noted at the beginning of the chapter, Stryker uses the metaphor of the atomic bomb to document Jorgensen's explosion onto the world stage as a critical epochal break. Deploying the atomic bomb as a literary device, Stryker consciously conflates "transsexual and atomic technologies" to make the following observation: "In the spectacular advent of Jorgensen's public womanhood we can discern a moment of rupture in the fabric of Western culture, a new event in our material circumstances, a point of ecstatic passage into the postmodern condition." Stryker critiques the framing of transsexuality (and gender fluidity) as a "fantasy figure," symptomatic of all that is wrong with postmodernity. For example, she critiques Jean Baudrillard's universalizing claim that within postmodernity everyone is a "transsexual" and that people in contemporary global culture derive pleasure from "playing with the commutability of the signs of sex."[71] As Stryker points out, Baudrillard "use[s] the figure of the transsexual to narrate a history of the second half of the twentieth century." However much she disagrees with his conclusions, though, in this instance she is sympathetic to Baudrillard's project. "The transsexual can, and often does, productively figure in attempts to make sense of recent as well as prospective historical experience," she writes.[72] Stryker uses Jorgensen's story to emphasize transsexuality's status as a vector through which the postmodern condition emerges.[73] Locating Jorgensen as the epicenter of this epochal shift, Stryker draws attention to how Jorgensen's short period working on the cutting-room floor of RKO studios influenced her understanding of her own body, which could be edited in a similar fashion. This bodily manipulation, Stryker observes, made it apparent that sex was malleable, "an operationalized surface effect achieved through performative means."[74] In "Black Telephones, White Refrigerators: Rethinking Christine Jorgensen," Dallas Denny also points to Jorgensen's autonomy in making history, describing Jorgensen as the "project manager of a bold social experiment" and "the driving force in her own sex reassignment."[75] Drawing on the work of queer and trans historians who see the protagonists of their accounts as making their own destinies rather than being the objects of science or medicalization, Stryker and Denny reorient transsexuality as a phenomenon that rewrites gender and history. To come full circle to the narrative of trans history I cited at the beginning of the chapter, this is the theory of Christine Jorgensen as ground zero.

Both Stryker and Denny see Jorgensen as an engine generating the progression toward contemporary transgender self-determination. To be sure, Jorgensen's actions changed many people's existences, both during her life and after her death in 1989. As empowering as this narrative might be, it is symptomatic of a historicism that conceals how many other people in the first half of the twentieth century demanded gender reassignment from doctors or experimented with hormone therapy. The logic of Jorgensen as ground zero falters on a predicament whereby the emergence of transsexuality begins to look like a logical historical progression, premised on either the development of medical technologies or the (early) transsexual subject's will to match his desire for transformation with access to those medical technologies. This may be empowering, for within this narrative transsexuality promises individual progress and mobility, as well as the potential for an individual to consume self-transformation as a commodity in late capitalism.

Just as pressingly, Jorgensen as a symbolic ground zero for postmodernity installs a teleology in which the history of nonmedicalized cross-gender practices stands in as a deep primordial past, the "not yet" of gender reassignment as a necessarily medical intervention. The 1950s emergence of more widespread access to gender reassignment technologies clearly marks a radical transformation in the history of embodiment. And yet to frame that moment as the groundbreaking historical moment in the history of transgender phenomena erases the somatic technologies used before medical-surgical and hormonal reassignment technologies became available. More to the point, framing the moment at which surgical and hormonal sex transformation hits public awareness as the advent of postmodernity tends to privilege surgical sex reassignment itself—which popular cultural and medico-juridical governmentalities already do. In effect, to imagine history this way is to run the risk of assuming gender nonconforming people before this time did not transform their bodies using the technologies they had available.[76] Do these pre-twentieth-century bodies form the "not yet" of transsexual postmodernity?

If these historical interpretations of Jorgensen frame her appearance on the world stage as the inauguration of postmodernity, they find a continuation in the valorization of the "cut" as transformative potential in more recent Deleuzo-Guattarian transsexual ontologies. For Eva Hayward, the cut is "a generative effort to *pull the body back through itself* to feel mending, to feel the growth of new margins." Hayward theorizes the cut as materio-discursive and, above all, ontologically generative. As she astutely points out, rather than privileging accounts that pose trans experience as determined by the form of the body (the binary trap of "preoperative" versus "postoperative," not to mention the primordialist reification of the supposedly natural male or female body), a generative ontological reading makes room for becoming and potentially limitless materialization to emerge as the figures for embodiment.[77] While Hayward frames the cut as metonymically related to how starfish regenerate their limbs that have been broken off, the cut as it relates to human bodies is definitively a surgical cut. For Hayward, this surgical cut is the condition of possibility. Because she writes in the present tense of philosophical abstraction, the cut also stands in for the historical moment at which surgical cutting became a possibility for gender nonconforming bodies.

It can hardly be coincidental that such phenomenological accounts of trans experience and history emerge at a moment in which a Deleuzo-Guattarian molecular becoming is privileged within critical philosophy and, with it, a simultaneous move to name the present as entirely different from the past. Whether this appears under the terms of post-autonomist economic speculation about post-Fordism and the primacy of immaterial labor or in new materialist and antihumanist accounts of science and technology that locate objects, microbiological processes, or affect-for-itself as the autonomous new paradigms for protopolitical agency (rather than the body of the worker, or any body, anywhere), the lesson remains the same.[78] Privileging such an abstracted and ahistorical notion of the cut, poetic and full of potential as it is, occludes the historical, economic, and racialized circumstances of the invention of and juridicomedical conditions governing access to GRS and other transformative technologies. The proximity and distance between the terms *gender nonconforming* and *transsexual* mark the existence of social fields in which the surgical cut is the least important vector of potentiality or becoming.

Reading an early draft of this chapter, Stryker pointed out that at the historical moment in which she and Denny were writing about Jorgensen, it was crucial to represent transgender people as autonomous, creative, and empowered. Feminists, leftist antipsychiatrists, and -psychoanalysts seemed all to agree that trans women were dupes of the medical establishment or outright colonizers of women's only space.[79] Writing the history of transgender or transsexual phenomena was not

yet a legitimate academic pursuit, particularly if the author was publicly identifiable as transgender. Thus the stakes of clearly delineating
a theory of transsexuality as autonomous were high. Nonetheless we
must question the primacy of stories about plucky individual self-
transformation, if only because they are so prone to appropriation.
For example, neoliberal policymakers have taken up such narratives
to rationalize the complete withdrawal of welfare and state assistance.
They are also used to punish those who cannot or will not invest in social mobility. In making this point I'm mobilizing Stryker's own work
in the new field of somatechnics, the emergence of which she's been
instrumental in facilitating. Somatechnics designates "the intercon-
nections between embodiment, technology, and bodily practice"; to
think with somatechnics means understanding that the "material intelligibility of the body (soma) [is] inseparable from the techniques and
technologies through which bodies are formed and transformed."[80] To
oppose trans epochalism involves resisting the assumption of endless
future-oriented horizons of malleability. Rather we can look for the
ways that somatechnic embodiment takes place in the past and in non-
modern spaces without posing them as the backward past preceding
the postmodern, technologized Global North. If flesh is endlessly malleable, we need to pay more attention to the malleabilities that have
characterized—and continue to characterize—nonmedical transgender embodiment. This is precisely a way to provincialize transsexuality.

As I argued in the introduction, many scholars (including Stryker)
have drawn attention to how whiteness remains the invisible background
against which transgender narratives, history, and cultural critique have
emerged.[81] Trans and queer of color critiques, drawing on transnational feminist scholarship, suggest the need to interrogate how liberal
models of recognition designate white trans subjects as those destined
for rights and admission into the liberal polity, while trans of color subjects are diagnosed as threats to the national sphere or those subjects
who need to be "saved" from the putative barbarism of their home nations. Here as elsewhere historical narratives designate which subjects
are worthy of consideration, or who "counts" as transgender forbears
and in what ways.

The predicaments of transgender whiteness, historicism, and modernity evident here are encapsulated in teaching history as part
of transgender studies. Since I moved to the United States in 2009,
it's been my privilege and dilemma to teach transgender studies at

five institutions. Stryker published *Transgender History* in 2008, which presents a fascinatingly detailed account of the emergence of twentieth-century transgender movements and, better yet, is accessible to undergraduate students encountering such material for the first time. Early on in the semester I offer a history lesson: What did gender nonconforming embodiments and practices look like prior to the contemporary moment my students and I inhabit? I begin with the United States. Reading the chapter "100 Years of Transgender History," I teach my students about the eruption of laws outlawing cross-dressing in US cities beginning in 1850, painting a picture of what life might have looked like for gender nonconforming people at the time of the Industrial Revolution. "100 Years of Transgender History" tracks the transmission of ideas about gender reassignment from Germany to the United States through Harry Benjamin's friendship with Magnus Hirschfeld and both figures' work with trans and gender nonconforming people, including Jorgensen herself. This history is ripe for provincializing, even from a US perspective: Europe seems to be where gender reassignment takes place first, before it occurs in the rest of the world. In the next class I undercut this vision of historical time by introducing my students to the concept of settler colonialism and having them read Deborah Miranda's "Extermination of the *Joyas*," which details how *jotas* and *joyas*—the names given to gender nonconforming people in seventeenth-century Spanish California—were exterminated and subjected to civilizing governmentality through internment at missions, Christianization, and a host of disciplinary controls aimed at eradicating gender nonconformity.[82] Miranda's work emphasizes the importance of place and colonialism in transgender history. In "Extermination of the *Joyas*," she offers a useful counterpoint to the victorious narrative of transgender history, illustrating how tightly historical narratives of gender nonconformity and sexuality are bound up with the history of imperial conquest, civilizing missions, and colonial governmentality. In one sense Miranda's work is unrecognizable as transgender history: she doesn't designate *joyas* as transgender, nor does she write about contemporary Two Spirit Native populations as transgender—or gay or lesbian, necessarily. (This makes it all the more valuable to teach, as students learn the difference between transgender as an analytical term and personal, or historical, self-identification.) Enmeshed in epistemologies of settler colonialism themselves, non-Native students tend to respond to this material with shock, leading to a conversation about how little they learned about conquest and US colonization at school. In turn this can lead to a discussion of how transgender studies needs to remain intersectionally grounded in understandings of racialized settler colonialism. I encourage my students to interrogate the framing of transgender (and transgender studies) as the new civil rights issue emerging in an allegedly postracial America. Crucially this means questioning the triumphalist narrative that frames past transgender heroes—nearly always white, apart from a token black and brown representative—as having vanquished medical restrictions and social stigma to provide contemporary trans people with the (few) rights and freedoms we enjoy.

Finally, provincializing transsexuality means moving through the predicaments of transgender racialization. To do so involves asking different questions of historical events than we have asked thus far. How did modern understandings of the scientific pliability of gender emerge in relation to settler colonialism in different geographical locations or in relation to so-called premodern or primitive gender-crossing practices?[83] For historical work this means looking not only at how knowledge of events in North America and Europe flowed across the uneven spaces of globalization, but also at how flows of knowledge, techniques of embodied transformation, and modes of identification have flowed toward both continents from other regions, and tracing the flows of all of these between different locations in the Global South. It might mean examining how concepts of transsexuality have been taken up in different locations, wholly disaggregated from their Euro-American medicojuridical roots, or conjoined with different medical and juridical frameworks governing gender variance or personhood. Finally, in focusing on North America, as I do in this chapter, it means understanding the emergence and consolidation of transsexuality in the United States as local rather than universal, as partial and contingent rather than inevitable. As I turn to a close reading of autobiographies featuring travel and immigration in chapter 2, these preoccupations remain as guides.

CHAPTER TWO

ON LOCATION: TRANSSEXUAL AUTOBIOGRAPHIES, WHITENESS, AND TRAVEL

The radicals of the industrial nations want to *be* the Third World.
—**Gayatri Spivak**, "Poststructuralism, Marginality, Postcolonialism and Value"

In 1958 a French surgeon and waterskiing devotee, Dr. Georges Burou, began performing vaginoplasties for trans women. Born in Algeria to French parents, Burou specialized in obstetrics and gynecology; he opened a maternity hospital and gynecology clinic in Casablanca in 1950, called the Clinique du Parc.[1] In 1956 Burou invented the penile inversion technique of vaginoplasty, using penile and scrotal skin to form the walls of the vagina. As the story goes, Jenny, an electrician from Nice who desired genital surgery, approached Burou and convinced him to operate on her. Later she met the famous showgirl Coccinelle, a performer with the Paris-based company Le Carousel. Coccinelle made her own way to Casablanca, beginning an abiding trend.[2] The English model April Ashley followed, as well as Le Carousel performers Bambi, Capucine, Amanda Lear, and others.[3] While Burou's innovative technique had become famous in Europe by the early 1960s, he would not gain official recognition from other surgeons until around 1975.

At the Clinique du Parc maternity wards and an abortion clinic took up the two lower floors. The third floor was set aside for trans patients. Burou offered a desirable, if expensive, alternative to the prescribed psychiatric evaluations and "real life tests" that were developing as standard practice for university- and state-based gender clinics in the UK and the US at the time; he did not share the general reluctance of surgeons in North America and Europe to perform trans surgeries.[4] For this reason many of the earliest European and American transsexual autobiographies feature a trip to Morocco to undergo surgery. April Ashley's memoir *April Ashley's Odyssey*, Coccinelle's *Coccinelle*, Renée Richards's *Second Serve*, Caroline Cossey's *My Story*, and Jan Morris's *Conundrum* all recount their authors' journeys to "the wizard of Casablanca." Triply rich in significations of the Orient, the remnants of postcolonial French culture, and the Bogart-Bergman film of the same name, Casablanca features in such accounts as a location that, through its very ambiance, transforms its transsexual visitors and renders them feminine.[5] The city's starring role in transsexual autobiographies offers an apt example of how racial and cultural difference erupts in imaginaries of gender reassignment through an orientalizing discourse that frames the locational backdrop of gender reassignment surgery as exotic and transformative.

As one of the main cultural forms through which transsexuality was narrated, autobiographies and memoirs help constitute how transness is articulated and recognized more broadly. For this reason autobiographies are central to understanding the geographical mapping of transsexuality, not only as a category of medicine but also as a category of personal and political self-definition. If accounts of Christine Jorgensen and Jorgensen's own 1967 autobiography offer an occasion for locating the historical instantiation of the journey-out-and-return-home narrative, as I discussed in chapter 1, post-1967 transsexual autobiographies and memoirs carry iterations of that narrative inflected by the historical and political times they appeared in: waning British imperialism in Morris's *Conundrum* and 1990s American liberal multiculturalism in Deirdre McCloskey's *Crossing* and Jennifer Finney Boylan's *She's Not There: A Life in Two Genders*. This chapter examines these transsexual memoirs in the context of colonial and racial anxiety and asks how travel, and the mediation of travel by colonial topographies, produces representations of a particular racialized, white version of transsexuality. I excavate the political and colonial economies concealed by figuring transsexual autobiographies as narratives with a universal structure and by treating travel as if it were an unmarked category.

In chapter 1, building on the work of Jay Prosser and others, I demonstrated that travel is central to the experience of transsexuality itself. Journeys in trans autobiographies sublimate the "quest for a gendered home" by constructing narratives through geographical movement, Prosser contends.[6] In this chapter I critique Prosser's assumption that "home" in a gendered or geographical sense has a universal or self-evident meaning. Making a genre intervention, I read accounts of gender crossing and travel as travel writing, taking into consideration the historical and generic traditions of much travel writing as a colonial, imperialist venture. In this move I draw on Mary Louise Pratt's methodology in *Imperial Eyes*, as well as critiques of orientalism beginning with Edward Said. For Pratt, travel books produced Europe's sense of itself in relation to the "rest of the world"; they enabled imperial power to know itself by obsessively surveying its peripheries.[7] I also use a transnational feminist studies and critical race studies lens to interrogate how white transsexual memoirists have deployed racial difference in varying ways to translate transsexuality's marginality for a mainstream readership.

In the first part of this chapter I show how autobiographical narrative emerged as a central form of verifying transsexuality in a medicolegal context and canvass theorizations of how transsexual autobiographies have contributed to transsexual life. Following this I rearticulate my theorization of travel and mobility in relation to autobiography and orientalism. Reading Morris's account of traveling to Casablanca for GRS in her 1967 memoir, *Conundrum*, I argue that while this document dramatizes and externalizes her parallel internal journey to become a "whole woman" (thus completing her journey from male to female), her own and similar accounts simultaneously record another order of exchange, reproducing the colonial boundaries of what de Certeau calls a "hermeneutics of the other."[8] In the second part of the chapter I offer a reading of a very different intersection between transsexuality and travel in McCloskey's 1999 memoir, *Crossing*. Rather than figuring herself as a traveler, McCloskey relates her experience of crossing genders to immigration and equates what she calls "gender crossers" with migrants. McCloskey is not the only transsexual autobiographer to deploy an immigration metaphor to account for her experiences: the original working title of Boylan's best-selling 2004 memoir, *She's Not There: A*

Life In Two Genders, was *Gender Immigrant*.[9] *Crossing* explicitly redefines transsexuality as a minority subject position equivalent to that of the immigrant, subtly recasting the dominant travel metaphor from signifying a first world, middle-class pursuit, to immigration, associated with marginalization and hardship. Finally, however, I argue that accounts marking the moment of gendered transformation in exotic locales and the later identification of gender variance with a racialized or mobile subalternity (trans people as refugees or migrants) represent two sides of the same coin. Both discourses share investments in the same project: to produce transsexuality as an intelligible category of existence within an epistemological framework saturated with modernity and to define trans people against the premodern, the uncivilized, and the other while simultaneously appropriating and circulating those attributes as cultural capital. At stake in these metaphorical linkages between gender reassignment and travel, I argue, are the shifting tensions between making a claim to marginality as a transsexual subject and the desire to domesticate or normalize that marginality.

Transsexual Autobiography: Sketching the Canon

To fully grasp the importance of travel in transsexual autobiographies, we need an appreciation of the historical conditions of transsexual autobiography's emergence. Early forms of autobiographical writing by gender nonconforming people were recorded in case histories by fin de siècle sexologists in Europe and the United States. Like other pathologized populations, gender nonconforming people were subject to what Foucault calls the "clinical codification of the incitement to speak."[10] Detailed autobiographical accounts of sexual inversion are contained in Richard von Krafft-Ebing's *Psychopathia Sexualis*, Havelock Ellis's *Sexual Inversion*, and Magnus Hirschfeld's *Transvestites*. These accounts were not understood as "autobiography" as such—sexologists used them to diagnose a variety of so-called sexual pathologies—but many gender nonconforming people read such accounts and identified with them. Later, gender nonconforming people wrote autobiographical letters to the pulp magazine *Sexology*, spurred on by the mass media's own sensationalist coverage of "inverts" and people who "changed their sex."[11] Other early autobiographical accounts, such as Lili Elbe's *Man into Woman: An Authentic Record of a Change of Sex* and Christine Jorgensen's *A Personal Autobiography*, were published to win the public's sympathy and counter negative mass-media coverage. Jorgensen's *A Personal Autobiography*, published in 1967, marks the first identifiable published autobiography of someone publicly recognized as transsexual. After 1967 a number of memoirs written by celebrities appeared, including volumes by Morris, Richards, and Mario Martino, as well models Caroline Cossey and April Ashley.[12] These texts were thought to be of interest to a reading public not only because they were written by transsexual individuals but because their authors were famous. By the early 1990s trans memoirs were being published by noncelebrities, including Mark Rees's *Dear Sir or Madam*, McCloskey's *Crossing*, and Claudine Griggs's *Passage through Trinidad*.[13] Also in the early 1990s a number of transgender-themed memoirs appeared that either critiqued the standard transsexual narrative or simply ignored its existence, including Kate Bornstein's *Gender Outlaw: On Men, Women, and the Rest of Us*, Riki Anne Wilchins's memoir and activist handbook *Read My Lips: Sexual Subversion and the End of Gender*, and the anthology *GenderQueer: Voices from Beyond the Sexual Binary*.[14] Here memoir and political writing often coincide: Wilchins (a member of the US activist group Transexual Menace) and Bornstein identify themselves as part of the transgender political movement and account for their personal writing as a strategy to educate and politicize readers.

Despite these important interventions, a normative transsexual narrative has remained ascendant in autobiography. This is partially because access to medical treatment has long depended on articulating that narrative to health practitioners, psychiatrists, and society at large. As transsexuality became a recognized phenomenon with a treatment protocol, being able to provide a coherent personal story became the condition that medical practitioners required from those desiring hormone therapy and/or gender reassignment surgeries. This coherent story forms a classical transsexual narrative: the early childhood feeling that one is trapped in the body of a gender one does not feel to be correct; traumatic episodes in which "abnormal" cross-gender behavior is punished, and hence performed in secret; the realization at some point that a name and a solution exist for people of this kind; and, sooner or later, consultations with doctors, psychiatrists, surgeons to align the physical body with the somatic experience of being a woman or a man—an always successful venture beyond which the protagonist begins a new life. Candidates for hormone therapy and GRS occupy a difficult position. To access treatment one has to echo this classical narrative, even and especially if one's own history does not reflect that narrative. Yet when trans patients repeat the classical account *too* faithfully they are derided by doctors as faking their case histories. Moreover a phobic obsession with rendering trans femininity as the most visible form of gender nonconforming life has meant that the abstract, gender neutral term *transsexual* often stands in for a particular trans feminine narrative of gender transition.

Given this history it would be a mistake to understand transsexual autobiographies as transparent accounts of an author's true experience. Yet this is precisely how autobiographies continue to be understood by popular audiences and within some transgender studies scholarship. Prosser writes that transsexual autobiographies are "produced out of a specific and stable subject position": the narratological conventions of autobiography depend on and are produced from the specificities and truths of that subject position.[15] As readers might recall from chapter 1, Prosser understands accounts of travel in transsexual autobiographies as a strategy of dramatizing the subject's gendered transition.

By looking at three autobiographies written by trans women, I risk unfairly targeting trans women's cultural productions while neglecting to examine how trans masculine memoirs present race, whiteness, and mobility. While I refer readers to the introduction of this book for a longer discussion of these issues, some words relating to autobiography are helpful here. Trans women have written the most popularly read and well-known transsexual autobiographies. These accounts tend to overrepresent the stories of trans women who access GRS. For example, the 2005 anthology *Sexual Metamorphosis*, a collection of excerpts from trans autobiographies edited by a non-trans man, Jonathan Ames (the coauthor of Richards's autobiography), overwhelmingly presents accounts of trans women who seek GRS. This is not the fault of trans women themselves but reflects a popular desire to consume such narratives—and reflects the hypervisibility of trans femininity within mainstream representations of transness and a heightened surveillance of female bodies. As I and others have remarked, this hypervisibility results in material and institutional violence. Nonetheless, as my reading of Jorgensen in chapter 1 illustrates, what can be understood as "transsexual autobiography" follows particular narrative conventions precisely because of the hypervisibility of trans feminine bodies.

In trans autobiographies GRS is a principal narrative convention. In fact it often is the litmus test defining a given autobiography as transsexual. The body serves as the site in which truths are (literally) manifested through the technologies of GRS. It is assumed that to be a transsexual always involves a host of physical and social transitions, including GRS (as if GRS involved the same process for everyone). Within transsexual memoirs a narrator's individual account of undergoing surgery and its aftermath cement a given text's status *as* transsexual autobiography. Additionally accounts of surgery tend to cement the underpinning of transsexual experience as a singular, straightforward movement from male to female or female to male through genital transformation.

Travel to obtain that surgery is another convention in trans women's autobiographies, one that is not reflected in autobiographies by trans men.[16] Again this is not to claim that trans women universally desire or are able to obtain gender reassignment. Rather the popular imagination, conditioned by a history of medical narratives valorizing GRS, understands this as the main turning point in gender transition. Transsexual autobiographies constitute one of the modernist sexual narratives Ken Plummer identifies with key generic elements, and those generic elements produce themselves as stages in the "natural" teleology of a gender nonconforming individual's gender transition.[17] Additionally such attributes combine to support the impression that transsexuality is a deeply rooted, ahistorical, and/or biological phenomenon.[18]

If one rejects transsexuality as an ahistorical phenomenon, however, one risks using a discourse of social constructionism to present trans desires for body modification as conditioned by medicine's heteronormativity, and trans autobiography as a hegemonic structure that incites the desire for body modification. In the 1990s this debate erupted between transgender studies scholarship and feminist theorists skeptical about transgender. In *Changing Sex* (1995), Bernice Hausman contends that well-known memoirs institute their own "discursive hegemony," often because of the recognizable status of the authors as publicly out trans people, or celebrities outed as transsexual. Hausman argues that transsexual authors produce "closed narratives," interpellating (trans) readers to construct their experience in the same way, with the same beliefs about the nature of sex and gender.[19] In the background lurks Hausman's belief that trans people's demand for "sex change" is produced by the medical technologies that emerged in the twentieth century to facilitate genital surgical transformation. In an incisive critique of Hausman, Prosser in *Second Skins* (1998) presents trans people's affective and somatic experiences of the need for body modification as far deeper than mere interpellation or identification with the medical industry. Prosser also forces antitrans feminists to grapple with the fact that transsexual autobiographies conform to particular narratives precisely because of their autobiographical nature. Autobiography as a genre "endows the life with the formal structure that life, itself, does not have."[20] For Prosser, rewriting life retrospectively as a step-by-step journey actually permits the transsexual subject to make sense of gender transition and to feel at home occupying her new gender presentation. As readers might recall from my discussion of *Second Skins* in chapter 1, Prosser argues that autobiographical narrativity is the tool transsexuals use to account for their somatic experience of body and sex, independent of actually existing autobiographies. Prosser astutely argues that writing an autobiography may permit some feeling of closure for a trans or gender nonconforming subject.

Neither Hausman's nor Prosser's perspective is sufficient for my purposes. By conflating generic conventions with psychic processes, both authors miss the opportunity to engage with the dynamics of autobiography as a multivalent discourse, inflected differently depending on geocultural and temporal contexts. Hausman assumes that the practice of reading trans autobiographical narratives must result in either wholesale identification with that narrative (in which case the reader must be transsexual) or active disidentification (in which case the reader must not be transsexual). There is no room for complex or partial identification here, or for disidentification.[21] Prosser, on the other hand, resorts to psychologizing narrativity. He claims that all transsexual psychic structures follow the same pattern; that is, all transsexuals are governed by the same laws of subject formation through linear narrative (childhood cross-gender identification, the discovery of and identification with transsexuality, a desire for body modification, etc.). He believes identification with the opposite gender and the subsequent desire for body modification involve a deep psychic structure that results in trans people presenting with the classical trans narrative. By making this argument, Prosser implies that trans identification is ahistorical and timeless. Moreover not all gender nonconforming people use this classical narrative to provide themselves with the same form of psychological closure.

As I argue throughout this book, understanding transsexuality as an ahistorical or biological phenomenon elides the racial and colonial underpinnings of transsexuality. It also obscures the historical emergence of trans autobiography as a genre. Transsexual autobiographies not only speak the truth of transsexual bodily desires and experiences but actively constitute and reproduce them *as* truth in nonmedical discursive formations that are just as powerful as sexological and psychiatric texts. If, to misquote David Halperin, transsexuality is a discursive, *transphobic* construction "that has come to be recognized as an object under the epistemological regime known as realism,"[22] the questions animating this chapter are thus: How do travel narratives in trans memoirs strategically shore up the constitution of the transsexual as an actual, living subject with a familiar, coherent life story? What kind of transsexual subject is produced through this move, and what racial and colonial topographies underpin it? To claim that transsexuality is a construction is not, of course, to claim that transsexuality is fake or a psychological fantasy. Rather, consistent with a Foucauldian methodology, it is to suggest that even the most deeply felt bodily experiences relating to gender and sexuality are historically and culturally mediated.[23] Or, to echo the words of Joan Scott, it requires that we question the constructed nature of trans experience and how trans subjects are constituted as different in the first place.[24]

Traveling Memoir

If transsexual autobiographies confer significance on relations of mobility between certain places, they do so in the context of particular understandings of place, home, and mobility. In this chapter I attend not only to how imagined and textualized places—Casablanca, Venice, Europe, Britain, and the United States—subtend identities but also the ways in which transsexuality has transformed particular places and furnished them with a significance they would not otherwise have. To make sense of these categories, we need a rigorous theorization of how identity, race, and gender relate to place. Feminist geography, especially Doreen Massey's work, is very useful here. In "A Global Sense of Place," Massey resists the notion of place as stable and coherent by pointing out that places are produced by social relations. For Massey, the identity of a place is conditioned by histories of imperialism and decolonization, global capital circuits, and nation-building efforts that seek to differentiate a place and its culture from its exterior.

Massey also calls into question the universality of mobility as something that all humans (and nonhumans) can perform in the same manner. While it is often assumed that within global capitalism capital moves freely while human mobility is increasingly regulated, this needs to be complicated. The smoothness or arduousness of mobility—the amount of effort expended to move—is conditioned by race, nationality, language, gender, and sexuality. Indeed, the unmarked capacity of whiteness and economic or social privilege to be mobile contribute to epistemological assumptions that mobility itself *should* progress smoothly and easily, without difficulty. As Massey points out, women's material mobility is restricted in various ways.[25] People without citizenship also have their mobility regulated, both to facilitate low-wage labor flows and to restrict unauthorized movement. This works in terms of flow across national borders but also flow through all kinds of urban and nonurban architectures, for example, through interactions with law enforcement and other street dwellers. As I illustrate in later chapters, this particularly pertains to gender nonconforming bodies and makes passing as non-trans a matter of life or death for many trans people. Massey also critiques the hegemonic understanding of global space-time compression in geography and cultural studies. Counter to claims that the compression of space and time created by the internet has universally "speeded things up," Massey contends that different social groups and individuals are placed in distinct ways in relation to time-space compression: "Some people are more in charge of [space-time compression] than others; some initiate flows and movement, others don't; some are more on the receiving-end of it than others; some are effectively imprisoned by it."[26]

Following on from this, we need to question the epistemological representation of travel as something everyone does or can do. "Travel" is usually understood as a leisure activity involving temporary geographical movement by car, plane, or boat, with implications of luxury, affluence, and ease. This is assumed to be a universal experience. Transnational feminist scholarship has questioned the historical and cultural specificity of that understanding of travel by pointing out how travel for some kinds of subjects is facilitated by colonial and capitalist global circuits.[27] As James Clifford observes in *Routes: Travel and Translation in the Late Twentieth Century*, the specific cultural, political, and economic conditions travelers move within determine how travel can be understood as liberating or disenfranchising.[28] At this point the distinctions and disjunctures between travel and other forms of mobility, such as immigration, become paramount. Travel is popularly defined through its status as a high-class pastime with significations of autonomy and privilege. That the term *travel* itself describes a universal form of geographical mobility reveals the hegemony of Eurocentric, imperialist forms of mobility, as Grewal observes. Grewal also points out that the deployment of travel as a universal practice elides forms of mobility that do not fit the imperialist formation, including migration, deportation, indenture, and slavery.[29]

In its universalized form, as Mark Simpson observes, travel relates to modernist themes of freedom, individuation, leisure, reflection, and detachment: "[It] treats as universal, as the common condition and capacity of all persons, what are in fact the dispositions, privileges, and values . . . of a particular social class under capitalism."[30] If travel aligns with the unmarked universalisms of the Enlightenment, and the stereotypical Western traveler is one who remains blissfully unaware of the inequalities and divisions enabling him to pass through "other" places, the immigrant is a figure simultaneously signifying aspirational reinvention and racialized difference. In the rest of this chapter the distinctions between travel and immigration map very different theorizations of what transsexuality is and how to produce it, quite consciously, as an acceptable and intelligible subject position. Transnational feminism's interrogation of the distinction between travel and immigration is indispensable here: as Kaplan observes, critiquing the distinction between travel and immigration and their appearance at particular conjunctures requires unpacking the uneven juxtaposition of both categories.[31] On one hand, in Morris's work we see an echo of the tradition of classical modernist British travel narratives of nineteenth-century imperialism. The equation of transsexuality with immigration in McCloskey's *Crossing* and Boylan's *She's Not There* depends on a different political form, that of liberal multiculturalism, what Jodi Melamed describes as the incorporation of knowledge about racial and cultural difference into state discourses that both prepared citizens to be multicultural and commodified racialized cultures.[32] Under the terms of this commodification, first world travelers can appropriate a racialized category of identity (immigrant) and racially unmarked transsexuality becomes legible by equating it with the displacement of immigration. Rather than modeling their memoirs on the European orientalist tradition of travel writing, as Morris does, McCloskey and

Boylan narrate their experiences of transsexuality through the melancholic introjection of racial others who are understood to have experienced the trauma of displacement. In both *Crossing* and *She's Not There*, introjecting and incorporating that trauma becomes a way for the white transsexual memoirist to account for the trauma and loss she encounters during transition. Marking the historical shift from a frankly imperialist, British-based vision of white transsexuality to an American liberal multicultural vision exemplifies how transsexuality is narrated differently in nations with different colonial and imperial histories and within different forms of governmentality. However, it also allows us to account for how liberal states have moved from categorizing transness as a unique condition to an identity equivalent to and to any other within neoliberal governance premised on competing formations of "diversity." In McCloskey's, Morris's, and Boylan's memoirs trans travelers' freedom to move still, somehow, goes unmarked. Investigating the racial logics that inform these three transsexual memoirs, I show how the classical transsexual subject is marked by whiteness and trace how these narratives shore up whiteness and racial hierarchies in their quest to make transsexuality legible. In all three cases racial difference is something consumable: a movable feast that renders white transsexuality legible and knowable.

The Trans British Empire: Jan Morris's *Conundrum*

Casablanca's reputation as the "sex change capital of the world" in the 1960s and 1970s appears on the surface to have been entirely coincidental. However, a confluence of factors made it the perfect location for practicing gender reassignment surgeries. Following a protracted struggle for independence with the French colonial regime that ended in 1956, Morocco was a popular tourist destination for rich, bohemian Europeans avoiding the growing presence of "vulgar" mass tourist economies in more accessible Mediterranean locales.[33] The cosmopolitan port city of Casablanca supported a large Moroccan middle class as well as the colonial French population.[34] Morocco had a reputation as more liberal and stable than other North African cities, which contributed to its cachet as an elite, exotic tourist destination. The capital until 1956, Tangier was frequented by artists, intellectuals, and bohemians from Europe and North America and a circle of famous gay men, including André Gide, Roland Barthes, Jean Genet, Paul Bowles, William S.

Burroughs, and Allen Ginsberg.[35] In the 1960s Western hippies began to travel to Morocco in large numbers.

In this environment Georges Burou's clinic—which provided obstetrics and gynecology services as well as abortion to the French population and foreign visitors—fared well. Abortion was illegal in France until 1975. While abortion was also criminalized in Morocco until 1975, the political turmoil of Moroccan decolonization and later national independence may have enabled Burou to operate in an atmosphere of legal oversight. He appears to have skillfully negotiated both this oversight and the privileges accorded wealthy French colonials to provide health services that were illegal for Moroccans at the time. In this context of an early reproductive tourism economy, GRS fit right in. Unlike with abortion, no formal laws existed in Morocco to prohibit gender reassignment surgeries. This allowed Burou's GRS practice to proceed without regulation at a time when such surgeries were becoming more regulated globally, and thus more difficult to obtain elsewhere.[36]

Burou's clinic catered to foreign visitors as well as middle-class Moroccans. One of these foreign visitors was Jan Morris. In 1974 Morris published *Conundrum*, a recounting of her life in relation to her gender transition. The *Daily Mail* called it "the best first-hand account ever written by a traveler across the boundaries of sex"; this description also appears on the front cover of the Faber and Faber paperback edition. Morris had already found considerable fame in Britain as a travel writer and journalist before *Conundrum*'s publication. She had worked as a journalist for the Arab News Agency for many years and published numerous popular travel books. *Conundrum* is both literary and self-consciously witty, written for an educated reading public that was already familiar with Morris as a literary figure.

The book opens with the classic childhood moment of transsexual realization: "I was three or perhaps four years old when I realized that I had been born into the wrong body, and should really be a girl." What follows includes a detailed account of Morris's deferral of gender nonconforming desires through her early adulthood, marriage, and career and her decision to transition in her forties. As in other transsexual memoirs, Morris's identification as transsexual unfolds through her discovery of earlier autobiographical accounts. In her early twenties she discovers Lili Elbe's *Man into Woman* in a bookstore. Reading that book gives Morris hope that, like Elbe, she too might someday achieve her dream of womanhood. However, a number of sexologists and psychiatrists assure Morris that she will grow out of it. Then, in 1954, she meets Dr. Harry Benjamin, who diagnoses her as a "trans-sexual." But he too counsels her to keep trying to live life as a man. Morris recounts taking estrogen on and off for years before deciding to undertake permanent hormone therapy in her late thirties. She describes how estrogen injections feminize her appearance. But hormones merely bring her to "the halfway mark": they turn her into "something perilously close to a hermaphrodite, neither one sex nor the other." Eventually she decides that she must put an end to ambiguity and obtain gender reassignment surgery: "I had reached the frontier between the sexes, and it was time for me to explore life on the far side"—as a woman.[37]

Psychiatrists overseeing her case at London's Charing Cross Gender Identity Clinic would not approve her for surgery unless she agreed to divorce her wife. Instead Morris sought GRS from Burou in Casablanca. Gender reassignment surgery for Morris is the definitive marker of womanhood, and her account of obtaining surgery confirms her understanding that gender is spatial and gender transition is a form of crossing over. Simultaneously the spatial and geographical attributes of the location in which she has the operation become overdetermined with transformational—and feminizing—qualities. Burou, she writes, "did not bother himself much with diagnosis or pre-treatment . . . and imposed no conditions, legal or moralistic." Thus, "as [Morris] had gone for so many consolations and distractions before," she ventures to Casablanca, or as she puts it, "foreign parts beyond the law."[38] Her account of her experience of GRS occurs in the final chapters of *Conundrum* and offers a richly detailed and unabashedly orientalist perspective on Casablanca.

Upon arriving in Casablanca, Morris draws attention to its status as a modern, "noisy and ugly" French colonial city. But she yearns for a more romantic, "authentically" exotic experience. The tension between reality and her desires permeates the following passages:

> It was really like a visit to a wizard. I saw myself, as I walked that evening through those garish streets, as a figure of fairy tale. . . . The office blocks might not look like castle walls, nor the taxis like camels or carriages, but I still sometimes heard the limpid Arab music, and smelt the pungent Arab smells, that had for so long pervaded my life, and I could suppose it to be some city of fable, of phoenix and

fantasy, where transubstantiations were regularly effected, when the omens were right and the moon in its proper phase.[39]

While Morris freely admits to the disparity between her wishes and reality—in fact the tension between them structures her retelling of this experience—she persists in depicting Casablanca as an exotic and premodern location. Her nostalgic projection of exoticism onto Casablanca finds specificity in her description of Burou's clinic. Here too she is not limited by fact. The Clinique du Parc turns out to be in the modern part of the city, but Morris sticks to her hope that the clinic will turn out to be "something smoky in the bazaar." Her account of meeting the clinic's administrator contains descriptions that echo not only the stereotype of the European tourist getting lost in a dark and labyrinthine North African city but also narratives equating the Orient with veiled women or the interiority of the harem: "I was led along corridors and up staircases into the inner premises of the clinic. The atmosphere thickened as we proceeded. The rooms became more heavily curtained, more velvety, more voluptuous. . . . There was a hint of heavy perfume. Presently I saw, advancing upon me through the dim alcoves of this retreat, which distinctly suggested to me the allure of a harem, a figure no less recognizably odalisque. It was Madame B—." This association continues into Morris's account of convalescence from surgery and her return home. The days spent in recovery from surgery seem to "loiter by, orientally." Fatima, the head nurse, is described as a "true figure of the seraglio," who works as hard as if she was "reporting directly to the Sultan." On the flight home to London, Morris describes feeling "like something new out of Africa."[40] Her literary response to the contact zone of Casablanca is to assume and appropriate its otherness, figuratively taking a part of it with her home to England.

Morris is not the only autobiographer to orientalize Casablanca in this way. The model and celebrity April Ashley visited Burou in the mid-1960s, and in her autobiography, *April Ashley's Odyssey*, she frames her narrative similarly. Ashley recounts arriving in Morocco alone and dressing glamorously to eat couscous the night before her surgical appointment, and she describes directing a taxi to take her past the clinic on her way back to the hotel. In an almost word-for-word repetition of Morris's account of precisely the same failed expectation, Ashley writes that instead of the "Egyptian temple" she had hoped for, the clinic looked "just like a clinic."[41] It is worth noting the conflation in both accounts between Casablanca and the authors' fantasy of Egyptian or generically "Eastern" temples, music, and bazaars. To the orientalist eye, the specific localities of North Africa merge into one homogeneous otherworld. The space, culture, and architecture of these specific North African locations merge into one indistinguishable Orient.

In his analysis of *Conundrum*, Prosser suggests that this urge to write Casablanca as a site of exotic and mystical transformation is a way for Morris to write sex reassignment as "a crucial gendered turning-point—in some sense, a transsexual boundary or border": "The orientalization of Casablanca, the rich description of the place itself, function as a metaphorical device for the subject's feminization. . . . Drawing on a founding myth of the West about the East's femininity, the autobiographer suggests that simply by being in this locale she undergoes feminization."[42] Thus, Prosser argues, the East figures as a stage on which the trans autobiographer dramatizes—indeed must dramatize—their final surgical transformation. However, rather than accounting for the orientalism with the desire of the transsexual subject for recognition, as Prosser does, we need a deeper analysis.

Racial difference structures the means by which Morris comes to understand herself as both female and different. In particular Morris's account of GRS in Casablanca cannot be understood without insight into the imperialism and blatant colonial paternalism of her perspective on North Africa and racial difference in general. This was not a perspective born of unfamiliarity; Morris was intimately familiar with West Asia and North Africa from her time as a British Army officer, during which she was stationed in Palestine and Egypt, and her time as a journalist working for the Arab News Agency. As Patrick Holland and Graham Huggan observe, Morris's ideas about gender and identity are overdetermined by an attempt across the entire body of her literary work to "recuperate and imaginatively repossess the British imperial world."[43] In *Conundrum* this takes place both through Morris's identification with a history of British travel writing and through asides about racial difference.

The language used to describe Casablanca in *Conundrum* mirrors Morris's entire literary and historical oeuvre in its tacit articulation of a British colonial ideology. Equating a geographically unspecific Orient with femininity was a hallmark of British imperialist philosophy, politics, and literature. As Rana Kabbani observes, European travel writers metonymized this Orient as a veiled woman: manly colonials and explorers could uncover the putative veil and plunder the sexual, economic, cultural, and imaginative riches beneath, in the style of Richard Burton's *Arabian Nights*.[44] If *Conundrum* codes the East as feminine, it also codes the Britain to which Morris belongs as masculine. Morris surveys, observes, and traverses with the wide-ranging eyes and feet of the colonial explorer. Her novelistic history of Great Britain, *Pax Britannica,* surveys the British Empire at the height of its reach across the nineteenth-century globe and in doing so, others have argued, fantasizes about the recuperation of that empire precisely at the point of its decline.[45] Indeed Morris regards herself as part of the tradition of great British travel writers. As she remarks in *Conundrum,* her "literary master" is Alexander Kinglake, the author of the 1844 epic travelogue *Eothen*.[46]

To grasp Morris's peculiar version of orientalism, it is worth briefly surveying Kinglake's text. *Eothen* is an imperialist Grand Tour of the Middle East and North Africa in which the explicitly racist and ethnocentric Kinglake proves his superiority over the Oriental through heroic quest.[47] Like T. E. Lawrence's *Seven Pillars of Wisdom* and Richard Burton's *Arabian Nights, Eothen* embodies the canon of popular colonial literature, part of the immense body of scholarship and institutional knowledge used to vindicate colonial expansion in North Africa and West Asia.[48] Kinglake himself regarded travel in the Orient as central to the Englishman's identity, reproducing colonial relations with the colonized subject of North Africa, whom Kinglake refers to as "a thing dead and dry—a mental mummy."[49] As Edward Said notes, Kinglake's perspective expresses both the comfortable assumption of national superiority and colonial will toward the Orient and a field on which the colonial subject can feel exceptional.[50] Like Kinglake, Morris tends to represent the Orient in the language of metaphor rather than description. This bears out Kabbani's observation that descriptions of the Orient were so overworked precisely because they had little to do with material places and much more to do with orientalist writers' desire for a malleable space in which to dramatize their own becoming.[51]

Cultural theorists have pointed to how the spatial logics of *home* and *away* consolidate European modernity in other contexts, such as class. "The paradox of Eurocentric identity," Jacques Rancière writes, "is that you must travel to disclose it. The Same can be recognized on condition that it is an Other. It is identical to its concept in so far as it is else-where. . . . Spatialization ensures that things and people stay at 'their' place and cling to their identity."[52] To illustrate this point, Rancière reads nineteenth-century narratives recounting travel in urban slums. Afterward he returns to the serene, open spaces of the European middle or upper classes. The purpose of journeys like these, Rancière writes, is to locate the ground that defines and enables the idea of modernity through its contact with the uncivilized or premodern. For Rancière, travel to the outside—the elsewhere or underside of capitalism—neutralizes the otherness that resides within the Western, male, white subject. The Paris slums externalize difference in a specific place and time, thus rendering identity safe. While Rancière's focus here is on the difference between the (lumpen) proletariat of the slums and an affluent, literate upper and middle class, his insight applies equally to the colonial encounters of the nineteenth-century travel writers who influenced Morris. As Kabbani observes, British colonial travelers imagined the Orient as a screen upon which Occidental fantasies of self-dramatization could play out.[53] On this screen the "real" other is erased—or never imagined to have an autonomous existence in the first place. Morris's account of gender transition echoes these coordi-nates but with the crucial difference that her identity shifts: in be-coming a woman, Morris nominally undoes the stability of the white, Western, male subject. However, this shift is mollified by displacing indeterminacy to the outside. Recall Morris's remark that on leaving Casablanca she felt like "something new out of Africa." This illustrates the theory of circumventing gender indeterminacy by way of displac-ing it, as I outlined in chapter 1. Read this way, Morris's movement from Europe to Morocco to Europe signifies a return home having ingested the Orient, domesticated and transubstantiated into proper feminin-ity. While the boundaries between male and female are permeable, what makes them permeable is the edict that the boundaries between here and elsewhere remain closed.

If the exotic character of Casablanca confers an affective sense of femininity on Morris, at the same time another transubstantiation is taking place. The city of Casablanca grounds and incorporates the difference—gendered indeterminacy, in-betweenness—that has until now resided in Morris. Substituting that indeterminacy for her new vagina, the sign of womanhood, the Casablanca experience prepares Morris for a return to the civilized world, in which binary gender is all-important. For Morris, home doubly signifies as womanhood and as Britain: not only the actual nation but the perspective, the civilization, and the culture of British imperialism. Indeed indeterminacy appears to be transferred to the East, the traditional receptacle for undesirable attributes in imperial culture. This geographical staging, wherein Morris's assumption of femininity depends not only on the assumption of femininity in the East but also on an exchange of indeterminacy for stable gender, structures the narrative.

Conundrum is also replete with asides about people of color in general, and blackness in particular, that assist Morris in her quest. In one chapter she admits to an abiding antipathy toward the non-Islamic parts of Africa: "I loathed the fetishes, the meaningless high jinks, the edible slugs, the tribal savageries, the arrogant upstart politicians, the ludicrous epauletted generals, the frightening art, the empty history." But this racist antipathy wanes when Morris can conceive of African culture as something that reflects her own psychological dilemmas. Hearing an Ashanti folk tale shifts her viewpoint, and she comes to see that "within the African mind there might be exact equivalents of my own conceptions. . . . I began to see that there could be African versions of myself, mirror-images of me, whose preoccupations were just as obsessive. . . . So over the years, on repeated visits, I came to regard black Africa as a solace." What Morris describes as a growing empathy transforms her understanding of blackness from something threatening and perverse to something benign or even useful, something whose main purpose is its "curative properties."[54] Here Africa is meaningless until Morris "discovers" its value and begins to extract or appropriate that value.[55] Yet Morris still understands this value as primitive and uncivilized: "I have come to see within the mystery of the African genius, veiled as it is by superstition, fear and resentment, something of the earth itself."[56] Morris stereotypically identifies African culture's "uncivilized" primitive closeness to the earth as fruitful for her own dilemmas of gender identity and difference. This passage resonates with Renato Rosaldo's term *imperialist nostalgia*, wherein racial domination can be rendered pure and innocent if it is represented as a love of what colonialism and modernity have destroyed.[57] Morris's representation of blackness is consistent with her characterization of all forms of racial otherness in *Conundrum*. Reading from a playbook as old as colonialism itself, she constructs the many continents she visits as a travel writer as a screen on which to project her own fantasies of self-improvement and transformation, without which such transformation would not be possible. As in her account of surgery in Casablanca, the black other is never imagined to have an autonomous existence. In fact the autonomy and immanent difference of the black other is explicitly understood as a threat to Morris's white British existence.

Additionally, *Conundrum* needs to be read within the historical context of its publication in the early 1970s. In 1972 Great Britain hardly represented a colonial British home in relation to the perceived otherness of the Orient. Independence and decolonization movements in South Asia, Africa, and the Caribbean led many once-colonized subjects to migrate to Britain in large numbers. This immigration flow challenged the equation of British national identity with whiteness. In fact, people of color were central to the ascendancy of British imperialism for centuries and had been present in the "metropole," if largely unacknowledged. However, as Stuart Hall remarks, the 1970s marked a moment in which "'race' had finally come home to Britain."[58] Meanwhile, the global economic crisis of the early 1970s inaugurated neoliberal economic policies and resulted in Margaret Thatcher's later election as prime minister in 1979. To echo Grewal's critique of Pratt's work in *Imperial Eyes*, the "contact zone" took place in those spaces designated by imperialism as the "peripheries" of the modern world *and* in the modern metropolis itself.[59]

Morris completely ignores these challenges to whiteness within Britain. She takes the upheavals occasioned by decolonization and the gradual dismantling of the British Empire as important only outside Europe. In *Conundrum*, her accounts of working as a journalist include a passage that surveys this immense political, economic, and cultural change. Morris never refers to decolonization or communism by name. But she recalls the wars, rebellions, and diplomatic squabbles ensuing from decolonial struggle as chaos intruding on order. For Morris, the 1970s marks the mourned passing of Britain's global imperial power, and she feels humiliation and defeat on behalf of her country: "I watched my own beloved [British] army floundering in degradation as it was forced, year by year, from its last imperial strongholds, now and then spitting back like a cornered animal." She quotes the famous British spy who defected to the Soviet Union, Kim Philby, laughing at a passage she had written about Britain's role in the 1956 Israeli invasion of Egypt as having a "despairing, pitiful dignity . . . like a thoroughbred gone wild among mustangs." In Morris's eyes, Britain is innocent and relatively powerless in its foreign policy—a wounded animal merely "spitting back" at the attacks on British rule in the Global South. These political upheavals are chiefly significant for Morris as affairs of a global and public masculine world she wants to flee: "It was like stepping from cheap theatre to reality, to pass from the ludicrous goings-on of minister's office or ambassador's study to the private house behind, where women were to be found doing real things." In moving toward gender transition Morris rejects the global stage and her masculine place in it. Meanwhile, she represents the Britain she understands as her abiding home as bucolic and timeless, as in the description of the Welsh country house where she lives in the final period before GRS: "up a bumpy lane, protected by ash trees, beeches and tumble-down oaks."[60] Morris's nostalgia for imperialism reveals a conservative desire for stability in the midst of social change. It also betrays a deep racial anxiety that decolonization might mean people of color must be recognized as more than a reflective screen for Morris' own fantasies. More important for the purposes of my project, Morris's late twentieth-century achievement of transsexual recognition and self-understanding through colonial metaphors and British nationalist imperialism foreshadows twenty-first-century exceptionalist homonationalism, wherein transgender rights and recognition are understood to be the accomplishments of a modern West, opposed to a queerphobic or transphobic premodern and barbarous other. (I take up homonationalist tropes further in chapter 3.)

Throughout *Conundrum* it is Morris's status as a travel writer and the privilege of mobility that allow her to make her transsexual journey. *Conundrum* tacitly understands travel as a given. To venture beyond the law and beyond national borders in such an autonomous manner requires proper interpellation into the sphere of the law to begin with, as well as the financial resources to escape the nation at will. It also assumes that these rights of passage are exclusive, premised on whiteness: the colonial other is never imagined as surveilling Morris's own Welsh home in the way she does Moroccan homes. In fact the freedom afforded by wealth and whiteness is *Conundrum*'s invisible narrative motor. Although Morris is socially marginalized by her transsexuality, she also occupies a social position that enables her to avoid many of the consequences of that marginalization.

As I argued in chapter 1, the epistemological structure of traditional transsexuality as a career or trajectory depicted and constituted by autobiography relies on navigation through transition as a temporary remove to a location elsewhere, followed by a return home. *Conundrum* equally locates home in the bucolic Britain of Morris's dreams and in her womanhood. Morris understands her capacity to traverse the globe as a given. She is the privileged upper-class traveler for whom the cost of flights, hotels, and recreation barely factor in her decision to go anywhere. She also travels autonomously, of her own free will; she understands the capacity to be geographically mobile as a universal attribute, part of what one does and must do as a transsexual subject.[61]

Morris depicts transsexual travel through metaphors of colonial and racial privilege. Several later North American memoirs highlight experiences of marginalization as trans, appropriating immigrant and forced mobility narratives. These later trans memoirs index the intensified instabilities of late twentieth-century capitalist globalization. In McCloskey's *Crossing* and Boylan's *She's Not There*, the trans person as immigrant is framed as embarking upon a no less heroic enterprise. Rather than representing the transsexual subject as unique and invisibly privileged, as Morris does, McCloskey and Boylan equate transsexual transition with immigration, remaking transsexuality into a minority, marginalized subject position.

Analogizing the Immigrant: *Crossing* and *She's Not There*

Morris's field of reference for mapping a transnational imaginary of gender reassignment is premised firmly on the distinction between Britain and its colonies. In shifting geographical and temporal focus to two memoirs that were written in the United States in the late 1990s and early 2000s, I turn now to a context in which imperial ideological strategies for differentiating the metropolis from the periphery have been replaced by very different ideological and material distinctions between mobility and racial difference. McCloskey's *Crossing* and Boylan's *She's Not There* were produced in the context of US liberal multiculturalism, which Melamed glosses as the institutional recuperation of the transnational civil rights and decolonial social movements that erupted during the 1970s and 1980s.[62] In particular, liberal multicultural discourse produced racial difference as part of a national tradition of cultural pluralism. Transsexual memoirs that appear in this period understand transsexuals—who are implicitly white—as a minority modeled on and analogous to racial minorities. Geographic mobility appears in the form of the American immigrant saga: a romanticized vision of immigrants as simultaneously displaced and nation-consolidating subjects whose experience is available for the white transsexual author to identify with and, in doing so, explain the displacement and loss of gender transition. This narrative obscures the exclusionary racial logics of the US nation-state and injustice of US immigration regulation.

The texts I read in relation to this argument are both well-received autobiographies by white, middle-class trans women who, like Morris, had achieved recognition in their fields prior to gender transition. Deirdre McCloskey is a well-known Chicago School economist; Jennifer Finney Boylan was already an established novelist before she published *She's Not There* in 2003. Both texts appeared after the mid-1990s explosion of utopian transgender politics and culture I gestured to in chapter 1. Yet neither book is stylistically invested in destroying gender binaries or playing with the textual limits of narrative in the manner of Bornstein's *Gender Outlaw* or Feinberg's *Transgender Warriors*. Instead both books read as straightforward literary autobiographies and present a conservative imaginary of gender and transsexuality. *Crossing* and *She's Not There* narrate their authors proceeding through similarly traditional steps in transitioning from male to female: social role change, hormone therapy, a variety of surgeries (including genital surgery), and successful and productive careers as women. For this reason, as with *Conundrum*, I read both texts as specifically *transsexual*, not transgender, memoirs.

In *Crossing*, McCloskey relates the story of her childhood, a straight male adult life, medical transition, her estrangement from her partner and children, and the social and emotional changes that accompany her entry into what she calls the "strong world of women."[63] While it follows many of the generic conventions of classic transsexual autobiography described in chapter 1, *Crossing* diverges from those conventions in some notable ways. The vast majority of events are narrated in the third person, intercut with short italicized sections written in the first person, capturing McCloskey's thoughts at the time. McCloskey refers to herself using different names depending on what stage of gender transition she is in. When she is living as male, she is Donald; during the period of gender transition she refers to herself as Dee; and in the last third of the book she refers to herself as Deirdre. McCloskey states at the outset that she prefers not to use the term *transsexual*. She categorizes transsexuality and transgender under the rubric of "gender crossers" and "gender crossing."[64] She uses the phrase *gender crossing* to refer to anyone with a nonnormative gender identity. And yet, because McCloskey's own biographical path traverses a medical and surgical transition from male to female, the term *crossing* comes to refer primarily to the process of medical gender transition.

McCloskey's tendency to equate transness with racial or cultural displacement is a constant throughout her book. She uses the metaphor of displacement primarily to account for her experience to nontrans people, both readers of the book itself and the non-transsexual characters to which she must relate her transition within its pages. On the first page she explains, "Gender is a good deal like foreign travel." She continues:

> Most people would like to go to Venice for a vacation. Most people, if they could magically do it, would like to try out the other gender for a day. . . . The Venice visitors as a group can be thought of as all the "crossgendered," from stone butch dykes to postoperative male-to-female gender crossers, all the traversers, permanent or temporary. . . . A few people go to Venice regularly, and you can think of them as the cross-dressers. . . . A tiny fraction [want] to *become* Venetians.[65]

It's this tiny fraction that McCloskey calls "permanent gender crossers," or transsexuals.[66] The way her trans continuum maps onto ideas about mobility here echoes similar conceits in *Conundrum* (especially the mention of Venice: Morris writes at length about her travels there). But McCloskey identifies with a particular fantasy of crossing: the story of the immigrant who endures exclusion and poverty, works hard, and is finally, triumphantly absorbed into American culture, in other words, the fantasy found in the tourist-targeted histories on display at the Ellis Island Immigration Museum in New York. She writes:

> On a trip to New York to see a friend after my own crossing I stood in the hall of photographs at Ellis Island and wept at the courage. Crossing cultures from male to female is big; it highlights some of the differences between men and women, and some of the similarities too. . . . My crossing was costly and opposed, which is too bad.

But my crossing has been dull, easy, comfortable, compared with Suyuan's or Giuseppe's outer migrations.[67]

The enormity of gender transition appears only translatable here through the metaphor of immigration. And yet just as she submits such a comparison, McCloskey immediately retracts it: her own transformation was "dull, easy, comfortable" in relation to those who, in the vision of Ellis Island, actually immigrated to the United States. The invocation of the names Giuseppe and Suyuan does particular work: these names stand in metonymically for the universalization of nonwhite subjects who, for McCloskey, are defined by their participation in the classical US immigrant saga. (The nationalist fantasy of assimilation that drives this immigrant saga is key, and I return to a deeper analysis of it below.) Cultural displacement is at the crux of this imagined comparison. Later, in a letter to colleagues informing them that she is changing her name to Deirdre and now needs to be regarded as a woman, McCloskey writes, "You cannot imagine the relief in adopting my correct gender. Imagine if you felt French but had been raised in Minnesota."[68]

Like *Conundrum, Crossing* shifts location regularly, following McCloskey as she travels around the globe: within the United States for academic conferences and cross-dressing conventions; to San Francisco and Philadelphia for various surgeries; to the Netherlands, where she lives and works in the years immediately after her "crossing"; to Sydney, where she undergoes genital reconstructive surgery; and home to Iowa. A key episode that assumes particular affective and narrative significance in the text occurs when McCloskey describes initiating long-cherished plans to live full time as a woman. As she gains approval from psychiatrists to begin hormonal and medical transition, her closest relationships begin to unravel. When she tells her family about her decision to transition, her wife and adult children cannot accept what is happening and eventually cut contact. Her sister, a psychology professor, decides that McCloskey is mentally unstable and has her committed to a mental hospital several times. Each time McCloskey manages to convince doctors that she is sane. To retreat from this upheaval McCloskey flies to friends in San Francisco who host her while she undergoes facial feminization and breast augmentation surgeries. Her stay in San Francisco allows her to circulate socially as a woman for the first time:

Dee dressed carefully in blouse and women's blue jeans, earrings, the reddish wig, with makeup to cover the worst damage from the electrolysis. Down the stairs and into the kitchen, a woman.

After Thanksgiving she moved to Marty and Esther's house, though no one knew. They were trying to keep the knowledge from Dee's sister. Dee's sleep was disturbed by fears of her sister's arriving suddenly with her state power, her police and psychiatrists and locks. Dee talked to a lawyer in San Francisco over the phone and prepared legally for renewed assaults, but in California the laws of commitment are not so easily manipulated as in Iowa or Illinois. If the police came to the front door of the house Dee planned to slip out the back. . . . Maybe.[69]

Following this, Dee arranges with friends in the Netherlands to take up a two-year visiting professorship in Rotterdam. When she leaves the United States for Holland, about to live full time as a woman for the first time, the narrative momentarily breaks out of the third person and into first-person authorial mode. The final sentence of this chapter bids farewell to the United States and stands out as a postscript to this string of traumatic events, which have also involved loss of contact with her sister, her ex-wife, and her adult children: "Goodbye for now, oh my sweet country, cruel and violent, loving and generous."[70]

McCloskey frames her loss as grief for a "lost homeland," writing herself as metaphorically experiencing a literal form of immigrant subjectivity. However implicitly, this final sentence also addresses a "you." On the face of it, that "you" refers to the United States ("oh my sweet country"), but this sentence could also be read as metonymically addressing the people located within the United States who have been personally cruel toward McCloskey. It is this attempt to narrate the trauma and loss of crossing that most clearly demonstrates the literary resonance of McCloskey's view of transsexuality as immigration. Rather than the matter-of-fact and practical tone in which she describes the routine business and leisure activity of an upper-middle-class academic elsewhere in the book, the descriptions of travel in these chapters are saturated with affect. McCloskey relates her excitement at the new life waiting for her in Europe and as a woman, yet also expresses grief and regret. At the one moment in which McCloskey the author allows the wall of third-person narration to fall and speaks powerfully in the first person, it is in a voice lamenting the loss of a geographical home.

She's Not There: A Life in Two Genders features a similar trajectory of global travel. Like McCloskey and Morris, Boylan began transition in middle age; in her account, living as a woman means coming out to her wife and children and potentially disrupting a successful career as a writer and professor. Boylan decides on the necessity of affirming her gender identity after long attempts at repressing or ignoring it. Her struggle to do so and manage her fear of losing her family and career forms the book's plot. As in *Crossing* and *Conundrum*, a pivotal moment occurs when Boylan finally resolves to "do something" about the persistent cross-gender feelings she's experienced throughout her life. This pivotal moment takes place as she spends a year on a fellowship in Ireland. In a chapter titled "The Troubles," Boylan recounts her fear of losing everything. She informs her wife, Grace, that she wants to cross-dress and begins to dress as a woman at home after their children have gone to bed. (Telling Grace that she is a transsexual comes later: "I didn't want it to threaten our marriage or our lives.") Despite this progress, Boylan recounts this period as a very difficult one. She deals with her dilemma "in the traditional Irish manner—drinking heavily, singing songs, and wearing sheer-to-waist pantyhose." Coming to terms with gender transition involves grief and isolation: "There was a sense of urgency and desperation in my heart. Slowly I was becoming aware of how little time might be left to me as a man. I feared that our return to America, in July, would begin a period of transformation and loss."[71]

In one scene Boylan recounts getting drunk at a traditional dance while she listens to Irish jigs and ballads:

> In the ballads I heard the constant theme of emigration. Surely they had me in mind when they sang about having to leave the land of one's birth because of the Great Hunger. Standing on the deck of a coffin ship, waving farewell to one's sweetheart. Making a difficult ocean crossing. Arriving at last in a new world, the land of promise, the land of freedom. But never quite fitting in, in the new land, always speaking with a trace of a foreign accent.
>
> Sometimes I think the best way to understand gender shift is to sing a song of diaspora.
>
> > Our ship at the moment lies in Derry harbor
> > To bear us away—o'er the wide swelling sea.
> > May heaven be our pilot, and grant us fine breezes

Til we reach the green fields of Amerikey.
Oh, come to the land where we shall be happy.
Don't be afraid of the storm, or the sea.
And when we cross o'er, we shall surely discover,
That place is the land of Sweet Liberty.[72]

On hearing this song, Boylan writes, she bursts into tears, convinced that the metaphorical crossing she is embarking on will result in losing Grace and the children, or a worse fate: "Surely, before I reached the green fields, I would perish in the storm. Or, even if I did successfully *cross o'er*, how could I live without the love of the girl I'd left behind?"[73]

In *Crossing* and *She's Not There* an encounter with immigrant stories—and an identification with immigrant experience—results in the protagonist's tears. Both texts understand transsexuality as having to give up family relationships, friendships, and professional life. Both McCloskey and Boylan turn to the immigrant as the figure who personifies their own sense of sacrifice, hardship, and fear of loss. McCloskey identifies with Suyuan and Giuseppe, while Boylan identifies with the Irish history of immigration to the United States.

For both writers, a national fantasy of the US immigrant is key, the myth that all newcomers to the United States begin at the same level and "are assimilated into the national fabric by dint of hard work, sacrifice, and a willingness to conform to 'American' norms."[74] This fantasy has at least two effects. First, it renders all experiences of immigration equivalent. Second, the United States is imagined to guarantee the freedom and liberty that other countries cannot. The fulcrum of this national fantasy is Ellis Island, where McCloskey stands and weeps "at the courage." McCloskey's romantic and melancholic introjection of crossing in her descriptions of visiting Ellis Island renders all immigration processes equivalent. Meanwhile Boylan is preoccupied with the romantic and mournful image of crossing a great sea and bidding farewell to loved ones, paralleling her fear of losing her own loved ones and crossing to female. Yet what drives Boylan's citation of the "song of diaspora" is crossing to the United States in particular, imagined as superior to other nations in which hardship and loss are the norm.

That two white trans women authors feel license to equate their own experiences of transness with those of immigrants reeks of cultural appropriation. Cultural appropriation describes what happens when cultural representation takes racial otherness as an artifact that is endlessly available for white subjects to mimic and incorporate. In the process instances of cultural appropriation flatten cultural difference and erase material histories of white supremacy. bell hooks wrote famously that within US popular culture, ethnicity and racial difference have become "spice, seasoning that can liven up the dull dish that is mainstream white culture." (One is reminded here of McCloskey's admission that her crossing was "dull" compared to Suyuan's or Giuseppe's.) As hooks points out, cultural appropriation assuages white feelings of lack while also offering the fantasy of reconciliation with otherness.[75] In *Crossing* and *She's Not There* immigrant identity circulates as a fetish, available for appropriation outside of its context. The value of the injury and subsequent triumph of the immigrant saga become commodifiable and transposable to white trans subjects who did not experience the structural disenfranchisement of the classical immigrant story—and who in fact are able to travel the globe at will, supported by university funds. In this way McCloskey's and Boylan's identification of transness with immigration or crossing relies on a liberal hybridist notion of difference, wherein, as Ien Ang writes, "differences may not be completely erased, but made harmless, domesticated, and amalgamated into a variegated yet comfortable whole."[76]

We should also look closely at the racializing dynamic of the affects with which McCloskey and Boylan narrate these passages. Both frame these moments of comparison with immigration as melancholic moments in which they mourn unresolvable losses and desire what Boylan calls the "land of promise, the land of freedom." Unable to articulate the loss of her previous life passing as male, McCloskey seems able to express the full extent of her loss only by mourning her nation of origin, the United States. Given this affective form, diagnosing McCloskey and Boylan as merely culturally appropriative is not sufficient. Instead I contend that narrating gender transition as the equivalent of the "song of diaspora" or the figure of the immigrant performs a racial melancholic move. Drawing on Freud, Anne Anlin Cheng shows how, in the United States, whiteness operates melancholically "as an elaborate identificatory system based on psychical and social consumption-and-denial." Cheng reads melancholia as a subject's grief for a lost object he cannot relinquish, causing the subject to consume or digest the object. Pushing on Freud's theorization, Cheng contends that melancholia necessitates "multiple layers of denial and exclusion" of the object that the subject must sustain to retain incorporation and simultaneously guard against the object's return. (If the object returned, it would be impossible to grieve or "have" the object internally.) In fact, Cheng argues, exclusion is the goal of melancholic introjection. The parallels with hooks's discussion of racial appropriation are apparent here. However, Cheng expands this discussion into a critique of US racial liberalism, in which, she astutely points out, the white subject does not desire the full loss of the racial other but rather desires to maintain racial others within existing structures.[77]

There is something very particular about the ways McCloskey and Boylan can imagine transsexuality (or transgender) within the US national imaginary. To dig deeper, I return to a consideration of how authors who consider themselves ambassadors for trans people translate transsexuality for a public readership assumed to be non-transgender. Under these conditions personal narrative cannot ignore the political quest for trans recognition, and in fact articulates itself principally *as* a call for recognition of a transsexual identity that is similar to, but distinct from, other identities formed within the liberal or neoliberal imaginary: gays and lesbians, immigrants, people of color, women, disabled people, and so on. Under the terms of this imaginary, one can inhabit only one axis of identification at a time: trans people can imagine themselves as immigrants precisely because they are assumed not to be racial others. Melancholic identification with the immigrant or the diaspora captures the imaginary immigrant racial other as a museum piece whose potential gender nonconformity, as well as her racial exclusion from the American nation, is necessarily denied.

It is equally important to think carefully about the specificity of the imaginary immigrant in McCloskey's and Boylan's national fantasy of immigration. For McCloskey, Ellis Island represents a multicultural "melting pot" that contributes to American nationhood, but which in reality assisted Western Europeans to immigrate to the US. Further, by choosing Ellis Island as the locus of her identification, McCloskey locates immigration firmly in the historical past: the Ellis Island immigration inspection station was closed in 1954. Both accounts are also saturated with the sentimentality of what Matthew Frye Jacobson names a "white ethnic revival," which marked a historical shift in the public language of whiteness. In the 1960s large numbers of white subjects began claiming particularist ethnicities, accessing their heritage as Irish, Norwegian, Polish, and so on. In the process white ethnic revival transformed the symbols of white immigration (such as Ellis Island) into monuments to the national imaginary.[78] Boylan's "song of diaspora" is an Irish ballad that moves her to tears; McCloskey's metaphor for displacement is feeling French in Minnesota. Thus cultural appropriation of otherness proceeds alongside a simultaneous claiming of immigrant heritage as the birthright of white US citizens. As Jacobson points out, the potent mythology that is romanticized here involves forgetting multiple histories: North American settler colonialism; the racial exclusions upon which US immigration policies have been, and still are, based; and the incapacity of the "nation of immigrants" myth to reckon with blackness and the history of chattel slavery.[79] Thus both authors simultaneously incorporate and introject the figure of the immigrant other through racial melancholia and deny racial difference in the service of a vision of a "united," assimilated, multicultural America. As Cheng astutely observes, this is precisely the double bind of racial melancholia: to be caught between rejection and incorporation.

Against Trans Analogy

To critique *Conundrum* for its imperialist underpinning, and to critique the introjection of the immigrant as racial other in *Crossing* and *She's Not There*, is not to dismiss their value as texts. These memoirs play an important role in the mainstream canon of transsexual autobiography; in fact their centrality in that canon is precisely what makes this critique necessary. It is important to remember how the canon comes to be, however, and to avoid blaming trans people for the cultural freight of the representations they produce. As chapter 1 made clear, white middle-class (and upper-class) trans women are made to represent transsexuality precisely because of how the American medical establishment and the popular press enshrined white trans femininity as the definition of *the transsexual* at the moment of its cultural emergence. Aside from the Caitlyn Jenner cottage industry, it is clear that lately the white, middle-class transsexual memoir has largely been abandoned in the public imaginary. The most popular trans memoir of recent memory is surely Janet Mock's *Redefining Realness*, while Laverne Cox's writing and public appearances in 2014 were covered as the "Transgender Tipping Point" in *Time* magazine. Mock is a black Hawai'ian trans woman;

Cox is a black trans woman. Both have publicly spoken out against violence toward trans women of color by individuals, police, courts, and the prison-industrial complex. In comparison to *Redefining Realness* and the enormous groundswell of transgender cultural production in the 2010s—novels, poetry, experimental music, dance, experimental and feature film, and all kinds of other genres of self-expression—the texts I read in this chapter might seem outdated.[80] Yet the recent focus on trans women of color in trans cultural representations evidences a historical shift toward neoliberal multiculturalism, in which trans people of color are championed as representatives of institutional diversity and required to perform more labor as such. In this light it is crucial to retain a historical context for the continual transformation of literary and cultural representations of transness.

Additionally, the deployment of analogy in *Crossing* and *She's Not There* offers a timely reflection of the growing use of analogy in the neoliberal imaginary of transgender rights. Within this imaginary, axes of difference are understood as equivalent precisely because with regard to the distribution of resources and rights in a liberal framework, each population can claim only one piece of the pie. Crudely put, claims for transgender rights and recognition can claim their legitimacy by comparing their plight to a population representing older segments of pie for which injustice is already recognized—and, often, imagined as resolved. In this way the transgender-as-immigrant analogy bears critical similarity to claims that "gay is the new black." When queer communities understand gay as the new black, they place black struggle for rights and restitution of histories of slavery and antiblackness in the past as struggles that have already been won.[81] The use of blackness as an analogy to other forms of struggle is not limited to queer communities, as Jared Sexton contends: "The metaphoric transfer that dismisses the legitimacy of black struggles against racial slavery . . . while it appropriates black suffering as the template for nonblack grievances remains one of the defining features of contemporary political culture."[82] Morgan Bassichis and Dean Spade further point out that "gay is the new black" erases the conditions of black injustice that still exist in neoliberal America and appropriates the "apparently satisfied struggle of black people."[83] In a similar manner analogies between transness and immigrantness consign immigrant struggles to a historical past, erasing the ongoing struggle for justice, rights, and more open borders by immigrants to the United States. More important, the analogy fails to acknowledge the many transgender immigrants who are criminalized and targeted by police, border patrols, and immigration officials in actually existing immigration enforcement.[84]

Of course Boylan and McCloskey articulate a "respectable" narrative of transness that does not involve criminalized activities such as sex work or being an undocumented immigrant. This too is central to the liberal imaginary in which *transgender* joins *immigrant* (and *gay* and *black*) in a claim on the state for rights and recognition. To access full rights in that imaginary a population must demonstrate its good citizenship. Indeed in 2013 Boylan wrote a column about the whistle-blower Chelsea Manning that specifically invokes dignity and responsibility in claiming rights. Critical of Manning for breaking her military oath, Boylan relates how a mentor once told her, "Trans issues [are] still so new to the American consciousness that any trans woman in the public eye [has] to behave in a manner above reproach." Passing this counsel on to Manning, Boylan hopes that Manning will "comport . . . herself with dignity and [accept] responsibility for her actions, [whereupon] she can show that a trans woman is a human being capable of reinvention and redemption."[85] One cannot imagine Boylan supporting a trans of color politics that is loud, fierce, or unapologetically black or Latinx in the world where only dignity and "responsibility" attract entry into the cherished sphere of full recognition. Transgender rights claims that rely on narratives of respectability almost always assume whiteness or seek to discipline trans of color populations into behavior that suppresses racial injustice and lays blame for violence, criminalization, and poverty on the individual trans subject.

As the second part of this book will show, colonial and orientalist visions of transsexual transformation, as well as visions of trans people as traumatized immigrants, circulate just as much within white trans cultural representations now as they ever did.

In excavating these fantasies within past autobiographical representations, we can see the limits of that narrative to account for gender nonconforming lives. If the dominant transsexual narrative depends on a geographical distinction between the *here* of Euro-America and the *elsewhere* of almost anywhere else, what happens to these distinctions when they collide with the materiality of globalization and immigration in the contemporary world? The critique I have made also points to the importance of not erasing the experience of gender non-conforming people who are caught in webs of disadvantage in terms of immigration itself. In chapter 3 I examine these trajectories within representations of migrating trans and gender nonconforming people in documentary film.

CHAPTER THREE

DOCUMENTARY AND

THE METRONORMATIVE

TRANS MIGRATION PLOT

What is put forth as truth is often nothing more than a meaning.
—**Trinh T. Minh-ha,** "The Totalizing Quest of Meaning"

Whether told as historical event or personal experience, representations of transgender life often depend on the power of truth claims. Autobiographical and historical claims to truth, or the real, furnish trans representation with urgency and value. This book focuses on representations of the "real" precisely to highlight such a dynamic. Documentary film offers a different, but related, form of truth-telling to autobiography. From sensationalist television specials to self-made video blogs uploaded to YouTube, documentaries present particular narratives as truth according to generic conventions that govern image, language, sound, and circulation. But as Trinh T. Minh-ha writes in the epigraph, what is offered as truth is often merely one possible interpretation—as she elaborates in the essay, a political interpretation.

The 2006 documentary *Bubot Niyar* begins with an outdoor night scene in Tel Aviv. In the darkness brown bodies are silhouetted in car headlights; junk metal and car parts lean against a concrete wall in the background. The camera catches gold lamé in the headlights, a yellow feather boa, glamorous humans grooming their hair and putting on high heels. We don't know where we are or for which performance the people on camera are preparing. Over this footage the film's director, Tomer Heymann, says in Hebrew, "I met the Paper Dolls five years ago near the Tel Aviv central bus station. They seemed different, out of place. Something about them made me curious." Cut to daylight: Heymann is riding a scooter, holding the camera so that we can see his face reflected in the rearview mirror. He rounds a corner and the camera rights itself to settle on a dim arcade, down which Heymann drives his scooter. The ambience is of a rundown urban landscape; as we will later discover, the central bus station district in Tel Aviv, where many migrant workers live. "Do you know where Giorgio's is?" Heymann calls to a shopkeeper. "I'm looking for Giorgio's beauty salon. A good-looking Filipino guy. Half-man, half-woman." We follow Heymann walking toward a storefront that turns out to be Giorgio's salon. Inside Giorgio cuts Heymann's hair and explains in Hebrew why his drag troupe is called the Paper Dolls. "If you cut paper like this, you get a doll. That's it. We're paper dolls because we're gay." "What does paper have to do with being gay?" Heymann asks. "It's not real," says Giorgio. "It's not a real man or a real woman. The paper isn't real. If you make a doll, it's not real, it's only paper." Heymann continues to interrogate Giorgio about his gender identity:

"Did you grow up as a boy or a girl?"
"As a girl."
"From the beginning?"
"Yes."
"How did you know you were a girl?"

This classic ethnographic arrival scene and subsequent interrogative conversation begins Heymann's exploration of the Paper Dolls, a group of Filipina migrant workers who form a drag troupe.

Bubot Niyar was made in Israel between 2000 and 2005. Directed by Heymann, a gay Ashkenazi Israeli, *Bubot Niyar* aired on Israeli television as a six-part television series. Subsequently Heymann recut the series into a stand-alone documentary; it screened to acclaim in a number of film festivals globally. *Bubot Niyar* documents the trajectories of several gay and transgender Filipino workers who worked in Tel Aviv in the early 2000s doing in-home care for elderly Hasidic (Orthodox) Jewish Israeli men. Israel has a long history of allowing overseas contract workers (OCWs) from the Philippines to enter on temporary visas, many of whom perform care work for elderly Israelis.[1] In fact the population of Filipino care workers in Israel is so large that the word *Filipini* in Hebrew is synonymous with *caregiver*. In *Bubot Niyar* the workers also perform in a drag troupe called the Paper Dolls.[2] Hairdresser Giorgio is one of the Paper Dolls, along with Jan, Sally, Chiqui, Neil, Cheska, and a few others. The film follows members of the troupe at work and as they perform. Drama ensues as Heymann arranges for the Paper Dolls to perform at Tel Aviv's biggest gay nightclub, TLV. When Israel tightens its visa restrictions for OCWs, Cheska is deported and the troupe breaks up as they leave Israel to find work elsewhere.

By opening with a conversation about gender and realness, *Bubot Niyar* presents a new spin on the queer preoccupation with trans embodiment as realness initiated by Jennie Livingston's 1991 documentary *Paris Is Burning*. *Paris Is Burning* famously presented a portrayal of Harlem's Black and Latinx drag ball scene. The film was one of the main 1990s queer cinema films to achieve commercial success, and it is also one of the most influential documentary films about queer and trans people of color. With its documentation of drag performances premised on categories of gendered "realness," *Paris Is Burning* became essential in gender and queer studies as a text through which to cultivate theories of gender performativity and performance.[3] Yet enduring debates have raged about the politics of racialized representation in the film: critics called the film sensationalized and exploitative and questioned the dynamic wherein a middle-class white lesbian film-maker could produce a document about poor and marginalized queer and trans people of color with questionable benefit to the participants.[4] bell hooks drew attention to Livingston's absence from the screen: "it is easy for viewers to imagine that they are watching an ethnographic film documenting the life of black gay 'natives' and not recognize that they are watching a work shaped and formed by a perspective and standpoint specific to Livingston."[5] hooks argued that Livingston's lack of acknowledgment of her status as a white filmmaker means she "assumes an imperial overseeing position." hooks contends is this is both antiblack and contradicts Livingston's "progressive" agenda.[6]

Contrary to *Paris Is Burning*, Heymann is a character in *Bubot Niyar* along with the Paper Dolls. We might think that Heymann's decision to feature himself so heavily in the film eschews the observational and ethnographic tone of *Paris Is Burning* for a more self-reflexive, performative documentary approach. Yet we would be wrong: for all the differences in directorial presence, Heymann's intrusive questioning and his own anxiety to emplace the Paper Dolls as one gender or another mean that *Bubot Niyar* uncomfortably reproduces some of the racial economies of representation criticized in *Paris Is Burning*. Yet different again to *Paris Is Burning*, *Bubot Niyar* features subjects who are marginalized because of their migration status, and for whom migration is narrated as the "route to upward mobility, freedom, and liberation. In this chapter I analyze documentary films that present transgender and gender nonconforming subjects engaged in transnational and rural-to-urban migrations, arguing that a central narrative governs trans and gender nonconforming representation in this genre: the metronormative migration plot. The metronormative migration plot dictates that migrating from rural to urban spaces or migrating transnationally can offer the possibility of self-fulfillment and the "freedom to be who you are": by moving, trans people can find bearable and worthwhile lives in which gender identity and sexuality are accepted or celebrated.

The films I analyze negotiate this plot by understanding migration as a transition between distinct spaces (and producing these spaces discursively): the divide between Global North and Global South and the divide between urban and rural. In doing so they contend with two myths about queer, trans, and gender nonconforming subjects: the exceptionalist assumption that the Global North is more livable than the Global South, and the metronormative assumption that urban areas are more livable than rural areas.[7] I discuss three recent migration documentaries that engage these myths in very different ways. Johnny Bergmann's *Gender Redesigner* (USA) tells the story of fAe, a white North American trans guy who moves from his hometown in rural Pennsylvania to the hub of US queer and transgender life: San Francisco. *Bubot Niyar* follows gay and trans Filipina care workers living in Israel who perform in a drag troupe called the Paper Dolls across five years, from 2000 to 2005. Sebastiano D'Ayala Valva's *Les travesti pleurent aussi* (*Travestis Also Cry*, France) traces the lives of two Ecuadorian *travestis*, Romina and Mia, who live in Clichy-sous-Bois, a suburb on the outskirts of Paris.[8] Mia and Romina work as street-based sex workers in the Bois de Boulogne.

Posing questions about the specificity of geocultural location, this chapter examines representations of trans and gender nonconforming travel in which the dominant narrative of a journey elsewhere, followed by a return home, finds limited or no traction. As I flag in the introduction, travel and migration as particular forms of geographical movement have very different ideological inflections. Caren Kaplan argues that while travel is understood as a bourgeois practice, associated with free time, affluence, pleasure, and whiteness, displacement or migration is widely understood as a one-way trip issuing from poverty or lack of opportunity, and is associated with loss, hardship, and nonwhiteness.[9] In chapter 2 I showed how several trans autobiographers have appropriated immigration analogies to make the hardship of transness intelligible. Here I attend to how representations of trans and gender nonconforming people produce those people as geographical *migrant* subjects. I critique the assumption that all trans people are indeed mobile: stuckness and immobility also feature in these narratives. However, the films I examine here refuse easy binary oppositions between dwelling and travel, home and away, and nation and diaspora.

Metronormativity, Urban and Rural Divides

The concept of metronormativity is key to understanding how trans and gender nonconforming subjects enter the global imaginary of documentary films about mobility. Jack Halberstam defines *metronormativity* as a spatial narrative of queer becoming that maps coming-out onto rural-to-urban migration. In the stereotypical metronormative narrative, the queer or transgender subject "moves to a place of tolerance [the urban] after enduring life in a place of suspicion, persecution, and secrecy [the rural]."[10] In the past few years an outpouring of US queer studies scholarship on queer rurality has rigorously dismantled the assumption that queer equals urban.[11] Scott Herring defines six axes in which metronormativity manifests: a geographical narrative plotting rural-to-urban migration; a racial logic positing urban whiteness as a normative ideal, thus erasing people of color from the "gay mecca"; a socioeconomic valuation of queer leisure-oriented urbanism; a temporal schema in which urban queers are assumed to be more "cutting edge" and "modern" than rural queers; epistemological, indexing the cultural overvaluing of urban worldliness; and an aesthetic norm pitting urban sophistication, hipness, and cosmopolitanism against rural ignorance, backwardness, and plebeianness.

While most critics of metronormativity focus on the United States, metronormative narratives of migration also work transnationally. Principally this is because cities are uneven spaces of globalization; the urban is a messy space of contradictory desires and investments in which the good life can be tenuous according to how one is racialized. For example, in the United States revitalization discourses designate urban areas as "diverse," defined by the proximity of cheap services and food made available by immigrant, black, and Native communities who live there. However, these same communities of color are understood to make such neighborhoods dangerous, necessitating more policing and redevelopment to raise property values and push out poor occupants. Gay and lesbian communities are considered vital to this cycle of revitalization, as they add value in the form of diversity and creativity but may be equally invested in urban gentrification and regulation.[12] Urban spaces are thus subject to what Jin Haritaworn, Adi Kuntsman, and Silvia Posocco call queer colonial settler fantasies, in which nonwhite and immigrant communities lend areas their multicultural cachet but are simultaneously displaced and criminalized.[13] Metronormativity also works transnationally to name some cities as more cosmopolitan or provincial than others. In a metronormative transnational imaginary, the urban centers of the Global North are associated with freedom and democratic choice. By contrast, cities in the Global South are often lumped with rural or suburban areas into homogeneous nations or regions, associated with poverty and/or religious or political oppression.[14] Popular imaginaries of global migration frame people migrating from countries in the Global South to northern Europe and the US as moving from an oppressive context to a liberating one. Inderpal Grewal and Caren Kaplan identify the shape of this narrative thus: "'Backward,' often rural subjects flee their homes and/or patriarchal families or violent, abusive situations to come to the modern metropolis, where they can express their true nature as sexual identity in a state of freedom."[15] As Eithne Luibhéid and Lionel Cantú Jr. observe, most accounts of queer migration cohere into narratives of movement from oppression to freedom, or "a heroic journey undertaken in search of liberation."[16] As they point out, migrants themselves do not necessarily understand their experiences in these terms, but a liberatory migration narrative is often the only one available. Queer and trans migration is particularly subject to this narrative precisely because gay and transgender rights, along with women's rights, are now used as markers of modernity in liberal democracies. This reduces the complexity of migrant experience to a story reflecting the nationalist fantasies of Western states as bastions of democracy. It erases the violence and discrimination experienced by migrating populations and erases their political resistance to those forms of power.

As multiple analyses of queer exceptionalism and homonationalism show, gay and transgender rights are now central to global geopolitics. The US government wields gay and transgender rights to justify itself as a global police force. In a 2011 speech to the United Nations, Secretary of State Hillary Clinton described the United States as at the forefront of efforts to combat homophobia, and reprimanded nations in which queer sex is criminalized. The United States itself did not entirely decriminalize sodomy until 2003, with *Lawrence v. Texas*. Clinton's speech coincided with a new US government strategy "dedicated to combating LGBT human rights abuses abroad."[17] Gay and lesbian rights here justify the post-9/11 US imperial fantasy and coalition with Israel, amplifying Islamophobic framings of Arab and Muslim countries as homophobic and transphobic.[18] This recuperation of lesbian and gay recognition and rights into the service of imperial war has been named homonationalism by Jasbir Puar and others.[19] In the context of Israel and the US alliance with Israel, pinkwashing, which I discuss in my analysis of *Bubot Niyar*, describes the branding of Israel as gay-friendly in order to obscure its colonial war on Palestinians.[20] Assemblages of homonationalism are certainly not limited to the United States, although they take different forms as the structures of nation and gender/sexuality inflect different histories and forms. Paola Bacchetta and Jin Haritaworn coined the term *homotransnationalism* to denote the forms of neocolonial encounters, affects, and sites that connect local scenes with national and transnational contexts.[21] In this chapter I analyze homotransnational discourses in the context of queer and trans documentary films.

Despite this common description of queer or trans migration as liberation, queer and transgender migrants from the Global South are interpreted simultaneously as threats to Global North nation-states and as possible candidates for liberatory freedom and the disciplining of "good" citizenship. Sima Shakhsari refers to this contradiction as the "politics of rightful killing."[22] While queer, trans, and gender nonconforming immigrants retain symbolic value in the US geopolitical imaginary as subjects to be rescued, this imaginary still defines such "rescuable" subjects as racialized, terrorist threats that must be extinguished in the logic of the war on terror. For Shakhsari, this means that trans and gender nonconforming migrants are both imbued with and stripped of rights simultaneously.

Queer and Trans Diaspora and Migration

I draw on scholarship on queer and trans migration and diaspora to investigate how these narratives are instrumentalized in documentary film. Importantly, this involves unsettling hegemonic notions of diaspora and migration. For instance, in *Impossible Desires* Gayatri Gopinath troubles the notion of diaspora as something that always unfolds through descent, thus "unmasking and undercutting its dependence on a genealogical, implicitly heteronormative reproductive logic."[23] For David Eng, the concept of queer diaspora reconceptualizes diaspora "not in conventional terms of ethnic dispersion, filiation, and biological traceability, but rather in terms of queerness, affiliation, and social contingency."[24] However, when queerness is articulated as a departure from the heteronormative confines of the family or from genealogical filiation, as in Eng's formation, this produces new binary oppositions: family versus queer sociality, filiation versus affiliation, and home versus destination. As Gopinath's work illustrates, home need not be a nationalist, heteronormative space in relation to queer diaspora. Gopinath's work itself focuses on texts that privilege queer home and kinship as a site of social organization. As in queer studies more generally, however, such analyses must also grapple with how demands for particular forms of labor organize migration along lines that actively undo both genealogical and queer, contingent forms of kinship.[25] For the current analysis, migration is thus always intertwined with the contingencies of labor markets. The condition of being a migrant both intersects and does not intersect with what Rey Chow, following Immanuel Wallerstein, calls the ethnicization of labor.[26] In wealthy nations, Chow points out, unskilled or devalued forms of labor are often performed by immigrant workers and those who are coded within a given nation-state as "ethnic" or "foreign."

The following analysis also shows that mobility and immobility are inextricably linked. Following Eithne Luibhéid, I define the migrant as "anyone who has crossed an international border to reach [a new home] . . . making no distinction among legal immigrants, refugees, asylum seekers, or undocumented migrants."[27] As Luibhéid points out, categorical distinctions among different categories of migrants reflect biopolitical governmentalities designed to control and modulate the movement of bodies across borders. Angela Mitropoulos refers to these processes as the proliferation of borders: "Arrayed beyond and around the obvious walls of migration control, the architectures and technologies of the border proliferate. These technologies seek to sort, expunge, confine and delay; to sift potential value from non-value; to fix the border inside and round both states and selves; to foreclose the future to versions of an infinitely stuttering present."[28] Definitions of permanent skilled migration and temporary guest work change according to labor shortages, while the definitions of asylum seeker and refugee change according to political exigencies and corporate demand.[29] In previous work I've stressed that this necessitates tracing the trajectories of migrant life without assuming one home and one destination, as migrants are embedded within vectors of global migration flow modulated by many national borders acting as filters.[30] National governments, international bodies, and localized nongovernmental organizations and institutions all contribute to global or local "regimes of mobility control."[31]

The documentaries discussed in this chapter deploy metronormative migration narratives differently depending on the protagonists' racial, economic, and juridical statuses. *Gender Redesigner*, which features a white trans masculine protagonist, frames transness as a becoming, a one-way transition that requires body modification and legal changes of name and gender designation to be "complete." By contrast, neither *Bubot Niyar* nor *Les travestis pleurent aussi* frame transition as a one-way trip, or even deploy gender transition as a narrative trope. Instead both films work within a narrative of racialized, queered migration, depicting it as the search for a location in which non-Western trans and gender nonconforming subjects can be free to "be who they are" and live out nonnormative sexual or gendered identities. *Bubot Niyar*, I argue, has a fundamentally ambivalent relationship to this dominant narrative: while its trailer depicts Israel as a place where the Paper Dolls are "free to be who they are," in contrast to the Dolls' native Philippines, the events of the film belie that depiction. This is evident in the stringent Israeli visa conditions they labor under and in the director's desire to manage the Paper Dolls' identifications within a Euro-American epistemological separation between gender identity and sexuality. *Les travestis pleurent aussi* focuses less than *Paper Dolls* or *Gender Redesigner* on the identities of its protagonists and more on the material constraints of multiple, intersecting interpellations and misrecognitions of race, sexuality, gender, and class that bind Romina and Mia to particular forms of life.

Reading Trans Documentary

In examining three films made and embedded in different geocultural locations, films that have circulated transnationally, I apply this book's transnational methodology to cinematic representation. As I explained in the introduction, my transnational feminist and queer methodology takes terms, knowledges, and forms of life as always already transnational. Just as the story of transsexuality's emergence begins with the transnational voyage of Christine Jorgensen, the historical legacy of that preoccupation with transnational mobility animates transsexual memoirs. That transnational epistemology works through an orientalist colonial imaginary to differentiate an individualized, technological, and medicalized paradigm of transsexuality from forms of gender nonconforming life that are marked as non-Western, traditional, and nontechnological. (In turn, these forms of gender nonconforming life, particularly trans femininity, are also understood as premodern and traditional in opposition to modern gay masculinity.) That distinction between liberal individualist narratives of transness and narratives about non-Euro-American gender nonconforming life is particularly important in this chapter, as I analyze its passage across three very different national cinematic contexts. My method is not cross-cultural or comparative; rather, I draw on the logic of transnational cinema studies to trace similar themes across geographically divergent filmic representations. Documentary cinema itself is transnational both in its range of subject matter and its production and circulation processes. I continue my strategy of provincializing trans narratives by attending to the specific political, historical, and geographical contexts in which representations circulate. As I note in the conclusion to this chapter, documentary highlights the connection between visibility in terms of *image* and visibility in terms of *political representation*, asking, Is visibility always good? When is visibility damaging, unjust, or violent?

In selecting documentaries to discuss in this chapter, I drew from a large international canon of documentaries featuring trans and gender nonconforming subject matter. Documentary film has become a signal form for the global production and circulation of knowledge and affective imaginaries about gender nonconforming people. While readings of fictional feature films abound in transgender studies, critical commentary on queer and trans documentary has not kept pace with the sheer numbers of documentaries featuring trans and gender nonconforming embodiments, culture, and politics.[32] The 1990s was the first decade in which trans documentaries were analyzed in large numbers. Queer film criticism in that decade focused on the representation of trans and gender nonconforming bodies in documentaries like *Juggling Gender* (Tami Gold, 1992), OUTLAW (Alisa Lebow, 1994), *Linda/Les and Annie* (Johnny Armstrong, 1992), and *Max* (Monika Treut, 1992) to dispute the logic of heteronormative binary sex.[33] This reflects the 1990s moment in which trans communities sought to reflect the truth of transgender life, similar to how historical narratives were deployed in the same manner. In a 1998 essay Christie Milliken argued that trans documentaries confound the dominant documentary logic of spectatorial pleasure through discovering the truth by inciting pleasure and curiosity in bodies that are simultaneously "fact and fiction."[34] And both Chris Straayer and Milliken imagined "transgender documentary" as inherently transgressive and antinormative. While these films appeared in a historical moment of independent media production and transgressive New Queer Cinema, an analysis that relies on axes of normativity versus antinormativity vis-à-vis gender and sexuality was, and remains, insufficient. With few exceptions through the 2000s, film scholarship has not kept up with the output of queer and trans documentaries.[35]

As I gestured earlier, debates about documentary films featuring trans and gender nonconforming bodies have always also indexed debates about the raced, classed, and spatial politics of representation. Partially as a result of Butler's reading of *Paris Is Burning* to theorize performativity in the 1993 book *Bodies That Matter*, the film also became the center of a debate within queer and gender studies about whether the black and Latinx queens featured in the film were aspiring to the cruel optimism of racial capitalism by expressing the desire to pass as women, be housewives, and consume luxury goods.[36] This also calls back to the critique I noted earlier of Livingston's position as a "neutral" observer. Documentary film is often understood to contribute to social change through its status as a window onto the truth. In a blistering critique of cinema verité, documentary filmmaking that avoids "artifice" to give an effect of realness and immediacy, Trinh observes that documentary film is defined against feature film through its status as the Real: "pure, concrete, fixed, visible, all-too-visible." She argues that this privileging of the real results in the emergence of an "aesthetic of objectivity": the look and feel that sustain viewers' sense that they are watching something that "really happened." Concomitantly, documentary makers develop what she calls "technologies of truth-telling" that can differentiate between "what is right and what is wrong in the world and by extension, what is 'honest' and what is 'manipulative.'" These technologies include synchronous sound and images; long takes with minimal editing; and shaky, handheld camera techniques that attempt to make viewers feel as if they are "really there." These techniques mystify the fact that, like all filmmakers, documentary makers dramatize and provoke events and interactions with their subjects to make the end result dramatically compelling. Trinh points out that these techniques obfuscate the layers of mediation that lie between documentary subjects and viewers; these layers include filmmakers and crew, editing, production, funding, and distribution, as well as the mediating processes of the medium itself. Thus, Trinh argues, the "socially oriented filmmaker" remains represented as the "mighty voicegiver" whose authority goes unquestioned.[37]

In relation to *Paris Is Burning*, critics extended the critique of Livingston as "mighty voicegiver" by questioning the politics of featuring economically and racially marginalized subjects who aspire to middle-classness without contextualizing the structural forces which rendered that aspiration unlikely (or the participants' consciousness of that fact). Many of these questions turn on the agency of the participants. For instance, Philip Brian Harper points out that the material conditions of film production and distribution meant that the Harlem queens featured in *Paris Is Burning* were forced to renounce the agency they might have had to document the drag balls through the legal process of signing release forms for Livingston's movie. In any case, racial and economic conditions meant that working-class black and Latinx queens and gay men did not have the resources to command their own creative agency in the same way Livingston did.[38]

Of course audiences may not have such a naive relationship to factual media representations. However, claims to reality inflect documentary with particular truth claims, especially when documentaries are seen to provide representations of marginalized bodies, identities, political movements, or events. In this way, Ardis Cameron argues, documentaries "shape categories of difference and erase the traces of representation."[39] Particularly relevant to my argument throughout this book, documentary generic conventions produce spectatorial subjectivity through spatial logics: discursive topographies of otherness distinguish home from away and, in doing so, mark the boundaries of the self in a manner similar to the ethnographic writing analyzed in chapter 1.[40] This may be motivated by various political agendas, for example to encourage a viewer to witness the other or to provoke viewers to transform their understanding of a given political issue. Meredith Raimondo shows how the AIDS documentaries *Pandemic* and *A Closer Walk* promote political transformation on the part of the viewer but do so by reproducing narrative and visual colonialisms. Raimondo argues that both films therefore reproduce imperialist logics that position viewers as educated global citizens and the subjects of the films—seropositive people almost entirely from outside the United States—as subjects who cannot escape their locations.[41] Raimondo's analysis offers an astute lens through which to examine how transnational politics filter through documentary framing and also to interrogate how sexuality, gender, migration, cultural difference, and transnationality intersect in the films read in this chapter.

Another layer of mediation that shapes the films I analyze is distribution and screening. One important market for film distribution is the college classroom. Classroom and library distribution sometimes enables documentaries to function as teaching aids for transgender 101 courses, which often present trans and gender nonconforming bodies as evidence of "gender transgression" and/or transsexual gender normativity, repathologized through a pedagogical and spectatorial scrutiny that assumes students are *not* gender nonconforming. This pedagogical impulse can rupture when documentaries form the basis for identification and community or classroom debate.

The market for documentaries about trans and gender nonconforming life is growing outside of the classroom, aided by a transnational LGBT film festival scene that presents and reflects trans experience alongside gay and lesbian experience. Queer film festivals are far from politically neutral spaces, however, and embody transnational politics. For example, the San Francisco International LGBT Film Festival takes sponsorship from Israel as part of the Brand Israel campaign that seeks to represent Israel as a gay-friendly modern democracy. Critics suggest that by funding LGBT cultural events, Israel is attempting to improve its international image and draw attention away from its colonial occupation of Palestine.[42] This issue of pinkwashing shapes the international circulation of the Israeli film *Bubot Niyar*. Film festivals are also a good litmus test to track how the global LGBT film industry understands the various participants of documentaries: Are those filmed for documentaries considered to be actors, worthy of payment and film festival appearances?

Trans Metronormativity: *Gender Redesigner*

Gender Redesigner, made in 2007 by Johnny Bergmann and shown on the gay cable channel LOGO, documents the gender transition of a trans man called fAe. Bergmann and fAe worked together on a television show pilot interviewing queer youth across the United States in 2002. The first shots in the film show fAe looking like a sporty butch lesbian, interviewing people at the New York Dyke March. Two years later fAe begins identifying as a man, and Bergmann starts to film fAe's transition. Bergmann narrates the plot, explaining the minutiae of transgender transition to the viewer, who is imagined to have no knowledge of such things. Bergmann explains transgender concepts in a hilariously deadpan, professorial voice-over. But Bergmann is also fAe's friend, and in interview shots he offers a more personal perspective on fAe's transition.

In the mid-2000s transgender masculinity had just become a popular interest in US queer culture, and *Gender Redesigner* is one of many documentaries made about trans men in that decade. It uses the vernacular of *transgender* rather than *transsexual* and is grounded in a white, middle-class queer and trans US subculture, totems of which include testosterone, chest surgery, gender fluidity, drag king shows, and dyke marches. In the film fAe narrates his desire to transition using elements of a very standard medical trans narrative, supported by Bergmann's voice-over. For example, Bergmann explains at the beginning of the film, "fAe's wanted to be a man her entire life. . . . Now she has decided to change her body to make it look more manly." (Bergmann uses female pronouns to refer to fAe until after he has chest surgery.) "I rejected dresses, dolls, and played sports," fAe explains as we see a slideshow of childhood photos. As he begins taking testosterone and has chest surgery, he reports feeling more free to express his feminine side—"I'm just a mixture. Not really one or the other"—yet the documentary stresses masculinity by filming him engaged in various masculine activities, such as house construction and looking at trucks to buy.

Gender Redesigner focuses on trans masculine subjects, in contrast to *Bubot Niyar*'s and *Les travestis pleurent aussi*'s focus on trans feminine subjects. In many ways their differences are reflective of the cultural codes that differentiate trans masculinity from trans femininity. They also reveal the racialization of trans feminine people of color, who are most often defined as subjects of *labor* rather than individuals. *Gender Redesigner* takes a white individual trans man as its subject. fAe's story of successfully finding himself through an interstate move to San Francisco is given value in itself. This is a common theme of documentaries about white trans individuals in general, both trans men and trans women: their life stories are understood as "relatable" and having value in themselves. The trope of the relatable individual confirms the individualism of liberal subjectivity. For example, *Funny Kinda Guy* (Travis Reeves, 2005) features Simon de Voil's transition and migration from Scotland to Australia; *My Prairie Home* (Chelsea McMullan, 2014) follows the Canadian musician Rae Spoon on a tour across Canada's prairies, reflecting on Spoon's childhood and family; and *Prodigal Sons* (Kimberly Reed, 2008) uses Reed's return to her hometown in Montana to open up a larger narrative about family relationships and sibling rivalry. By contrast, films that feature trans and gender nonconforming people of color, such as *Bubot Niyar* and *Les travestis pleurent aussi*, often portray a cohort or community deemed at risk. Trans of color subjects of documentary are often understood as located in a geographically bounded neighborhood and/or an international pattern of migration and labor. In these instances the documentary form has a sociological function: its goal is to capture a milieu, or a field in the ethnographic sense. *Paris Is Burning* works in precisely this fashion, as does *The Aggressives* (Daniel Peddle, 2006), a documentary about New York–based black trans masculine people. *Bubot Niyar* and *Les travestis pleurent aussi* portray a drag troupe and a cohort of gender nonconforming sex workers, respectively. One could argue that these forms of storytelling merely reflect the reality of white trans privilege versus the material exploitation of trans people of color. However, decisions about setting and character reproduce the terms through which viewers can imagine different kinds of trans life.

While all three of the films I examine portray migration, *Gender Redesigner* specifically tells the progress of fAe's transition in a narrative of rural-to-urban migration. After a prologue featuring a lesbian-identified fAe interviewing marchers at the New York Dyke March in 2002, a chronological plot takes shape. fAe's age is never specified, but he appears to be in his early to mid-twenties. Bergmann explains at the beginning of the film that fAe has moved home to western Pennsylvania and begun identifying as a man; fAe is living on his parents' farm outside Pittsburgh and attending massage school. Bergmann meets fAe at Pittsburgh's airport and returns home with him. We see the Pittsburgh skyline and then a tractor mowing a hayfield as fAe says in a voice-over, "Pittsburgh is traditionally kind of conservative, because it's smack dab in the middle of a rural area." A number of fAe's friends and family back up this statement, including fAe's athletic, straight-looking brother: "The mentality around here isn't very open to new things. Gay and lesbian just came in and is being accepted around here but as far as trans is concerned it's a very radical step." fAe's parents do not participate in the film, but Bergmann films around their house and farm. Much of the establishing footage we see here is of fields, traditional red barns, farm equipment, and shots of fAe driving along rural roads (figure 3.1). fAe doesn't appear to have a job and is living with his parents to save money. While fAe himself seems quite happy with this arrangement, Bergmann seems bothered. "You should move to New York with us," he tells fAe. "I can't move to New York. I have to live for free at my parents' house," fAe replies, with a self-mocking laugh. Bergmann's voiceover elaborates, "It's another hour and a half of driving to get to the family farm, which is pretty much in the middle of nowhere." We cut to Bergmann, this time in front of the camera. "fAe is now doing this transition thing in rural Pennsylvania. Who transitions in rural Pennsylvania?" he scoffs. "I wouldn't do it."

Events in the film underscore the difficulty of transitioning in a rural location. Two days before leaving for chest surgery in Ohio, fAe realizes he should have sent the surgeon a certified check as a deposit or his surgery may be canceled. He manages to avert the check's cancelation but has to drive for over an hour to get to the bank and get the certified checks made. The bank closes at 4:00 p.m. Suspenseful music plays as we see footage of fAe driving down a dirt road. He looks stressed out. "So, I have to drive to another town. . . . Just cutting it a little close is what we're doing here." As if to highlight the fact that they're in a

3.1 fAe Gibson driving in rural Pennsylvania, from *Gender Redesigner*.

rural area, the bank is called the Farmer's National Bank. He makes it there on time. Afterward, back in the car driving home, fAe explains that he knew the bank clerk and that even this routine financial transaction could mean being outed as trans. "I was a little worried about how people in this town would react to [my transition]," he says. "[The bank clerk] had to write down the names that were going on the certified checks, which were like, 'University Plastic Surgery Center.' . . . So they're gonna know that I'm getting some sort of plastic surgery. And probably the fact that I have sideburns, y'know, it might be a giveaway." He gives Bergmann a wry smile. "This just put into motion the gossip I suppose, because I'm already looking more manly than I usually do. But now my business is out there."

Sometime after chest surgery fAe decides to move to San Francisco with his friend Jen. Beforehand he goes to the courthouse to get his gender and name changed. "I'll be legally a man in California!" he says. We cut to fAe talking logistics on the phone with Jen, and then to him dancing in front of the camera, humming a show tune. Clearly he is excited about the move. He, Jen, and the film crew plan to drive two cars and a truck, bringing furniture and belongings as well as two dogs and a cat on a five-day road trip across the United States to San Francisco. "One possibility is that I go totally broke," says fAe. "The other possibility is that I fall madly in love and I stay out there forever." Footage of the truck moving through prairies and desert landscapes is intercut with fingers pointing to various places on a US map. The camera captures the truck in front of a neon sunset somewhere in the Southwest. During a visit to the Grand Canyon and more on the road footage, fAe talks at length about his anticipation of a new life. Maybe he will date again after a long break: "I'd like to meet new people as my current self." Bergmann follows fAe and Jen as they arrive in San Francisco and begin moving their furniture into their new apartment. fAe's mood is upbeat.

The film cuts to one year later, when Bergmann returns to San Francisco. fAe and Jen are in a band called the Sex Combs. He is happy and involved in band rehearsal, yelling queer lyrics about "pussy face" into the microphone and banging a tambourine. "Being one weirdo amongst western Pennsylvania is different than being part of a nice group of weirdos out here," he says. Over footage of fAe throwing a ball for his dog at Ocean Beach, fAe says, "I love being a dude in San Francisco and having it not be, I'm not questioned." Bergmann corroborates in the voice-over: "He just looks so masculine! So much like a man!" This very straightforward narrative of rural-to-urban queer and trans migration is not complicated by the film. In the final minutes of *Gender Redesigner*, fAe relates that he passes so easily in San Francisco, even other trans guys can't tell. He has reached the life he had aspired to, of "just being himself." The anonymity granted by urban space is an important factor in this sense of fulfillment: fAe can now pass as a man without being recognized at the bank or the grocery store as he once was in Pennsylvania. He is also visible as a potentially queer man in the queerest of global cities. We don't learn how fAe is making a living in his new home or how he pays the exorbitant rent of a San Francisco apartment.

Gender Redesigner's narrative resolution depends on an assumption that living in rural areas is dangerous or impossible for trans people: even if fAe had a home and a job in rural Pennsylvania, the film presents his life as immeasurably better once he arrives in the gay metropolis. As Lucas Crawford has pointed out, many trans and gender nonconforming people find a way to live in rural areas aided by "unconventional allies, lovers, and mentors."[43] Counter to *Gender Redesigner*'s focus on fAe's passing as a man, Crawford suggests the concept of imperceptibility to account for the state of living in a rural space where everyone already knows you and where a previous history makes "passing" unlikely. For Crawford, imperceptibility unsettles the classic one-way transgender plot and the ways that urban theories of gay and transgender becoming cannot "see" some trans and gender nonconforming bodies. *Gender Redesigner* presents a narrative in which the stakes of living rural are neither high nor particularly dangerous. Despite this the film never acknowledges the forms of rural gender nonconforming life that exceed transgender as an explicit identity category or a narrative of trans urban fulfillment.

The narrative of rural-to-urban migration presented in *Gender Redesigner* is also highly racialized. The film is most interested in the story of fAe's individual transition. That narrative is understood to have an intrinsic value: it situates fAe in the classic American individualist fantasy of liberal reinvention and materializing dreams of a better life. fAe does not relate being stuck, and the way mobility is represented confirms the fantasy: *You can have it all. You can pass, if you move to the big city.* Individual white trans advancement here stands as the achievement of a United States that can harbor liberal as well as conservative enclaves, within which the founding racial violence of the nation-state is concealed. As with the narratives of white transsexual transition I examined in chapter 2, individual fulfillment is privileged as a narrative with intrinsic value and is a marker of economic and racial privilege. There is no sense that fAe is forced to migrate to San Francisco for economic reasons or that he is in search of work. In fact the various mobilities of the film—moving to New York for college, driving to Cleveland for chest surgery, and moving to San Francisco—happen with only vague mention of finances or work. By contrast, the nonwhite gender nonconforming subjects in *Bubot Niyar* and *Les travestis pleurent aussi* are defined by their economic status as migrant laborers, and their gender nonconforming identities are presented as continually sutured *to* labor.

Overseas Contract Workers in Israel: *Bubot Niyar*

I first saw *Bubot Niyar* at the 2006 Melbourne Jewish International Film Festival. I was surprised to see a film about Filipina trans drag performers on the program. At the time even Jewish lesbian and gay subject matter was considered peripheral in Melbourne's Jewish intellectual community. After *Bubot Niyar* ended, the mainly middle-class, middle-aged audience filed out. A collective mood of self-congratulation seemed to reign—"See? We're so down with the gays!"—as well as a palpable sense of discomfort. *Bubot Niyar* presents a contradictory vision of Israel and a contradictory vision of gay globality. On the one hand, Israel is presented metronormatively as a bastion of gay rights. The Paper Dolls are diasporic outcasts leaving their oppressive homes in the third world for the more progressive and welcoming first world. The marketing in particular works to tell this story. On the other hand, *Bubot Niyar* reveals that the queer Filipino workers in the film are socially excluded because of their migrant worker status and their gender presentations. Israel is clearly a hostile place for them in many ways, and eventually it becomes uninhabitable. While the film confronts this contradiction and evokes the viewer's sympathy for its subjects, Heymann's depiction of the Paper Dolls never quite overcomes a desire to manage them, to dictate how their gender presentations should be understood and also to literally manage their budding careers in Tel Aviv's gay scene. This management is noticeably colonial. The contradictory narratives of metronormative gay pride and compassion for racial and sexual outsiders mask the fact that the Paper Dolls are never permitted to exist as subjects in the documentary outside of these two narratives. In previous work I have engaged much more deeply with the politics of affect and labor in *Bubot Niyar*, particularly about the careers of the Paper Dolls after the film was released and Sally's death in the United Arab Emirates in 2011.[44] Martin Manalansan has also written extensively about Jan's disaffection in performing care labor, arguing for scholarship on feminized global care labor to denaturalize the heteronormative association of feminine bodies with caring.[45] While I am unable to do justice to these readings in this chapter, I focus on the manner in which the film produces two possible lenses through which viewers can look at the Paper Dolls, foreclosing the troupe's (and possibly viewers') refusal of metronormativity and other worlds they might create.

The titles in *Bubot Niyar*'s trailer tell an uplifting and dramatic tale of transnational queer migration: "They were outsiders / Looking for family / Finding love and acceptance / In a different world / As who they are." Images of drag shows, outrageous costumes, makeup, rainbow flags, camp gestures, and Pride parades flash to a house music beat, positioning the film within the global queer imaginary. Israel here represents a fantasy of the global queer metropolis, where everyone may access the freedom to "be who they are" under Western liberalism. This fantasy of freedom works on two registers: freedom from the heteronormative and gender normative constraints of the family, and freedom from a traditional political conservatism coded racially as nonwhite. Most important, the music track and the frenetic blur of colorful images tell us that this film is uplifting. This is confirmed by the blurb about *Bubot Niyar* on Heymann's website:

> In a small apartment in southern Tel Aviv, a group of Gay Filipino migrant workers meet every weekend. Throughout the week they work as caregivers of elderly Orthodox Jews in the Tel Aviv suburb and on weekends they performed [*sic*] before an audience of Filipino migrant workers across Israel on their drag-queen show, called The Paper Dolls. In spite of the chaotic Israeli reality, where fear of terrorist suicide bombers competes with the fear of the "Immigration Police," the group members succeed in expressing their true selves. They see Israel as an open and free place, where they can enjoy sexual and cultural liberty.[46]

This summary is echoed in many reviews of the film. For example, in his *LA Times* review, Kevin Thomas states, "[Despite] widespread Israeli antipathy toward the transgendered and suspicion of immigrants in general . . . the transsexuals [*sic*] enjoy a more liberal atmosphere in Israel in contrast with that of their native country."[47] This is echoed by film studies scholarship. For example, Niv Cohen writes, "Israel is described . . . by [the Paper Dolls] as a place of relative sexual liberation, especially when compared with their native land."[48] *Bubot Niyar* was made in 2006, several years before the term *pinkwashing* was coined to describe concerted campaigns by the Israeli government and Israeli culture-makers to present the country as "relevant and modern" and to divert attention from a decades-long imperial and racist war.[49] Touting Tel Aviv as a global gay tourist destination has been a significant part of Brand Israel. This brand appears in a range of media, including Michael Lucas's 2009 porn film *Men of Israel*, 2011 Israeli advertising campaigns in the UK and Germany, and Tel Aviv's 2012 hosting of World Pride. Despite being released before the emergence of Brand Israel, *Bubot Niyar*'s marketing foreshadows exactly that line. It argues that Israel is an "open and free place" and that the gay and trans Filipino domestic workers there are merely living out the logical desire to migrate somewhere more open. This narrative is impelled by the logic of metronormativity.

Despite the film's alignment with a metronormative vision of Israel as a gay paradise, however, no one in *Bubot Niyar* ever claims that the Philippines is sexually oppressive or unfree. In fact the Paper Dolls understand Israel as conservative. Filmed partying at Eilat's first Gay Pride Parade in 2001, Sally says, "When I was in the Philippines, we thought Israel was a sacred place, that everything is closed, people are religious, primitive. It's very surprising that there is a Gay Pride Parade." Footage of Sally dancing with another troupe member, Neil, follows (figure 3.2).

Throughout the film Heymann appears preoccupied with understanding the Paper Dolls as outsiders who can never overcome their precarious status as gender nonconforming people and OCWs. He mediates the viewer's sympathy for them while reproducing an ethnographic gaze, constantly "putting them in their place" as racially other. For instance, the early scenes I describe above invite the viewer to enter a landscape marked as foreign and enigmatic. The poorly lit footage of drag queens and the camera's high-angle framing perform an archetype of ethnographic film: the arrival scene featuring the entrance of the ethnographer into a foreign place. In ethnographic film

3.2 Sally and Neil dancing at Eilat Gay Pride, from *Bubot Niyar*.

3.3 Jan leaving the stairwell where he dressed, from *Bubot Niyar.*

arrival scenes also align the ethnographer and the viewer. Like Heymann, the viewer is presumed to be, or invited to spectate as, a tourist. Consistent with this arrival scene, elsewhere the Paper Dolls are presented as objects of the camera's and of Heymann's gaze, inciting a voyeurism that the film's presumed audience is also asked to perform. This voyeurism is mediated through the Paper Dolls' clear racial and sexual difference from their environment and through their status as overseas workers who are exploited and subject to inhumane immigration restrictions. For instance, Heymann focuses on how the Paper Dolls negotiate dressing up femme, but rarely as a moment of liberatory enjoyment. Jan presents as male in the apartment he lives and works in, but he wears dresses and makeup to go out in Tel Aviv with his friends.[50] Heymann films Jan leaving his apartment and proceeding to change into femme garb and apply makeup in the stairwell before he walks out into the street. "I get dressed downstairs here," he says in the stairwell. "Not upstairs. I'm so embarrassed." Jan exits the stairwell completely transformed, but with a morose, almost wary expression (figure 3.3). In another scene Heymann films Chiqui and Neil pushing wheelchairs on the streets of B'nai B'rak, a Hasidic neighborhood. Their bodies are marked as different not only by the brownness of their skin but by their long hair, jeans, and colorful shirts, in contrast to the men wearing traditional black Hasidic suits. The camera captures children staring and adults averting their eyes. Chiqui says, "When the bus enters B'nai B'rak, I feel different. They look at me like I'm small, like dirt, something like that." This scene not only highlights Chiqui's racial difference, but undercuts the image of Israel as queer-friendly and "tolerant" by drawing attention to the racism of many Israelis.

Bubot Niyar additionally regards the Paper Dolls as victims of an oppressive transnational labor market. This is consistent with a liberal transnational imaginary that decries the exploitation of overseas contract domestic workers but does not question the regime of global imperialism that sustains these chains of care. In Israel as elsewhere Filipinos are symbols of global overseas contract work. In contrast to the upbeat, glamorous world of performances and Pride marches foregrounded by the film's trailer, the scenes featuring the Paper Dolls at work emphasize the painstaking and monotonous repetition of the labor they perform. Some of the Paper Dolls have elderly employers with dementia who are physically incapacitated: they must be fed, bathed, taken for walks, given physical therapy, fed again, and put to bed. Others, like Sally, have a role more like a live-in housekeeper. One of the principal subplots of the film is Sally's relationship with her employer Haim: Haim respects Sally's gender identity as feminine and buys her gifts, and they are depicted as being very close. But when Haim dies of cancer, Sally's visa is canceled and she must return to the Philippines.[51] When the Central Bus Station is bombed and the Israeli government begins a campaign to deport immigrant workers, Tel Aviv becomes a space that is violent, threatening, and inhibiting for all the Paper Dolls. Cheska loses her visa and cannot leave her apartment for fear of being arrested by immigration police; eventually she is detained and deported. Heymann films himself visiting Cheska in the detention center and even records a message from her to the other Paper Dolls. Chiqui tells his employers he wants to resign, and they retaliate by claiming he has stolen jewelry. "She's accusing me that I took it but the thing is, I know she's just upset," says Chiqui. "That's why she told me like that." Despite this, he has to leave: "I really want to stay here, but I don't have a future here. Even after so many years, you can get nothing here. Like if you went to another country you can have your citizenship, you can build your home. You can settle your own. . . . Not like here. Here we're really strangers." These predicaments illustrate that the very capacity to be mobile and to migrate also involves stuckness and immobility. The Paper Dolls' migration may be a choice, but it is circumscribed by their national status as Filipino and by the constant transnational just-in-time readjustment of demand for overseas work-ers and deportation campaigns.

While all of these events are filmed in the style of cinema verité, with Heymann appearing to merely document the "truth," Heymann also takes on the Paper Dolls as a project to manage. During the time he is filming them, Heymann arranges for them to audition for Shirazi, the owner of a popular gay nightclub in Tel Aviv. Each member of the troupe puts on her best act: a highlight is Sally, who performs a raun-chy version of the traditional Jewish folk song "Havah Nagilah." After the audition it emerges that Shirazi is willing to hire the more "pro-fessional" performers (who also happen to be the most conventionally attractive) and rework the show entirely for a performance at his club. Shirazi meets with the Paper Dolls to break the news gently. In English he says, "This Friday we're gonna do something very nice. . . . People know that it's Paper Dolls but we mix into the party. . . . All the deco-ration is not Philippines. It's something from the—" "Asian?" Chiqui interjects knowingly. "No, no," says Shirazi. "Japanese. . . . The decora-tions are gonna be Japanese." Shirazi has the Paper Dolls wear kimonos, apply white geisha-style face paint, and choreograph new "oriental" dance moves. While those troupe members who survive the audition seem pleased to be performing for a larger audience, it's evident that the new costumes and the orientalist theme create tension. Never-theless the performance goes ahead, to the house music track "Paper Dolls" heard in the trailer: "We're not real, we're just paper dolls." At this point we encounter the only other trans person in the entire film, an Israeli drag queen. She is sitting in the dressing room after watch-ing the Paper Dolls perform. "They're not *real* Manila drag queens," she bitches. "I know real Filipino drag. They're just trash from around the Central Bus Station." Meanwhile Shirazi enters the dressing-room and instructs the Paper Dolls to stand at the club's entrance and bow to people walking past with palms pressed together in a Thai-style *wai*. "Come with me and I'll tell you what to do," he says. As Chiqui listens, the camera captures both his awareness of Shirazi's racism and a silent but building anger (figure 3.4).

It is unclear what the Israeli drag queen means by "real Manila drag," but she, like Shirazi and other club patrons, clearly believe the Paper Dolls are lower-class, tacky "trash." Her rejection of the Paper Dolls as unfit for a "famous" gay club combines their status as overseas domestic workers and as feminine subjects. Even their drag style is unacceptable

Come with me and I'll
tell you what to do, okay?

3.4 Chiqui reacts as Shirazi instructs the Paper Dolls to "hostess" in the club, from *Bubot Niyar*.

to Shirazi and has to be "modernized" into a pan-Asian pastiche that draws from the one Asian nation-state Westerners think of as having ultramodern cachet. In the mainstream gay scene they are just another act competing against ripped, masculine, white go-go dancers. In this situation being Filipina is not recognizably oriental enough. The Paper Dolls' racial difference and gendered and sexed indeterminacy is merely a commodity, but evidently not a valuable enough commodity on its own: it has to be supplemented with a more familiar pastiche of Asianness.

While the film itself positions Shirazi and the anonymous drag queen as racists, Heymann himself appears to see the Paper Dolls as somewhat unsophisticated subjects who require his intervention and guidance. In addition to literally managing the Paper Dolls' drag career, Heymann also manages them symbolically, as the camera films him adjudicating the configuration of sexuality and gender he thinks they should embody. This is particularly evident in his interactions with Sally, who presents everywhere as a woman. For two of the years she lives in Tel Aviv, Sally has a boyfriend who doesn't know she is trans. Heymann seems to feel very close to Sally, often flirting with her. Two scenes in which they talk illustrate how Heymann manages Sally's gender and sexuality. In the first scene he stands outside an apartment building with Sally after a Paper Dolls show. We have just seen the drag troupe perform for the first time. With no prelude Heymann abruptly says, "It's strange for me, I'm not used to seeing such things." Sally stands next to him, expressionless. "Strange in what way?" she asks. He shrugs. "Sometimes I even find it a bit repulsive. Like, aren't you ashamed, shaving your entire body and all. . . . Aren't you ashamed of that?" This time it's Sally's turn to shrug. "Nothing to be ashamed of."

In a later scene Sally and Neil are in a hotel, in various stages of undress. Wrapped in a towel, Sally reads a Yehuda Amichai poem from the book her employer has lent her, "Songs for a Woman." Heymann asks, "'Songs for a Woman' is your favorite poem?" "Yes," she replies from the bathroom, where she is applying moisturizer. "Because I'm a woman, right?" She smiles at the camera teasingly. Heymann calls from the bedroom, "No, you're half a woman." Neil laughs, and the camera operator follows Sally as she walks into the bedroom toward Heymann. "You don't say! Who told you so?" she says. "How much of a woman are you?" asks Heymann. "A real woman," she replies. "C'mon Sally, half a woman?" Heymann persists, his humor deflating into earnestness and anxiety. "One hundred percent," Sally says smiling. At this point Neil interjects, "One hundred percent? But you've got a wee-wee!" "Who said? Did you taste it? See it?" Sally replies. Applying eyeliner at the mirror, Sally begins to sing a song in Hebrew.

Sally maintains a breezy, tongue-in-cheek attitude during this exchange, deflecting Heymann and Neil through humor but also refusing the genre of the literal that might lock her description of herself into the realm of fact, or "truth." Nonetheless, Heymann's anxious questioning implies not merely that she is a drag queen—a male who "dresses" as a woman—but that her *everyday* gender presentation is mere surface, not real. Additionally, the nuances of translating Filipino concepts of gender and sexuality (which might remove us beyond the category of "woman" or "man" altogether) disappear here. Heymann's insistence that he be able to define what Sally is attenuates her own capacity to define herself as she pleases. What enables him to do this so freely is their different biopolitical status. Heymann is a white-skinned man and an Israeli citizen; Sally is always already a foreign worker, subordinate to Heymann's desire to manage both through her femininity and her racialization as Filipina and non-Israeli. Despite their closeness Heymann performs the tolerance and compassion of what Ghassan Hage calls the "good white nationalist." In good white nationalism, the racial other is tolerated but still requires management, by the nation-state or by individuals.[52] Heymann later performs his nationalist management of Sally's gender by literally directing her in a photo shoot (which is also a moment of explicit direction for the movie itself). After Sally's and Heymann's joking exchange we cut to the same room, an undetermined amount of time later. Sally and Neil are now both dressed. Neil is on the bed with Heymann, posing for a photo. Heymann says, "Now it's Sally's turn. C'mon Sally. How about a picture, just you and me. Like husband and wife, Sally." Sally climbs on the bed while Neil holds the camera. Heymann puts his arm around her and they spoon. The difference between Heymann's nondescript, straight-acting masculinity and Sally's femininity could not be more stark here. "Your hair smells good. What did you put on it?" he asks her. Sally says nothing. Her expression is neutral. Again, the light flirtation of this exchange masks its power: Heymann has just refused to allow Sally to self-identify, even jokingly, as a woman. As if to emphasize the point that Sally is subordinate to Heymann's and the film's categorizing anxiety, Heymann drapes his arm over her in a way that is simultaneously proprietary and flirtatious.

For Hage, the gesture of "welcoming" or "including" migrants into the multicultural nation affirms the white national citizen as manager and the migrant as an object to be managed.[53] This desire to include is thus ambivalent and premised on white supremacy. Hage points out that all kinds of nationalism manifest in desires to literally manage the *bodies* of migrants, ranging from directly violent acts, such as attacking Muslim women who wear headscarves, to indirectly violent but seemingly innocuous acts, such as suggesting that migrants work on their pronunciation or work on their appearance to "blend in." While Israel's dominant political imaginary indexes liberal multiculturalism far less than Australia, the country Hage is writing about, both nations share settler colonial discourses. Israeli settler colonial fantasies regard racialized immigrants and indigenous Arabs and Palestinians as threats to national sovereignty. Israeli negotiations of racial and cultural difference are complex and take place through multiple filters: Filipino OCWs subsist as outsiders to the Zionist Israeli nation-state alongside Mizrahi Jews, recent Russian Jewish migrants, Arabs, and an increasing population of African migrants (some of who are Jewish, some not).[54] In *Bubot Niyar*, Heymann positions himself as a conscientious ethnographic filmmaker who is intimate with the Paper Dolls and aligned with them politically. But his anxious questioning of their gender presentation—and Shirazi's exoticist placing of them as subservient Asians in the nightclub—shows how wide the power differentials are between them.[55] Yet the Paper Dolls are not merely the victims of this racializing managerial domain of representation. Hage emphasizes that while white nationalist projects might understand migrants as objects, migrants do not understand themselves as objects. In the scene I discuss above, Sally persists in declaring that she is a woman, or like a woman, despite Heymann's insistence that she is not.[56] The Paper Dolls refuse the racial and gender logics ascribed to them, even if they do so smilingly or silently.

Uncannily Heymann's adjudication of Sally's gender echoes the repudiation of the figure of the *bakla* in Filipino gay culture, where, as Bobby Benedicto argues in *Under Bright Lights*, the "present" of modern gay globality is premised on disappearing femininity. But perhaps this is not so uncanny. For as several other episodes in the film show, Sally and the other Paper Dolls are constantly being put in their place: as Southeast Asian migrants, as domestic workers, and as feminine, all of these marking them as déclassé and undesirable. To understand this it is necessary to expand on what *bakla* means and to whom. *Bakla* is a Tagalog term; Benedicto defines it as an unstable term, a "sexual tradition that conflates homosexuality, lower-class status, and transvestism or effeminacy."[57] Other Filipino studies scholars have defined *bakla* in various ways: as a subculture specific to lower-class beauty parlors and service workers, as a form of "psychospiritual inversion," or as a relationship to performance.[58] In *Global Divas*, an ethnography of gay Filipino men in New York City, Manalansan defines *bakla* as "encompass[ing] homosexuality, hermaphroditism, cross-dressing, and effeminacy."[59] Manalansan argues that his diasporic informants recuperate bakla: rather than its being a premodern antecedent to gay, they reinvent it as an alternative modernity.[60] Benedicto interprets Manalansan as saying that bakla for diasporic Filipino gay men becomes a way to retreat from the racializing logics of the mainstream gay scene, where Asian men are already coded as feminine and where they feel they do not belong.[61] Benedicto writes specifically about Manila, however, in contradistinction to Manalansan's ethnography of the Filipino gay diaspora. The Paper Dolls are neither the gay elite informants that occupy Benedicto's autoethnography nor the middle-class Filipino gay men living in New York City of Manalansan's *Global Divas*, who are reinventing bakla for their own purposes. However, Benedicto's complex emplotment of bakla as an image that becomes "unattractive" as the

Manila gay scene comes to understand itself as more global and more modern is important to a reading of *Bubot Niyar*. Just as bakla is considered to be somewhat tacky and antithetical to gay modernity, the Paper Dolls are read by multiple characters in the film as "trashy" and "repulsive." Even if the film itself does not support those readings, it defines the Paper Dolls through their work status as caregivers and their play status as drag queens. Both of these definitions enclose the Paper Dolls in the gendered and racialized status of other. This racialized gendering marks them as premodern subjects who, though the film may represent them as aspiring to gay modernity and metronormative self-fulfillment, may not ever fully arrive.

I want to finish this line of argument by thinking carefully about what we do not see in *Bubot Niyar*. In the shortened feature-length version of the documentary, we never discover what Chiqui, Giorgio, Sally, Cheska, Jan, Neil, Rika, and the other Paper Dolls did for work before they came to Israel. We don't know what class background they come from (although at times we might guess); we don't know if, before becoming care workers, they worked as doctors, hairdressers, accountants, or call center workers. We aren't told whether any of them performed drag in the Philippines or took up drag performance later as migrants. Apart from Sally, who talks briefly about dating, we never hear about the protagonists' sexual lives. While the film *Les travestis pleurent aussi* is much more explicit about its protagonists as sexual beings, this too takes place while defining them via labor and immigration status: precarious, undocumented sex workers.

A Foothold in Europe: *Les travestis pleurent aussi*

Les travesti pleurent aussi opens with photographs of the filmmaker Sebastiano D'Ayala Valva with several trans women. They look like family photos. Following the title sequence, Mia, or "La Mujeron" (the Big Woman), applies makeup in her bathroom mirror. The camera follows her as she gets dressed. "I feel good about the way I am," Mia says in Spanish over these images. "I'm neither a woman nor a man. I'm just a person, that's all. An ordinary person just like any other. I can't tell you if I feel like a woman or a man, just another person." She continues to talk in voice-over as we cut to images of her spraying a weave with hair lacquer and applying eye shadow in a tiny apartment bathroom: "I do this to make it shine, to give it more life. It must shine a lot for the

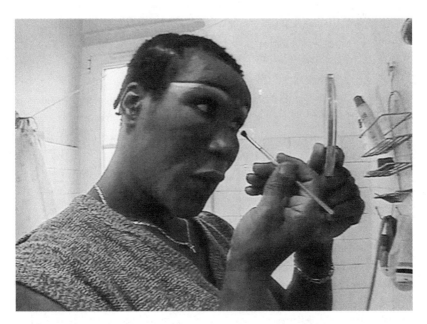

3.5 Mia applying makeup in the opening of *Les travestis pleurent aussi*.

colors to stand out. I left home when I was sixteen, I'm now thirty-four years old and I say this with no shame, I can't read or write, because there are many of us like this in the world, but not all of them really want to get ahead" (figure 3.5).

After this classic iteration of a transgender mirror scene, the film cuts to the streets of Clichy, an outer suburb of Paris.[62] The camera settles on numerous gay men and trans women walking along the street. Mia's voice-over continues, interpreting the environment for the viewer: "Here in Clichy, there are Arabs and some French, but mainly faggots and lots of *travesti*. All the way down the avenue to Place de Clichy, it's full of travesti. They all live in the hotels around here." Compared with the explicitly ethnographic arrival scene in *Bubot Niyar*, this method of setting up a documentary's spatial zone is more subtle. However, the scene does similar work: the film situates us in a place marked as foreign because of its inhabitants. Then we cut to Mia's friend Romina. She is sitting cross-legged on a window seat in her apartment, explaining gender identity and sexuality to the camera. "We are the third sex," she says. "Travestis, transsexuals, and lesbians are the third sex. It's the magic of seeing a woman with a male sex or a man with a female sex. It's magic."

Les travestis pleurent aussi follows the everyday lives of Romina, Mia, and Mia's non-trans sister Issy, all of whom are Ecuadorians in Paris earning a living from street-based sex work. The director puts together the dramatic events of their lives to shape a loose plot. Issy arrives from Ecuador and starts doing sex work, eventually getting arrested in a deportation raid. Romina leaves her husband, who resents her doing sex work, only to return a couple of weeks later. *Les travestis pleurent aussi* uses a similar cinema verité style as *Bubot Niyar*, but the feel is more gritty because of D'Ayala Valva's extensive use of a handheld digital video camera. Like other trans documentaries, this one feels the need to communicate the details of how its gender nonconforming protagonists identify and perform gender presentation. Refreshingly, however, *Les travestis pleurent aussi* successfully sidesteps the entire narrative of global diasporic queers finding self-fulfillment through migration in which the diasporic queer or trans subject finds the good life in the metropolis. In *Les travestis pleurent aussi*, however, there is no narrative resolution, no happy ending, and most notably no "good life." Rather than presenting a myth about the promise of transnational queer or trans migration, the film offers a deliberately bleak picture of the precarious existence of queer immigrants in Europe. In fact D'Alaya Valva avoids setting up drama in the form of editing to construct a plot: the rhythm of the film is cyclical and repetitive, evoking a sense of trappedness or immobility. In offering a visual document of lives in which freedom's promise has broken down, *Les travestis pleurent aussi* pushes past the metronormative stereotype into an attempt to represent what Lauren Berlant calls the post-Fordist "bad life": "a life dedicated to moving towards the good life's normative/utopian zone but actually stuck in what we might call survival time, the time of struggling, drowning, holding on to the ledge, treading water."[63] Rather than being depicted as actively engaged in the search for a better life, Mia and Romina are clearly aware that it is a fantasy. Instead the film shows both protagonists absorbed in the task of continuing to live and surmount the difficulties of living. However, by defining Mia, Romina, and Issy so thoroughly as a parable of the "bad life," *Les travestis pleurent aussi* forecloses their capacity to represent or merely *be* anything else for the viewer.

Like *Bubot Niyar*, the protagonists in *Les travestis pleurent aussi* rarely refer to themselves using the Euro-American language of *transgen-*

der. They call themselves *travestis*. In a Spanish-speaking context the meaning of the term is contested. It circulates within Latin and South American countries, including Brazil, Mexico, Argentina, and Ecuador. In scholarship *travestismo* sometimes appears as a metaphor for the embodiment of national colonial identity, and sometimes it is understood as a denaturalization of gender. (As Vek Lewis points out, this is similar to how queer studies has deployed *transgender*.)[64] In English-language anthropological studies of Brazil and Mexico City, travestis are considered "transgendered prostitutes": female-presenting people assigned male at birth who generally do not wish to have genital surgery but who may modify their bodies with silicon and hormones. Don Kulick, for example, writes, "Travestis do not wish to remove their penis, and they do not consider themselves to be women."[65] Contrary to this positivist account of what the travesti is, the Argentinian travesti activist Lohanna Berkins defines *travesti* by discussing its context and historical formation. Different from the Euro-American *transgender*, *travesti* has been reappropriated by travesti culture and politics from a psychiatric definition. It is often associated with sex work because gender nonconforming people are excluded from the labor market and thus sex work is often the only way for them to earn an income. Berkins explains that while the term *travesti* therefore carries a history of pathologization and social stereotypes, *travestismo* is defined by travestis themselves: "Many Latin American travestis demand the option of a position outside the binary and our aim is to destabilize the male and female categories."[66] As we see in *Les travestis pleurent aussi*, the term also circulates transnationally in Latin American migrant communities, carrying the same contestations and contradictions.

Questions of identity, however, are eclipsed in *Les travestis pleurent aussi* by questions of politics, particularly the politics of sex work, global economic injustice, and border controls. At the time the film was made, Nicolas Sarkozy was waging a campaign for president of France by whipping up anti-immigrant sentiment. As interior minister, Sarkozy had passed legislation to crack down on street-based sex work with an increased police presence, body searches, and raids on known sex work strolls. Sex work itself was not criminalized; rather the raids were used to increase pressure on undocumented immigrants, who were widely seen as undesirable specters of poverty and as threats to French national culture.[67] As Mia and Romina explain in the film, however, they migrated to France because Ecuador is so poor it is impossible to earn a living or support a family there. Like many migrant workers, their goal is to send remittances back to their families in Ecuador.

D'Ayala Valva's decision to feature Mia and Romina as the main characters highlights class and racial differences within the Ecuadorian immigrant population in France. Mia is black and illiterate; his family work as farm laborers. He and Issy live in a hotel, as they are unable to find an apartment in Clichy. Mia never articulates ambitions beyond sending money back to his family: "Every day I do the same thing. . . . Not for me, but for my family. It's my family that counts above all and I'm here to fight for them. I don't care if I catch a disease, I'm not scared of dying." Mia, a former boxer, dresses in feminine clothes only to work. At home he wears sweats. He does not appear to enjoy sex work.

In contrast, Romina lives in an apartment with her Portuguese husband and her terrier. She points out that her apartment is more luxurious than what many of the trans sex workers in Clichy can afford. Most travestis, she says, live in hotels, which charge exorbitant weekly rates for small rooms. "It's difficult for us," she says. "First we are foreigners. Second, we are transsexuals, and third, most of us are prostitutes. For a transsexual, it is still very hard to get accepted." She does the housework, the shopping and cooking, and does street-based sex work at night. "The routine is the same, whether you live in a hotel or an apartment. I do the cleaning, I do the shopping, I walk the dog, I cook for my man." Romina clearly comes from a somewhat affluent background; she tells D'Ayala Valva she studied medicine in Ecuador and is fluent in several languages. She doesn't say why she chose to do sex work rather than more socially acceptable careers but instead lists her financial goals: sending money to members of her family and saving to buy a car and a house in Ecuador. Romina flirts outrageously with D'Ayala Valva, boasting about her husband, her regular lover, and her "current flame." Like Mia, she articulates a pragmatic attitude to sex work. "There are moments when I like prostitution," she says. "To be a prostitute with the bad weather, the police, is difficult. But I do enjoy some moments. You know why? Sometimes you are stressed out and you need something new. . . . You're there working and then you meet a guy"—she pauses and fans her face, smiling—"who takes you to seventh heaven. He's good looking and I get paid."

Issy becomes a central character in the film alongside Mia and Romina. However, her face is never shown. "When I first arrived I saw the hotel and many travestis," Issy says in voice-over as the camera films her back, walking along a street. "I'd never seen such a thing. I was terrified." Issy also did not know Mia was a travesti. "I nearly fell over backwards although I'd been told. In the pictures he sent to Ecuador, he wasn't dressed as a woman. . . . For me, he's still a man." She explains that one night Mia was working but couldn't find any clients. Their rent was due the next day, so Issy decided to start doing sex work too. D'Ayala Valva accompanies Issy to the Bois de Boulogne, where she rigs up a tarpaulin to work in, keeping a branch nearby to fend off attackers. Like Mia, Issy does not tell her family in Ecuador how she is making a living. She sends the money she earns to her children in Ecuador. While Issy does not say this explicitly, it is clear that she understands sex work as repugnant. "I'd like to tell them I work in a wood," she says, "but I can't, because of my son." Worse, she says, the family may know they are doing sex work but not care. "Out of sight, out of mind."

D'Ayala Valva's decision to feature Issy in the film alongside Mia and Romina does two things. First, it refutes the assumption that trans and gender nonconforming sex workers are without family: Issy and Mia share each other's lives and secrets. Second, it implies that status as an undocumented sex worker is similar for trans and non-trans people. "We give emotional comfort," says Issy as she shows D'Ayala Valva the place where she sees johns in the Bois. As sex workers, Issy, Mia, and Romina all do a form of feminized affective and embodied labor, if we define affective labor as work that involves emotional care—which many have argued sex work certainly does.[68] Issy, Mia, and Romina occupy a similar social position as the care workers in *Bubot Niyar*: no matter their legal sex designation, capitalism understands them as equivalent, capable of performing feminized labor. To survive they must capitalize on the capacities and skills they have or that they find most rewarding. In contrast to *Bubot Niyar*, which understands the Paper Dolls as defined by their sexual identity—as gay—and through their birth-assigned designation as male, D'Ayala Valva is far less interested in these details. As racialized migrants, Issy, Mia, and Romina are also defined by the forms of border crossing they can access. Whether migrating through particular visa categories or as undocumented immigrants, they are all vulnerable to racial profiling, criminalization, and harassment by police and immigration security forces. In fact the filtering of bodies according to racialization and immigration status partially defines Mia's, Romina's, and Issy's roles as workers, thus subjecting them to uncertain conditions. Their criminalization as racialized immigrants makes it impossible for them to fight collectively for a living wage or for betting living conditions in general. As many have argued before me, this implies that effectively combating violence against trans and gender nonconforming people does not lie with hate crimes statutes or legal recognition of transgender people but with much broader measures: decriminalization of sex work; loosening immigration restrictions and national border controls; and making welfare, health care, and social safety nets available to all people regardless of immigration status.[69]

As I note above, *Les travestis pleurent aussi* constructs a very flat affective range. The editing and cinematography create a sense that Mia's, Romina's, and Issy's lives are unrelentingly repetitive. While it features migrants, a sense of stuckness and immobility pervades the film. In fact although the protagonists sometimes articulate a sense that things will get better or that they will "win the game," the film seems to think the opposite. Although D'Ayala Valva filmed over three years, the chronology of events is unclear, and the director makes no effort to introduce diegetic continuity. Daytime and nighttime shots are cut together without any apparent order. Romina has blonde hair in some shots and black hair in others. Consistent with classic cinema verité style, D'Ayala Valva shoots long takes and includes lengthy silences. The film returns again and again to shots of Romina and Mia performing household tasks: vacuuming, doing laundry, cooking, shopping for groceries. The same slow, gloomy flamenco guitar track plays between dialogue scenes, adding to the sense that time is standing still. No dramatic tension or plot animates the narrative. The two most suspenseful episodes take place right at the end of the film, when Romina leaves her husband and Issy is arrested. Minutes later, during the ending title sequence, we discover that Romina went back to her husband and got a breast enlargement, and Issy was released from prison after a few weeks.

While this slow, repetitive temporal rhythm repudiates a metronormative global queer narrative, *Les travestis pleurent aussi* has its own normative tendencies. The film belabors Mia's, Issy's, and Romina's precarious location as undocumented sex workers and the difficulty of their lives so heavily that it is difficult for the viewer to imagine how they might define themselves differently. In the few scenes where they socialize with friends, the friends are not named or identified, although D'Ayala Valva reports that he initially immersed himself in the scene of travestis living in Clichy, and that social scene functions as the film's setting. In one scene Mia marches in the Paris Pride parade and poses for photos with admiring and/or fetishizing white French parade-goers. But Mia does not talk about his relationship to the white Parisian queer scene or whom he likes to date or fuck outside of work. In fact Mia rarely mentions play or leisure at all. Rather he talks about work, how much to charge for a trick, how much money he sends home to his family, and the everyday difficulties of paying rent and surviving. Early in the film Mia is shown arguing with a hotel manager about paying the rent. He turns to face the camera and says, "We're illegal, so they do what they want. But I left my own country because I didn't want to be treated badly. It's worse over here. You have to kill, steal, anything to pay the hotel. Fifty euros a day." Off camera D'Ayala Valva asks, "And how do you do it?" Mia replies, "With my work. I have to prostitute myself. I suck, I fuck, I get fucked. I have to suck or get sucked. What for? Touch men's asses, get touched by men. For what? To pay the hotel. I have no savings. We don't send any money to our families. There are no jobs, no places to live. We're illegal immigrants."

If this exchange lays bare the realities of living in Europe as an undocumented trans sex worker, it also defines Mia as that identity without allowing for him to have desires or dreams that exceed that identity. In the process the film risks turning Mia and Romina into one-dimensional characters whose predicaments represent the entire underclass of trans immigrant sex workers in France. The viewer is not imagined to experience these predicaments; rather the film provides an educational moment. Recalling Trinh's invocation of the documentary filmmaker as the "mighty voice-giver" whose authority goes unquestioned, it is helpful here to interrogate the representational conventions by which D'Ayala Valva also, at moments, becomes the "voice-giver" to vulnerable victims of circumstance. Implicitly viewers are directed to take this "educational" moment seriously and to feel compassion for the other. The film does not question whether this compassion can be effective in dismantling the systems that produce the injustice Mia, Issy, Romina, and the other unnamed travestis in the film experience.

D'Ayala Valva returns again and again to Mia talking about the working conditions of street-based sex work. Paradoxically these scenes also undo the viewer's identification of Mia as a victim of circumstance by acknowledging that she is a political subject. Filmed catching a cab to

a street corner and walking the stroll, Mia explains, "When I first arrived, I had trouble. A travesti made me pay for a spot. He told me
I had to respect him because he had been in Paris longer. He wanted
200 euros a night, but I could hardly pay for the hotel, I couldn't give
him 200 euros. I have a 'husband' to support. And that husband is my
mother." Later Mia is filmed on a street, at night, advising someone
new to the area about the going rates for various sexual practices. "You
should charge twenty euros," she says to the unnamed woman, "but
not ten or fifteen. Because if you work with us, you have to follow the
rules." The rules here are about cooperating in an informal network to
ensure that everyone charges similar rates and that sex workers do not
undercut or exploit each other. While explicit collective bargaining is
impossible given the informal nature of street-based sex work, Mia has
a political analysis of the situation and acts politically to enforce higher
rates within the community she inhabits.

Migrating Subjects, Subjects of Migration

To conclude this chapter I briefly consider all three films together,
recalling Rey Chow's observations about the ethnicization of labor.
Chow argues that being coded as "foreign" within any given nation-
state often coincides with performing the most low-valued labor. "The
experience of migration," she writes, "simply highlights and amplifies
the connection between commodified labor and ethnicization. . . . The
ethnic as such stands in modernity as the site of a foreignness that is
produced from within privileged societies and is at once defined by and
constitutive of that society's hierarchical divisions of labor. A laborer
becomes ethnicized because she is commodified in specific ways."[70]

Chow is talking about particular forms of labor here, but she is
also talking about the representational modes through which labor
is made visible. We can see the effects of this commodification taking
place even within the production of the documentaries I have written
about in this chapter. To be interpellated as a migrant, a foreigner, is
to participate in the commodification of one's body and to be forced to
negotiate agency and mobility within the scene of commodification. To
be a trans or gender nonconforming migrant on film means that one
must contend with the narratives of queer and trans migration that
posit the Global North or the urban metropolis as a liberatory space,
while also contending with the unjust reality of global labor migration

and national border security in general. Racialized gender nonconforming subjects must necessarily contend with their subjectivation as laborers. White trans subjects have the luxury of being defined as individuals whose migration narratives embody complex desires, dreams, and motivations about self-transformation.

This becomes particularly apparent when we compare the differences between the documentaries. While *Gender Redesigner* features a migration narrative that only briefly intercepts questions of labor, *Bubot Niyar* and *Les travestis pleurent aussi* both gain their status as films *about migration* by filming protagonists interpellated into ideological systems that racialize them simultaneously through their nation of origin and through the forms of labor they can (or are required) to perform. fAe, the white trans guy in *Gender Redesigner*, is not defined by his work status or by his citizenship. He is not interpellated into the same form of migration as the Paper Dolls, whose lives are shaped by their capacity to perform care work for and establish familial relationships with their individual employers, or Mia and Romina, whose gender variant bodies and particular value enable them to make a living in Paris, despite not having the right papers to travel. Representationally fAe can just "be a person": the documentary represents his individual narrative of transition as legitimate, and the film inserts pedagogical information about transgender transition.

Bubot Niyar and *Les travestis pleurent aussi* offer two very different examples of documentary filmmakers participating, or not, in the circulation and production of migrant subjectivation. Heymann's attitude toward the Paper Dolls is always ambivalent; while he workshops his own aversion to their femininity, he also attempts to manage how they articulate their sexual and gender identities. The question Heymann always wants to raise in *Bubot Niyar* is the relationship between his gayness and the Paper Dolls' gayness; he is invested in differentiating how similar and different they are from him, the film's representative normative gay subject. In *Les travestis pleurent aussi* D'Ayala Valva presents subjects of migration without explicitly attempting to manage their identities. However, Mia and Romina are still, somehow, objects of a gaze assumed to be outside of the world they inhabit. The camera still functions as the instrument of an ethnographic gaze looking at gender nonconforming migrant sex workers, the abjected standard-bearers of the intersection of poverty, queerness, and racializing marginalization under global capitalism. Just like the Paper Dolls, however, Mia and

Romina refuse abjection; they are no one's heroes. Rather they would like to raise enough money to participate in capitalism—to buy houses back home, to rest, to live the good life—but they are also philosophical about that fantasy's impossibility.

I have analyzed these three documentaries about trans and gender nonconforming migration to illustrate how racialized and class differentiations between gender nonconforming subjects who migrate come to bear on the framing of migration by both filmmakers and trans subjects themselves. I have argued that despite the reality that many kinds of people migrate for many reasons, to be interpellated as a migrant is to be ethnicized as nonwhite because of the labor circuits within globalized modernity. As the films presented here show, the narrative of gender travel I read extensively in chapters 1 and 2 is specific to particular geocultural locations and domains of experience, wherein whiteness enables subjects to imagine elsewheres that facilitate rather than complicate their desire to live as one's chosen or desired gender, free from violence or constraint. *Gender Redesigner* certainly demonstrates this. While the protagonists in *Bubot Niyar* and *Les travestis pleurent aussi* also imagine elsewhere spaces as facilitating their desires, the reality of the spaces they migrate to, and the opportunities they can access, are very different. However, we should be careful not to assume that skin color or class necessarily defines what one can experience as a trans person. Experience always exceeds the boundaries of identity categories. It is just as crucial to acknowledge that experience is not a self-evident order of speaking truth. The narratives available shape what we imagine is possible, which in turn shapes how we might resist or rewrite those narratives.

PART II

Whereas the first part of this book offers a historical and representational context for how mobility inflects trans subjectivity formation and critiques its geographical and racial specificity, the second part interrogates trans and gender nonconforming mobilities by asking how gender nonconforming subjects themselves articulate mobility in their everyday lives. In these chapters I practice a methodology that I call "following the actors"—patients, care workers, surgeons, and sometimes myself. Rather than beginning with an analysis of large-scale institutions, "following" foregrounds how individual trans and gender variant people (including myself) use mobility to negotiate the contradictory regulatory assemblages that make up the transnational medical, legal, and administrative systems through which we access body modification technologies, health care, and juridical recognition or misrecognition. I argued in part I that mobility animates the production of meanings about transsexual and transgender life. In part II, I examine the material mobility of knowledge, people, and capital that constellate around gender confirmation surgery practices. I investigate how trans and gender nonconforming people use mobility to skillfully negotiate the inconsistencies among transnational, national, and local health care formations. I draw on Inderpal Grewal and Caren Kaplan's

transnational theorization of sexualities and genders to map different medical traditions and conceptions of the body in relation to colonial and postcolonial histories and the contemporary asymmetries of
transnational capital.[1] I interrogate the micropolitics that often constitute such health care decisions as "choices." In the process, I reveal the
messy relationships between individuals, the emergence of markets,
state regulation of gender reassignment, and the circuits of medical
epistemology and individual and community information-sharing that
constitute how gender reassignment somatechnologies are made available, paid for, and experienced. Gender reassignment surgeries are a
transnational assemblage. In revealing how trans subjects negotiate the
absence or insufficiency of health care in their home countries through
travel, I map the asymmetries that haunt trans life everywhere. These
asymmetries include vast mobility differences between affluent and
poor trans subjects, disturbing racial asymmetries in the quality of
care available, and transnational differences in understandings of what
trans health care involves and how body modification intersects with
transgender embodiment. The first part of the book provincializes gender reassignment by investigating historical, literary, and cinematic
narratives, and this part provincializes gender reassignment by tracking material practices of travel, mobility, fixity, and immobility.

CHAPTER FOUR

GENDER REASSIGNMENT AND TRANSNATIONAL ENTREPRENEURIALISMS OF THE SELF

We should think of consumption as an enterprise activity by which
the individual, precisely on the basis of the capital he has at his disposal,
will produce something that will be his own satisfaction.
—**Michel Foucault,** *The Birth of Biopolitics*

In early 2005 my friend Tom asked if I'd ever heard of surgeons practicing top surgery in Thailand. At the time my own chances of finding the resources for surgery appeared slim: I had sought a gender dysphoria diagnosis and been rejected and was in the first year of graduate school, with no savings. But I continued to research surgeons and surgery techniques. Tom and I swapped tips over email about Australian surgeons with good reputations and which surgeons elsewhere in the world might be affordable. Like finding any medical specialist, finding a decent surgeon is a combination of word of mouth and luck. And unlike in the United States, gender reassignment surgeons in Australia rarely advertise and are inaccessible without a doctor's referral and a gender dysphoria diagnosis. Later that year Tom told me he'd found a surgeon in Bangkok. Dr. Sukit Worathamrong specialized in reconstructive surgeries for trans men, both chest reconstruction surgery and phalloplasty. Apparently the cost would be far less than in Australia. Dr. Sukit required less psychiatric documentation, and the surgical and nursing care were reputed to be just as professional as in any hospital in Australia.[1] At the time I was researching the availability of gender reassignment surgeries in the Asia Pacific region for this book and volunteering for a trans and genderqueer support and advocacy group. Nearly every trans woman I encountered in Australia—friends, acquaintances, and those I eventually met through ethnographic fieldwork—had at least considered traveling to Thailand if they were interested in GRS.

I did in fact travel for chest reconstruction, but to the far north of Australia rather than to Thailand, after the long process of getting psychiatric approval and a shorter process of going into debt to finance it. Trans women and surgeons chiefly established Thailand's status as a global hub of GRS in the mid-1990s through email listservs and online forums. Media coverage and surgeons refer to Thailand as a Mecca of transgender surgeries. Medical experts in gender dysphoria have often seen traveling overseas for GRS (to Thailand or anywhere else) as a way of circumventing the intensive psychiatric assessment and "real life" tests stipulated by the World Professional Association for Transgender Health (WPATH) and the American Psychological Association.[2] However, trans women and an increasing number of trans men seek reassignment surgeries in Thailand for many other reasons: cheaper services; better techniques; Thai surgeons' reputation as being more accommodating and sensitive to trans people; and, among the more entrepreneurial surgeons, a "care package" that equally emphasizes first-rate hospital care and luxury treatment.[3] While Thailand has a large population of gender nonconforming people, many of whom obtain aesthetic or reconstructive body modifications, the most famous and premium clinics in Thailand provide GRS to non-Thais from all over the world: North America, Europe, Australia and New Zealand, South Africa, and other nations within Asia, such as Japan and Korea. These clinics are part of Thailand's growing transnational medical travel industry. *Medical travel* refers to an emergent and global profit-driven market that facilitates travel to obtain cheaper or less-regulated health care in different countries.[4] Yet these clinics also constitute a niche market with a history independent of, but coexistent with, broader circuits of medical travel in Thailand and in Asia more generally. Many GRS clinics are housed within private hospitals catering to a large non-Thai medical travel population. These hospitals are a destination for many people globally who cannot or who choose not to access gender reassignment surgeries close to where they reside. A few surgeons specialize in surgeries for trans masculine people—chest reconstruction, phalloplasty, and so on—but the majority of Thai gender reassignment surgeons cater to trans women.

The factors contributing to Thailand's popularity as a destination for GRS are complex: restrictive and expensive legal and medical regulative regimes in trans subjects' nations of origin; political conditions within Thailand, including the government-sponsored popularity of medical travel; and transnational economies of health, tourism, and affect circulating within and across Southeast Asia. In this chapter I explore the material obstacles to obtaining decent trans health care, and in chapter 5 I examine Thailand's status as a fantasy destination in which those material obstacles appear to melt away for some racialized subjects and reemerge to obstruct others. Theorizing Thailand as a GRS destination and as a persistent subcultural fantasy reveals how the transnational trajectories that gender nonconforming people embark on are always produced within the grammars we use to understand our experiences and desires. Just as Casablanca became a center for GRS in the 1960s, so Thailand has become such a center in the later twentieth- and early twenty-first centuries.

Information about surgical technique at Thai gender reassignment clinics is distributed directly via Thai surgeons' marketing websites. These are all in English; since non-Thai interest in Thai GRS surgeries peaked in the mid-1990s, the Thai clinics marketing themselves to a non-Thai clientele have maintained English-language websites. The key to successful marketing in this niche industry is relating a large volume of information about each aspect of the surgery process. This encourages the prospective patient to feel that she is in control of a procedure that is carried out in a distant country, where she may lack support networks of family or friends. More important, Thai surgeons market their product in a style that constitutes the patient as the discriminating consumer of a luxury service who should know about every aspect of the process in advance.

This synergy between very technically knowledgeable patients and informative websites does not exist in a vacuum. It exists in a framework of private transactions for services rendered, embedded in a globalized medical travel market. In this framework of postmodern health care, patients become individualized consumers engaging in calculations of risk and purchasing power—even if they understand health care as a right while they materially understand it as a commodity. This entrepreneurial consumer framework is very different from the gatekeeper model of obtaining GRS, a model prevalent in Australia (see the introduction for more detail). Individual trans and gender nonconforming people negotiate the contradiction between the gatekeeper model, in which they are interpellated as a subject of psychiatry who is dependent on medical authority to approve them for somatechnological body modifications, and a biomedical entrepreneurial consumer framework, in which they are interpellated as consumers of body modification as a commodity. When we denaturalize the figure of the transsexual-as-patient that dominates understandings of transgender health care in the Global North, we see that what appear to be a contradiction may not be so contradictory after all.

In framing this argument I draw on Marcia Ochoa's observation in her ethnography of Venezuelan femininity in beauty pageants and trans culture, *Queen for a Day*, that Venezuelan *transformistas* she knew narrated their experience as different from North American assumptions about the "transgender body" and Anglophone transgender studies' preoccupation with the same. Ochoa points out that Venezuelan medical authority functions differently than North American medical authority; in Venezuela one can access pharmaceuticals and surgical procedures without a medical infrastructure of intensive regulation or psychiatric assessment protocols. Further, genital reassignment surgery is not necessarily a desired outcome of body modification procedures for many *transformistas*; rather they employ logics of aesthetic correction and corporeal satisfaction or happiness.[5] Ochoa thus provokes transgender studies to examine body modification procedures beyond the normative conception of medically authorized "sex change." This is instructive for transgender studies scholars who study locations and political-economic frameworks outside the Global North, for transnational transgender studies scholars with projects that straddle multiple regions (like this one), and particularly for US scholarship. After all, US trans subjects also invest in multiple frameworks or understandings of somatechnical body modification. Although biomedicine is now dictated by free market neoliberalism and individuals are constructed as voluntarist "health consumers" for whom active responsibility for health is an imperative of citizenship, in the arena of transgender health this individualized consumption is unevenly distributed and works in tandem with older discourses of psychiatric power in which patients are anything but autonomous. This chapter therefore intervenes in critical conversations about neoliberalism and biomedicine, in particular the assumption that neoliberalism has universally destabilized discourses of medical authority.[6] As Christoph Hanssmann argues, medical authority is not as universal and monolithic as we often assume, but rather "diffuse and capricious, whether ostensibly supportive or putatively violent."[7] I show in this chapter how such medical authority is also racially and economically stratified.

I frame gender reassignment surgeries as part of a suite of somatechnical body modifications, conceptually attached to other forms of surgical and nonsurgical body modification inside and outside of the "medically necessary." It is equally important to localize or provincialize what gender reassignment itself means in the context of global assemblages of health care and national configurations of biopolitics. I provincialize surgical body modification and detach it from transsexuality to show how transsexuality as a concept enfolds assumptions about health, bodily autonomy, and the equation of a given case history with particular forms of medicalized body modification. Medical and social science literature on transsexuality often treats this enfolded concept as a universal, when, as I show in chapter 1, it is specific to a North American identity narrative premised on upward mobility and self-transformation. The medical model of transsexuality has most influenced understandings of the protocols necessary to make surgical body modification available. Different national, regional, and transnational configurations of health and medicine result in subtly different configurations of transsexuality and surgical body modification. Thus the first part of this chapter explores these at length to contextualize the transnational disjunctures patients traveling to Thailand for GRS must navigate.

I continue with an analysis of how, as they attempt to obtain a gender dysphoria diagnosis, trans people become embedded in patient subjectivation—subject to the medicalization of transsexuality, which puts surgery candidates in the hands of medical practitioners and their diagnostic discretion. I draw on my own experiences here, using ethnography and autoethnography to frame the micropolitics of medical authority and clinical procedure. By contrast, in their dealings with Thai gender reassignment clinics those I interviewed are embedded in a mode of consumer subjectivation I call "entrepreneurialism of the self." I discuss consumer subjectivation in Thai clinics through close readings of clinic websites, which build synergy between surgery candidates' imagining themselves as accessing choice as autonomous individuals, and the clinics' assumption that prospective customers are discriminating and intelligent consumers. Drawing on Kane Race's work on biomedicine and consumption, I read these websites as a domain of consumer enunciation where consumption is thought to confer agency—in opposition to the constraints experienced within the medical model.[8] Finally, I argue that although the gatekeeper model and the consumer model may seem oppositional, neither offers total freedom, for the very incoherence of these two forms of subjectivation is central to the circulation of capital.

Clinical and Individual Entrepreneurialisms

The feedback loop of clinic marketing websites and the consumption practices trans subjects use to research and decide on surgery is an entrepreneurialism of the self. Distinct from the entrepreneurialism of corporations or institutions (for example, the Thai GRS clinics that market GRS medical travel), *entrepreneurialism of the self* describes a discourse of individual neoliberal rationality. Foucault used this phrase in his 1979 lectures at the Collège de France in which he takes up North American neoliberalism in the work of the Chicago School economist Gary Becker. Foucault uses Becker's theory of consumption to explain the reemergence of *Homo economicus* within neoliberalism as an "enterprise activity by which the individual, precisely on the basis of the capital he has at his disposal, will produce something that will be his own satisfaction."[9] Colin Gordon adapts Foucault's term to describe consumption as a process of enterprise and investment in the self, in which life is a process of constant improvement.[10] However, notions of individual entrepreneurialism are useful for me here. Such a definition is close to Wendy Brown's understanding of neoliberal rationality, in which all human action is imagined in terms of its capacity for entrepreneurial gain, "conducted according to a calculus of utility, benefit, or self-satisfaction against a micro-economic grid of scarcity, supply and demand, and moral value-neutrality." Brown argues that neoliberal rationality does not coerce individuals into shaping their behavior in this way, but that institutional structures reward calculation. By implication those institutional structures also penalize behavior that does not competitively seek self-satisfaction. This entrepreneurialism of the self interpellates us into an ideological framework where to succeed, or to interface effectively with the state and/or the market, we must "provide for [our] own needs and service [our] own ambitions."[11]

Feminist science and technology studies scholars have theorized the entry of neoliberal rationality into medicine and health as biomedicalization. For Adele Clarke, Janet Shim, Laura Mamo, Jennifer Ruth Fosket, and Jennifer Fishman, biomedicalization describes not only the commodification of health but also how the "proper management of [health conditions is] becoming [an] individual moral responsibilit[y] through improved access to knowledge, self-surveillance, prevention, risk assessment, the treatment of risk, and the consumption of appropriate self-help/biomedical goods and services." Clarke and colleagues gesture at an entrepreneurialism of the self when they talk about how biomedicine imposes "new mandates and performances that become incorporated into one's sense of self," such as being proactive, neorational, and prevention-conscious.[12] Biomedicalization, then, describes the emergence of easily accessible, online information about health care, the consumption of which involves developing expertise about one's own health, health risks, and conditions, as well as the technical details, risks, and benefits of particular medical procedures. Crucially, online media, such as web forums discussing the skill and reputation of individual practitioners, are said to expand our capacity for assessing and comparing the standards and availability of particular forms of medicine. Tania Lewis points out that accessing health information online, in which individuals are cast as "DIY selves," enables those who perform their own health research to become adept at self-care as self-management.[13] The greater autonomy imagined to be conferred through online research is consistent with other challenges to medical authority, including the patient rights movement and community health frameworks, both of which sought to equalize the power differences between doctors and patients, particularly in mental health, women's health, HIV prevention, and environmental health.[14] However, unlike these collective and social justice–oriented movements, consumer health models present patient rights as individualized: DIY selves may lack the capacity to work cooperatively except through information-sharing.

Neither Clarke and her coauthors nor Lewis mention that these entrepreneurial subjectivities are accessible or inaccessible depending on racial or biopolitical categorization of life into valuable or disposable populations. Remedying this, Janet Shim invents the term *stratified biomedicalization* to describe how biomedicine surveils and intervenes in racially marked groups by "the explicit targeting of racialized populations and essentializing notions of their behavior, as in epidemiology's focus on 'ethnic' groups and the 'cultural' behaviors."[15] This is an excellent conceptual tool to investigate how the question of who counts historically within Euro-American medicine as an appropriate subject for GRS is racialized. As I have stressed in previous chapters, treatment protocols reward trans subjects' aspiration to the markers of whiteness and respectability while penalizing those who do not aspire to upward mobility or who labor in informal economies, such as sex work. And as I show in this chapter, having the resources to imagine oneself as an expert in comparing GRS techniques, recovery times, and hospital care is differentiated in terms of racialization and class, as well as financial stability and physical ability.

In analyzing GRS, I am not privileging surgical (and hormonal) bodily transformation at the expense of nonsurgical or nonhormonal trans embodiments. Not all trans people want or get GRS. The majority of trans people cannot afford it—although at least in countries with subsidized health care, it is within easier grasp. By researching the mobile practices of those who make that choice, and *can* afford it, I foreground the political economies of access to trans and gender nonconforming people's bodily modifications. As I argued in chapter 1, mobility is a form of cultural capital. For those able to accrue it, mobility confers an expanded sense of the world's potentialities and their potentiality as bodies and selves. I track transgender medical travel to analyze the precise ways in which that particular form of mobility reproduces itself, how it works, and how it forms a domain of knowledge around choice and freedom. As will become clear, the discursive domains of autonomy that confer mobility on some trans and gender nonconforming subjects always interlock with discursive domains that deny mobility to other subjects. In this chapter disenfranchised subjects are those who, for one reason or another, must comply with the medicalized protocols of assessment, diagnosis, and patient surveillance of gender variance. Nonetheless even being able to choose to travel overseas to obtain a necessary or desired surgery presents a somewhat precarious form of autonomy.

Transnational Disjunctures in Gender Reassignment Somatechnologies

The missing element in many analyses of neoliberal biomedicalization and entrepreneurialism of the self is how these processes differ across nations, regions, and space. Anglophone transgender studies scholars have not paid enough attention to how transnational and local specificities in the biopolitical management of health care inflect different subjective experiences of transness and trans health care, both between different spaces within the English-speaking world and between other regions, especially those in the Global South. In trans studies thus far, these disjunctures have been attributed to the terminological break between transsexual and transgender: *transsexual* articulates a medicalized version of gender nonconforming life, attached to "passing," hormones, and surgery; and *transgender* has been taken up as more gender fluid, playful, or deliberately opposed to medicalization. However, this split does not take into account how transsexuality is understood differently when the medical procedures and treatment protocols that compose it happen within different structures, how trans and gender nonconforming subjects engage with medicine differently to access body modifications, or how gender reassignment surgeries are understood outside of Euro-American definitions of gender. To trace these formations I examine how gender reassignment and gender dysphoria have emerged in different health care systems.

The multiple configurations of how access to GRS is regulated inconsistently in different locations are affected by large, unwieldy structures and infrastructures. National assemblages of governance affect what constitutes citizenship or personhood (and gendered personhood in particular). This includes histories of medicine and psychiatry, as well as the economic management of health and medicine: the different formations of publicly funded health care, health insurance, privatization, and welfare or safety nets in different nation-states and localities. Histories of racial capitalism, slavery, colonialism, and imperialism inflect the biopolitical management of welfare and public health and the very capacity to make distinctions between public and private. So too do religious and cultural values. Further, these different structures are not merely static institutions but rather institutional assemblages that shift and mutate as they interact with political forces and activist attempts to modify existing structures or to create alternative health care provisions.

One of the most obvious differentiating factors influencing access to GRS is the question of regulation: Is it publicly or privately available? Who administers or regulates such access? One formative and transnationally popular model is a clinical team approach, in which different specialists discuss particular patients under the aegis of a larger health system (a hospital, university, or public health institution, for example). This approach emerged in the United States in the 1960s in gender identity clinics attached to universities: Johns Hopkins University, UCLA, Stanford, Northwestern, the University of Washington, the University of Minnesota, and a few others.[16] The clinical team model was simultaneously taken up in many other locations. However, there are some instructive particularities to the health care systems under which these programs emerged.

In the United States, due to the absence of a comprehensive state or national public health care system, only university clinics and teaching hospitals could support public- or state-funded gender reassignment somatechnologies. Even these could not have functioned without the support of private donors—notably Reed Erickson's Erickson Educational Foundation.[17] Clinicians involved in US university clinics thus had a relatively high degree of autonomy. They were answerable to public and expert opinion but not necessarily to larger administrative or regulatory bodies. Patients heard about university clinics by word of mouth or through private referrals (often from Harry Benjamin) rather than an official or universal referral process. Following a backlash in the late 1970s against gender reassignment as treatment for gender dysphoria—a critique that arose partially from the left antipsychiatry movement—the majority of US university gender identity clinics were shut down.[18] As a consequence trans health care was relegated to the private sector.

The privatization of US trans medical care in the 1970s had a large impact on the scope and form of access to psychiatric and therapeutic diagnosis, as well as to gender reassignment somatechnologies, as Meyerowitz observes.[19] In one sense this opened up access. As more physicians became willing to offer gender identity disorder diagnoses, hormone therapy, and surgical procedures, privatization opened the way for many more trans people with financial resources to find body modification.[20] Importantly, this access was contingent on the discretion of individual providers and surgeons regarding treatment protocols and requirements for surgery. It became common for trans and gender nonconforming people to access nongenital procedures such as chest reconstruction surgery, breast enhancement, or facial surgeries without a years-long "real-life experience," hormone therapy, or even (sometimes) a gender identity disorder diagnosis. However, privatization also restricted access in important ways. Access to health care for low-income individuals was influenced by larger economic processes: a sharp increase in the overall cost of medical treatment in the 1970s, tied to high inflation in the midst of a recession, and government withdrawal from redistributive and regulatory health care programs in the 1980s under the Reagan administration.[21] The growth of a profitable private industry of specialist GRS is also attributable to the overgrowth of medical specialization and retreat from and underfunding of primary care and preventive health care services (particularly for poor communities and communities of color) in the same period.[22] Medicaid and Medicare, the programs available for low-income patients, did not include coverage for any form of trans health care until 2014.[23] Instead, alternative trans health care for low-income individuals emerged within independent and philanthropically funded health clinics begun by women of color, feminists, trans people, lesbians and gay men, and AIDS activists during the 1970s and 1980s. These same clinics became responsible for developing harm-reduction treatment protocols as an alternative to the requirements designed by the Harry Benjamin International Gender Dysphoria Association.[24] As such, trans health care has always formed a part of other services: primary care, HIV prevention and treatment, and other harm-reduction or informed consent practices. These large-scale institutional trends have shaped the gamut of trans and gender nonconforming identifications and cultural practices. They have enabled trans identification to be detached from surgical and hormonal body modification, while, inversely, making the somatechnics of surgical and hormonal modification available in the absence of self-identification as trans.

As Ochoa's work in *Queen for a Day* illustrates, outside North America it is neither exceptional nor unusual for gender reassignment somatechnologies to be widely available in the absence of medical protocols or diagnosis. Latin and South American countries with a large reconstructive and cosmetic surgery industry provide somatechnologies aimed at transforming gendered embodiment on demand as part of a mass aesthetics of femininity; this includes silicone implants and liquid silicone injected into the skin to "contour" buttocks or breasts, as well as hormones and facial surgeries.[25] In Southeast Asia too, largely unregulated facial surgeries and orchiectomies (removal of the testes) are popular among gender nonconforming populations who may not interface with a medical protocol of gender dysphoria, even if such a protocol is practiced within some medical arenas.[26] (I expand on the differential provision and discontinuities of gender reassignment somatechnologies within Thailand in chapter 5.) These practices accompany diasporic immigrant populations into the Global North, as they are available through informal economies and word of mouth.

In contrast to this emergence of private or free market availability of somatechnologies, nation-states that take up a clinical model of gender dysphoria within socialized health care tend to institutionalize the clinical team model and thus centralize access to gender reassignment somatechnologies. For example, the UK's National Health Service (NHS) oversees the Charing Cross Gender Identity Clinic. Referrals to the clinic must come from a "community mental health team" or a psychologist, also under the aegis of the NHS.[27] While the NHS subsidizes physician consultations, hormone therapy, and surgery, this creates a level of governmental oversight unheard of in the United States. This state-run clinic model circulates internationally in an ad hoc manner. Toronto's Clarke Institute of Psychiatry, a state institution and the only program providing access to GRS in Canada, provided the model for a similar program in Hong Kong.[28] Hong Kong's Gender Identity Team was established in 1989 and included a psychiatrist, psychologists, a surgeon, a social worker who made house visits, a geneticist, and an attorney.[29] Australia's system works in a similar way, about which I elaborate more below. Iran presents another national model that exists within the structure of socialized and state-run health care.[30] The history of GRS in Iran exemplifies a situation of state-administered gender reassignment that emerged within an entirely different legal and theological context. Afsaneh Najmabadi's *Professing Selves* details how in 1973, an Iranian magazine reported that a man in the province of Shiraz had undergone surgery to become a woman. The patient had consulted the Legal Medical Organizations in Tehran and Shiraz, which had permitted the operation to take place. As Najmabadi observes, later candidates for GRS in the 1970s followed this process of psychological consultation and applied to the local Legal Medical Board. At this point trans people seeking surgery were considered separate from cross-dressing men who did not obtain surgery. As reports of surgical "sex change" in Iran emerged over time, dominant medical discourse changed course and began to understand gender reassignment as related to cross-dressing and what Najmabadi calls "women-presenting males"—in other words, morally unsound "sexual deviancy." In 1976 the Medical Council of Iran banned sex change surgeries. Following the ban some doctors advised trans people to go overseas to obtain surgery, but others continued to perform surgeries. In 1983, however, this ban was repealed: Ayatollah Khomeini delivered a *fatwa* stating that "changing sex with a doctor's approval is not prohibited."[31] Najmabadi notes that medical opinions on GRS were transformed by this new theological recognition and by advances in prosthetic and reconstruction surgery that emerged from Iran's war with Iraq in the 1980s. This new need for training and specialization in reconstructive surgery expanded the acceptability of trans surgeries. Currently to access GRS in Iran requires assessment from the Tehran Psychiatric Institute and approval from the Legal Medical Organization of Iran. This permits insurance coverage as well as minimal state subsidization of the surgery.

Subjects' capacities to understand themselves as trans or gender nonconforming in particular ways are influenced by these diverse national and transnational configurations of health care. In a medical environment in which body modification is available only to subjects who present as embodying "real" maleness or femaleness, subjects are more likely to self-identify within these boundaries. Conversely, in a context such as the United States, where body modification is available independent of case history or identification, nonbinary and genderqueer identities are often more visible. This does not take into account the transnational circulation of gender nonconforming identities such as transsexual, transgender, nonbinary, and genderqueer. But it may explain why European and Australian trans activists tend to fetishize North America as a location wherein anything is possible and where nonmedicalized trans communities flourish much more extensively than elsewhere.[32]

The other question that arises in considering the discontinuities between transnational gender reassignment somatechnologies is that of agency or patient demand. Euro-American scholarship on gender reassignment somatechnologies generally assumes they become available through patient demand and are premised on patient consent.

Instances in which this is not the case are particularly important to consider in provincializing the history of GRS. In South Africa at the end of the apartheid era, in the 1990s, GRS was available at a very low cost to coloured trans women and drag queens under the public health system.[33] Amanda Lock Swarr details this publicly funded "specials" program, which provided very low-cost sex-reassignment surgeries, but without adequate aftercare or follow-up. Publicly subsidized GRS under South African apartheid was subject to similar problems as publicly subsidized gender identity programs elsewhere: long waiting lists; expectation of patients' conformation to rigid gender stereotypes; no choice of physician, psychiatrist, or surgeon; and so on. White trans people could access expensive gender reassignment surgeries privately, but only if they had the financial means. In fact during the 1990s trans people in South Africa with economic resources often disdained the surgeons working in South Africa and traveled to Morocco for surgery with Georges Burou; in subsequent decades Thailand became their destination of choice. By contrast, Swarr's informants, both medical workers and trans people, characterize the specials program as "experimental" and rife with surgical complications; indeed Swarr describes how rumors of disfigurement and extreme complications abounded in Cape Town's drag community.[34] Swarr argues that the service was made accessible because it was convenient for the South African state and medical establishment to align individual appearance with administrative gender classification. In making this claim Swarr rejects the notion that increased availability of GRS is always premised on patient demand or that demand equals consent.

Simultaneously GRS was part of a different and much more explicit regime of medical abuse and experimentation in the South African Defence Force (SADF) during the apartheid era. As Swarr narrates, the SADF subjected gay, lesbian, and gender nonconforming conscripts to aversion therapy, such as chemical castration, experimental drug "therapies," and surgical treatments, including GRS. Swarr quotes journalists who claim that nine hundred conscripts had forced gender reassignment surgeries between 1969 and 1989. As Swarr points out, exposés by South African journalists and other scholars frame military conscripts who had gender reassignment surgeries as gay men and lesbians, not transsexuals, forcibly "reassigned" to shore up heterosexuality. While Swarr was unable to interview anyone who had surgery under this program, she does point out that some of the conscripts who received reassignment surgery may have identified as trans or gender nonconforming. Here a heteronormative, medicalized understanding of transsexuality accorded with the apartheid state's preoccupation with controlling racial and sexual norms and coincided with an unprecedented amount of power given to medical practitioners to experiment on racially subjugated populations. More broadly this illustrates how gender and sexual norms are produced through the biopolitics of race and vice versa. However, this program was deemed inconsistent with the emerging democratic norms of the postapartheid era and was discontinued after the transition to democracy. Rather than understanding these historical shifts as contradictory or anomalous, Swarr argues that violence toward gender nonconforming people in South Africa is "inherent to the transitional state and the contradictions of rights claims." Swarr notes elsewhere that South African psychiatrists and surgeons incorporated the work of liberal US medical perspectives on transsexuality and gender reassignment into their emerging treatment protocols.[35] Although Harry Benjamin, John Money, and other US-based experts advocated a conservative logic of prescribing GRS only for "true" transsexuals, they did not suggest that gender reassignment could "cure" gayness or lesbianism. Indeed sexual orientation was considered to be entirely different. Although medical experts in South Africa outwardly subscribed to the model of gender reassignment, at least some surgeons practicing GRS under apartheid interpreted these protocols as a way to eradicate homosexuality.[36] These contradictions illustrate precisely why gender reassignment somatechnologies need to be understood as procedures and technologies that change across space and time, deployed for different purposes and under the guise of contradictory and sometimes opposing ideologies.

Trans and Gender Nonconforming Health Care in Australia

Also a settler colonial state founded on European invasion, Australia offers a remarkable contrast both to the provision of gender reassignment in South Africa and to the Thai example I discuss later in this chapter. Australia is an ideal place to examine how geographic location alters the forms of biomedical subjectivation that inflect gender reassignment imaginaries because the English-language vocabularies of trans and gender nonconforming embodiment are very similar to those circulating in North America, but health care itself is managed quite differently. This creates different forms of stratification and access and different forms of subjectivation *as* transgender, transsexual, or gender nonconforming. Gender reassignment in Australia is influenced by its history as a settler colony and its political and racial economies, as well as governmentality in the realm of health care. In previous work I have shown how Australian transgender legal and political struggles have turned on trans subjects reproducing gender normativity, white masculinity, and national capital in the form of racialized cultural practices: barbequing, playing sport, or engaging in home renovations.[37] This is because Australia's history as a British colony inflects a public discourse of whiteness that, until recently, reproduced British cultural traditions and institutions in an effort to be part of the West, despite a geographical location that is more proximate to Asia. Australia regards itself as politically and culturally egalitarian, a value that is accorded greater weight by the successful introduction of welfare reform after World War II, ensuring a social safety net that includes unemployment benefits and universal health care. Thus twentieth- and twenty-first-century Australian culture encodes the myth of a "fair go" or "mateship," values of fairness and working-class solidarity. However, this egalitarianism is racialized, as exemplified in the figure of the Aussie battler, an icon of Australian white working-class masculinity whose putative battle echoes settler anxieties about conquering and transforming the land, extinguishing Indigenous occupants.[38] Australianness has also traditionally encoded heteronormative notions of reproducing the white, or culturally assimilated, nuclear family in the service of responsible citizenship. This is a far more communitarian and less individualist discourse of national citizenship, rights, and recognition than is found in the United States. As in the United States, Australia controlled immigration throughout the nineteenth and twentieth centuries: the White Australia policy restricted immigration to northern Europeans by setting arbitrary language tests designed for potential immigrants to fail.[39] After the dismantling of the White Australia policy along with a new era of immigration from regions outside of Europe in the 1970s, a state-sponsored discourse of cosmopolitan multiculturalism emerged. State governments consciously rewrote Australian national identity as encompassing cultural diversity and tolerance and involving (at the very least) symbolic reconciliation with Indigenous communities, if not full acknowledgment of the violence and genocide of European invasion.[40] This was always more of a projected public discourse than a reality, and recent governments have reverted to a nostalgic white nationalism.

The cosmopolitan openness to diversity that survives is imagined on the basis of not only race and ethnicity but also gender and sexuality: same-sex relationships are accorded the status of civil partnerships in Australia, and a strong antidiscrimination discourse focuses on sexuality or gender identity in addition to race, age, gender, ability, and so on. This too, however, is tenuous in relation to the right's nostalgia for traditional Christian values and white supremacy, in which sex and gender diversity appear as threats to the sanctity of the nuclear family and the nation. Similar to the visibility of transnormative subjects in the US public culture, transgender subjects who are publicly visible in Australia tend to be white and to express a normative desire to be "just like everyone else," while drawing on the narrative of the battler or the "fair go" to make a claim for recognition.

Access to gender reassignment somatechnologies in Australia is overwhelmingly medicalized. This is consistent with a state-run system in which most hospitals and public health centers are managed by government and in which doctor visits and essential hospital treatment is paid for by the state. Depending on location, particularly in large cities, it is relatively easy to find a primary care provider one can see regularly. Pharmaceuticals are also state-subsidized for people on low incomes, the unemployed, single parents, and the elderly. Although private hospitals exist and those with higher incomes can purchase privatized premium health insurance, the federal government has a central role in managing all aspects of Australian health care. Socially controversial biomedical procedures are thus highly regulated, including access to assisted reproductive technologies, surrogacy, stem cell research, and transgender and intersex health care, encompassing treatment of people with intersex conditions and treatment of children who identify as transgender.[41] Accessing hormones generally requires finding a trans-literate doctor who is willing to prescribe them.[42] Historically, HIV and queer community health practitioners have been willing to prescribe hormones on an informed consent or harm-reduction basis. It is expensive to locate hormones or other body-modifying substances on the gray market, as Australia is an island and importing is highly securitized. As I write in the introduction, until 2007 the main Australian clinic providing gender dysphoria diagnoses and surgical procedures functioned on a model of true transsexuality. Some states have legislative regulations governing gender reassignment; others do not. In most areas a medical consensus exists about where to refer patients for surgical procedures; the clinic I describe in the introduction and that many of my informants talk about in this chapter is a key conduit for referrals of this type.

It is important to add a few words about the history that shapes contemporary white Australian cultural perspectives toward Asia, including Thailand. Desires to mold Australia as a civilized and modern bastion of European values at the time of federation in 1901 gave rise to an assemblage of laws and regulations known as the White Australia policy. As in the United States, the White Australia policy accompanied attempts to deport Chinese and Pacific Islanders, many of them indentured laborers, who had immigrated to the colonies during the nineteenth century. Across Australia's history Asian nations' emergence as global and economic forces has been regarded as a looming threat or crisis for the Australian nation.[43] In the 1950s and 1960s this panic focused on China and Vietnam as sources of potential communist invasion, but as the White Australia policy was dismantled in the 1970s and neoliberal economic deregulation followed, nationalist xenophobia rewrote itself as protecting jobs for Australian (read: white) workers and limiting Asian investment. During a brief cultural moment in the 1990s, the Keating government initiated more political and economic ties with Asian nations to claim Australia as a part of Asia, but such an idea never took popular hold. Many white Australians imagine Asia—and Southeast Asia in particular—both as an exotic and easily reachable location for inexpensive leisure travel and as a potentially threatening site of excess or violence, a space where "anything goes."[44] Because Thailand depends on the profusion of private enterprise to support tourist and service economies, that country is a place Australians go to access gray market services that cannot be found within Australia. This includes sex tourism and medical services, but also pharmaceuticals, particularly anabolic steroids. When I visited Thailand for fieldwork, Australian friends asked me to bring back large quantities of Valium, which was easily available without a prescription from pharmacies in Bangkok. Thus the perception of gender reassignment somatechnologies being more unregulated and accessible in Thailand is consistent with popular Australian discourses about Thailand more broadly.

Interrogating Resistance to Medical Authority

All the trans women I interviewed who were obtaining GRS in Thailand had first researched its availability in Australia. Some had researched other nations as well. Many had participated in the program at the Monash clinic to obtain psychiatric approval for GRS, despite knowing they weren't interested in being operated on by the surgeon affiliated with it. Emma, for example, was born in Vietnam and moved to Australia in the mid-1990s, in her twenties. When I met her in 2006 she had been living in Melbourne for ten years. She was familiar with the Thai gender reassignment market; some of her friends in Southeast Asia had obtained surgery in Thailand. After one appointment with an Australian surgeon, however, Emma decided to travel to Thailand. By the time she could afford surgery she had been on hormones for several years; she had been living as a woman since long before moving to Australia from Vietnam. By this time she didn't want to wait an additional two years for psychiatric evaluation. Additionally Emma felt that her autonomy was compromised by having to see a psychiatrist. "This is my decision," she said. "I don't want anyone to tell me whether I can or can't [transition gender]. I am not crazy, I don't need anyone else's approval."

Karen grew up in Southern California and moved to northern Australia in her thirties. A white, middle-aged medical professional, she had a teenage daughter from a previous marriage and had gone on and off hormones for many years before she decided to seek GRS. Karen responded to my call for participants in 2006 and I interviewed her at her clinic in the outer suburban area of a large city. Her profession meant she brought considerable medical expertise to her surgery consideration. To begin the surgery process Karen first consulted a therapist in her own city, who suggested she schedule an interview with the Monash clinic in Melbourne. She paid for the cost of flights and accommodation to get to Melbourne for this appointment. She had heard stories from other trans women who had been through a similar process about what she might expect: "I came prepared for Dr. K., because everybody told me that, you know, that she was moody and all over the place and that if she's in a good mood, everything's wonderful, and if she's not she blows you out the door and tells you to come back in a year. So when she was kind of off the wall . . . I was kind of expecting that and it didn't bother me." Dr. K. approved Karen for a further appointment with the in-house surgeon at the Monash clinic. She flew to Melbourne once more to consult this surgeon. She described the consultation: "He seemed kind of intimidated by me for some reason and about halfway through the interview, he got this funny look on his face and he said, 'You're obviously intelligent.' And I thought, wow . . . [*at this point she dissolves into laughter*]. What a weird thing to say. I was asking very medically oriented questions." Then Karen asked about any complications in patients he'd operated on in the past and asked to see photos of his work. The surgeon did not respond well:

> If you could have seen the look on his face, I mean it was like he, at this point he was really shaking. Because then he had to say, "Well, I've had"—what do they call that syndrome? He'd had to amputate the leg of one of his patients. Compartment syndrome. And he listed a couple of other things that had happened. And he became very defensive. And then I asked him if I could see some pictures of his work. And that elicited an even more. . . . He begrudgingly brought out this book and he was very careful to look through the pages and get just to the page he wanted and then open it up. Luckily for me, the phone rang right as he did that and he left the room so I had a look.

Karen had been researching a Thai surgeon while participating in the gender clinic program and eventually booked a date for surgery in Thailand. Simultaneously, despite her misgivings, she made an appointment for surgery at the Monash clinic. If something went wrong with her preferred option of Thailand, she would have the gender clinic's services to fall back on.

Elizabeth had a similar experience. We met in a small hipster café in Melbourne's downtown in early 2008. She was white and in her mid-thirties and had lived in Melbourne all her life. Elizabeth was happy to "name names"; as she saw it, taking part in my research offered the opportunity to talk back to a medical system that had made her life extremely difficult. Like Karen's and mine, Elizabeth's case was overseen by Dr. K. She followed the routine outlined by the gender clinic: seeing a psychiatrist every three months until the "real-life experience" component of the WPATH protocol has been fulfilled and the patient can be approved for genital surgery. Elizabeth said her original appointment was in 2001, but she was not approved to have surgery until late 2006. Unprovoked, she offered a very negative opinion of the clinic: "I found the conduct of one particular psychiatrist, Trudy Kennedy—and

I'm going to name her—to be absolutely amateurish. Actually opposite of professional, downright destructive, from her attitude. That's all that needs to be said there. I know I'm going to be anonymous here, so that's why I can say it. It's quite harsh words but I want to say it."[45] Like almost every GRS candidate I met, Elizabeth was researching other surgery options online. She decided that she wanted vaginoplasty with Dr. Chettawut Tulayaphanich in Bangkok. When she told Dr. K. this, Dr. K. was displeased and, according to Elizabeth, stalled her in "meaningless" appointments for the next two and a half years. When she did eventually get approved for surgery, the clinic would not give her the written statement diagnosing her with gender dysphoria and approving her for GRS. Elizabeth came to the conclusion that to get what she needed, she would have to resort to deception.

> They refused to give me [the] letter, and I had to say, "Look, I want a letter for my parents. To show them what I've just gone through." She continued, "[The letter] was addressed to me, but on the premise that I was going to give it to my mum and dad to say, "Look, she's been approved."" . . . [The people at the clinic] were worried that I'd take off and go see another surgeon.

Elizabeth made plans to travel to Thailand for an initial surgery in 2006, but also made an appointment with the in-house surgeon at the Monash clinic. "I went through all the psych tests," she said. "I even went out to see [the surgeon] and even scheduled a tentative date for the surgery. Knowing full well that I'd cancel it all." She felt anxious about whether her surgeon in Bangkok would contact the psychiatrist and discover that she had obtained the approval letter under "false pretenses." To cover her bases, she found another psychiatrist who was willing to write her a diagnosis letter, as well as other doctors:

> I got a letter from my case worker, a clinical case worker, and then I got three doctors' letters: two from the Monash clinic, two different doctors there, and then one from my GP. . . . I sent them off as PDFs with my email. I think Dr. Chettawut was like, "This is so over the top," but he was very grateful for it, and I just wanted to make sure that all the paperwork and make sure I was going to get through.

As readers may recall, I was Dr. K.'s patient around the same time that Elizabeth was seeking approval for surgery. The clinic dismissed me for posting on a public blog about my first appointment; years later Dr. K. wrote me a surgery approval letter in return for a promise I would "say positive things" about the clinic and to desist from my activist work in trans health care, which she believed was undermining the gender clinic's legitimacy. These accounts, and in particular Elizabeth's experience of negotiating a system that actively punished her for desiring the autonomy to select the surgeon she perceived to be the most skilled, illustrate the practical disempowerment some patients experience in their interactions with a capricious, inconsistent, and outdated regulatory system. Their articulations are corroborated by the only existing qualitative study of trans people's health in Australia, published in 2008.[46]

However, Karen, Emma, and Elizabeth did not necessarily regard themselves as disempowered. Despite the abundant evidence of malpractice, erratic and unrealistic standards for patient behavior, and the well-known fact that getting approval for surgery through state-based clinics is extremely difficult, they had already made a choice to reject medical authority or to use it creatively in seeking what they desired. I too did not consider myself disempowered so much as temporarily hindered in my plan for chest reconstruction surgery.

In pointing this out I want to destabilize the assumption that trans and gender nonconforming subjects who resist medical authority are universally heroic or that a "real" form of trans subjectivity exists that is not captured by psychiatry. As Dean Spade points out in a key essay on medicalization, "Mutilating Gender," the disciplinary power deployed by gatekeepers reproduces normative gender by mandating the successful narration of the transsexual narrative.[47] Trans studies' foundations lie in rejecting and offering an alternative to that norm-producing logic. Yet the strategies people use to resist medical authority are not universal, and they do not refer us to a universal trans, gender nonconforming, or nonbinary subject whose gender identity "escapes" subjectivation. In fact, for my informants and myself, a different form of neoliberal subjectivation preceded interpellation into the treatment protocols in which we were understood as psychiatric patients. In understanding that outdated models of transsexuality bore little relationship to our own lives and in simultaneously seeking out alternatives while we participated in the gender clinic program, Emma, Elizabeth, Karen, and I envisioned ourselves as consumers who were forced to behave like patients strategically to assemble the medical care we wanted on our own terms.

Dissatisfaction or Disempowerment

This point is borne out when we investigate the idioms my informants used to describe how they regarded the gender clinic system and surgeons who perform gender reassignment surgeries in Australia. They tended to phrase their issues in terms of dissatisfaction. Gemma, for example, lived in Sydney and was an activist in the trans community and the Sydney arts scene. A young, queer white woman, she had not consulted the Monash clinic, concluding from hearing friends' experiences that it was "negative" and "conservative." She had considered obtaining surgery in Sydney but decided her first choice was Thailand. Gemma spoke about her decision to travel to Thailand as a calculation made on the basis of comparing surgical skill and her affective relation to the surgeon: "It's extremely important, of course, to make sure you make the right choice. . . . And that it feels right. I'd heard quite a bit of negative feedback [about a surgeon in Australia]. . . . I just really didn't feel very comfortable [with him]." But Gemma also made a considered calculation about the value of her money and the service she would receive:

> Look, for the price, I could go to Thailand, with my partner, business class, stay at nice resorts, see a world-renowned surgeon who I know has fantastic results, and all for the price of going to bloody Concorde Hospital [in Sydney], getting second-rate care with a doctor I'm not entirely happy with, and I'm not enamored with his results. And [it would] still be about the same price. So it was really a no-brainer.

"Bloody Concorde Hospital" is not an institution that disempowers Gemma by providing less than adequate services here; it is an option she is not happy with. Therefore she takes her business elsewhere.

The dissatisfaction might be with the gatekeeping clinic process itself, but it also involved assessment of the surgeon's technique or manner. Many trans and gender nonconforming people seeking surgical procedures research "results"—photographs of surgeries or YouTube videos showing off surgical results at various periods of time after surgery. In other words, trans patients generally enter a surgeon's office knowing in detail what techniques the surgeon uses. Karen's original consultation with the Monash clinic's surgeon was an appraisal; she already knew the standard she desired. After hearing the surgeon talk about his procedure of asking patients to donate blood before surgery (a nonstandard routine) Karen said, "I thought, this guy is overcompensating for the fact that he had one bad experience. And so that pretty much made my mind up that I wasn't going to go that route." Elizabeth contrasted the "amateurish" treatment she received in Melbourne with Thai surgeons' technique and the gradations of price and results available in Thailand. She had researched photographs of various surgeons' vaginoplasties before seeing the Monash clinic's surgeon, with whom she decided not to proceed: "I noticed that the Australian results mirrored the low end of the Thai. I wanted above that. . . . [When I looked at a photo of the gender clinic surgeon's results,] even though it's meant to be not a very good outcome, it's one of the best outcomes I've actually seen, looking between the legs of people in Melbourne." The fact that the gender clinic psychiatrists penalize people like Elizabeth for articulating a desire to choose their surgeon indicates to patients that the psychiatrists see GRS as a required part of social transition, regardless of the physiological outcome, rather than a procedure involving minute gradations in technique, depth, sensation, and aesthetics. In comparison to the information on Thai marketing websites, which detail all of these elements as well as patient care and recovery, the Melbourne gender clinic discourages patients from understanding themselves as consumers.

The question that emerges, then, is how individuals with different access to imagined mobility and choice articulate their experiences. A very different narrative emerges when the person involved is immobilized or cannot envision multiple options for accessing somatechnological body modifications. At the time I was researching, Aden, a trans man I knew through the advocacy group I co-organized, kept a blog called *Fat Sexy Gender* in which he recounted his experiences with the gender clinic program. By the time he was writing his blog I had stopped attending meetings, but we encountered each other socially and followed each other's online journals. Aden has a chronic illness; it is difficult for him to sustain the everyday activities naturalized as normal for nondisabled people. He also self-identifies as fat. After he had changed his pronouns, name, and social gender presentation, Aden saw numerous doctors and was referred to the Monash clinic program in the hopes of getting hormones and surgery. He waited for three years for approval to begin hormone therapy or be referred to a surgeon. In a blog post called "Big Fat Stupid Doctors," he relates his frustration with the clinical team treating him:

I am transgendered. To transition from female to male in my city I need to go through a gender clinic. I have no choice. There is only one clinic. I cannot go anywhere else.

This clinic is bigoted in ways that would astound you.

I have been told (to my face) that I need to lose weight before I will be allowed to transition—and when I explained that I cannot exercise I was told that I can "take pills for it nowadays." I have been told (to my face) that I should wait until my chronic illness that I have had for ten years gets better before I transition.

I've also been scowled at, looked down upon and scoffed at for being bisexual, polyamorous, and unemployed (even though, you know, I AM DISABLED.)

All this is coming from medical professionals, ladies gents and others. These people control my health. These people get to decide whether or not I get to have medical treatments that will save my life (in this case by stopping me committing suicide).

I am being denied medical treatment.

Aden writes that he eventually "realized that complaining won't help with this particular lot . . . [and that he would] have to jump through their hoops." To this end he consulted a primary care provider for help with losing weight. The doctor lectured him about his weight, advised him that walking would aid the chronic illness that made him unable to walk, and finally proposed prescribing him an amphetamine to help with weight loss. After this Aden posted a few more entries on his blog and then stopped posting altogether in 2010.

Aden, Elizabeth, and Gemma all express frustration at the limitations placed on them. However, they articulate that frustration in fundamentally different ways. Gemma describes her frustration alongside a certain relief at having a better option. Elizabeth recounts how "amateurish" she found the clinic's policies and immediately moves on to discuss Thai surgery techniques. Aden's articulation of frustration is flat: this is taking place in the present, without respite. His frustrations echo my own frustrations in the period when I had been kicked out of the Monash program and could not access chest surgery at all. It is coincidence that the examples of trans people trapped in the medical model I offer here are trans masculine subjects, while those who accessed surgery elsewhere are trans feminine subjects; I refer the reader back to my opening anecdote, in which Tom exercises choice in traveling to Thailand for chest surgery. At the time Aden and I both attended trans and genderqueer support group meetings, where we vented about what was happening, the traumatic effects of this on our daily lives, and how to politically resist such treatment. Aden's frustration at being denied treatment was compounded by his anger at the pathologization of his weight and sexual practices and the trivialization of his disability. Aden's case illustrates how medical practitioners use their patient's entire life and history (not only their gender identity "issues") to make their assessments. In doing so medical practitioners exercise psychiatry's power, which historically carries the capacity to institutionalize and to prescribe treatment, especially in the case of patients deemed insubordinate or noncompliant. This form of biomedical power has its roots in racial governmentalities, as in the diagnosis of "protest psychosis" given to black protesters in the American civil rights movement, the history of medical experimentation on Aboriginal, black, and immigrant people in Australia and elsewhere, and various governmentalities designed to pathologize and "cure" sexual and gender deviance (including the South African example mentioned earlier).[48]

This stark reminder of psychiatry's coercive history is useful, for it offers a guide to the disjuncture between the totalizing extension of psychiatric power and how, for particular privileged populations, health care is understood to be beneficial and aligned with choice and self-determination. My own and others' rage and disempowerment burns so deeply because we do not regard ourselves as patients at all but as consumers of health care. In matters of general health we are able to choose a medical provider who aligns with our particular preferences. Key to a sense of radical disempowerment or capacity to overcome disempowerment, therefore, is the ability to imagine oneself otherwise or not: in other words, the cut between mobility and immobility.

Mobilizing Consumer Enunciation

The availability of gender reassignment medical travel in Thailand is governed by a markedly different paradigm that barely, if ever, approaches patienthood in its traditional sense. The material conditions that enable individuals to access surgeries are mediated by a prevailing sense that trans and gender nonconforming subjects should have autonomy over the conditions of their surgical transformation, and that such autonomy is natural or commonsense. As I have argued, self-determination over somatechnical modification is key to a critical transgender politics that takes the urgent demand for body modification as the evidence for its necessity. However, it is equally crucial to denaturalize this sense of self-determination. To this end I explore how Thai GRS clinic marketing websites augment and incite consumer entrepreneurialism. For a trans person seeking reassignment surgery in Thailand, the project is not merely to decide between having surgery at home and having it in Thailand. Once you make a decision to consider Thailand as an option, a number of surgeons can be researched and compared; the question is deciding which one. As Elizabeth said, "You can purchase from a base line, basic result up to a higher level result. You can go from a fixed price, to a price on application. . . . It's like, whatever you feel like on the day. And so then, also the surgery results, you got what you paid for."

Clinic websites hail their visitors as consummate, savvy consumers. These consumers are expected to want to know everything about the surgical procedure in advance. They must weigh the skill and reputation of each surgeon and develop expertise in evaluating the relative merits of accommodation, aftercare facilities, and leisure activities. This form of information gathering and knowledge circulation about GRS confers on patients the fantasy that they are able to make an entirely autonomous and informed choice. Thus they experience the process as restoring sovereignty over their own bodies and over the trajectory of gender transition. Sovereignty over one's own body is particularly important given the complexity of the surgical procedure and its significance in terms of psychic or affective gendered embodiment.

For example, on the front page of the Suporn Clinic site, a photograph of Dr. Suporn Watanyusakul accompanies a short blurb explaining which surgical procedures Suporn performs and what kind of information can be found on the site. The site offers a menu, under which various aspects of GRS are explained. Under SRS (sex-reassignment surgery) one can find a list of Suporn's conference presentations, the text of his 2002 address to the Royal College of Surgeons in Thailand, a summary of his vaginoplasty technique, and a timeline detailing modifications to his surgical technique. Another submenu, "Results," offers a slideshow of images of patients' genitals after surgery, as well as a visual demonstration of one patient's vaginal depth.[49] Similarly comprehensive information about other procedures is available under the headings FFS (facial feminization surgery) and AM (augmentation mammoplasty, or breast enlargement). Under the "Scheduling" tab, users are informed about the clinic's booking policy, what patients need to supply prior to surgery, the minimum length of time on hormone therapy before Suporn will operate, and required referral letters and identity documents. A separate information section outlines how payments should be made; advice on arrangements for traveling to Thailand such as visas, airline bookings, and how to get from Bangkok airport to the clinic; and what forms of documentation will be provided by the clinic for patients after surgery. Additionally the site offers information about the standard of hospital care, recreational and social activities that take place at the clinic, and services included in the total cost of surgery. This includes accommodations in a hospital during recovery, medications, a courtesy mobile phone, meals, and transportation.[50] This level of detail is consistent with other Thai websites promoting medical travel, both for GRS and other procedures.

A sense of entrepreneurialism is implicit in the very detailed descriptions Karen, Elizabeth, Gemma, and others gave about their shopping techniques, specifically what attracted them to one particular surgeon and not the other. Karen related a complex process of choosing her Thai surgeon (which happened alongside arrangements she made with the Melbourne gender clinic surgeon). She joined an online email list for non-Thais seeking GRS in Thailand. She also gathered word-of-mouth information from a transgender support group where she lived and reported being able to look at a friend's new vagina, after recovery; the friend had traveled to Thailand herself for genital surgery. Karen's research culminated in traveling to Thailand to meet her "number one" surgeon candidate: this was to check out the Thai hospital but also to ensure the surgeon himself was personable and "wasn't looking at [her] like some kind of freak."[51] Gemma had gone about "researching [her] options fairly exhaustively." "I looked at Monash as an option, going to New Zealand, some other Thai doctors. I'd seen a few people's results and listened to their stories and heard their experiences and planned it out really carefully. And as well [I thought about] what I could afford and what the timeline was like and so on. And ah yeah . . . Dr. Suporn eventually came out on top."[52] Researching Thai gender reassignment surgeons through internet message boards, information sites, and surgeons' websites and reading other trans women's surgery journals and examining actual vaginas to look at the result were central to every participant's experience of making this decision.

Most of these research methods are internet-based. All the women were conversant with the techniques used by Thai GRS surgeons, how they compared with other surgeons globally, and the distinguishing hallmarks of a surgeon's individual technique. Asking informants how they chose a surgeon resulted in extended discussion of technical details: the amount of skin particular surgeons use in constructing the labia in vaginoplasty, the survival of penile tissue nerves, whether the penile skin is placed inside the vagina or used to cover the clitoris, the time taken between different vaginoplasty procedures (some surgeons operate in multiple stages with recovery periods in between), and what this means for healing and postsurgical sensation.

Entrepreneurialism, of course, is all about value, not only the value of one's deal but also the value of one's surgery experience itself, and the value of one's new embodiment. For clients of the Thai clinics, thinking about value—particularly their own value as Westerners with disposable income—was never far away. For example, Elizabeth talked extensively about her "buying power" as an Australian citizen spending Thai baht. When I asked Elizabeth to elaborate on what she meant by "buying power," she told me about her choice between two Bangkok hospitals and a surgeon who changed from one Bangkok hospital to another:

> Dr. Preecha's aftercare was fairly good, I mean, he works out of the BNH hospital [in Bangkok]. Fantastic. I went there and had a look at it. But the Piyawate Hospital beat it hands down over the BNH. [Piyawate] might be a public hospital, but the nursing staff were far more attentive. I mean you've got all the décor at the BNH, and you've got the looks at the Piyawate, it looks like a four star hotel, the Piyawate. Obviously the BNH looks like it's a five star. They've got the nice rooms and stuff like that, beautiful recovery rooms. Of course Preecha's now swapping over [from the BNH] to the Piyawate. Because of the BNH's emphasis on show and glamour, and not on care, not really pulling it together.[53]

Elizabeth's anecdote reflects the generalized do-it-yourself nature of health care in post-Fordist capitalism. In the context of her experience negotiating diagnosis in Australia, she rejects the notion of herself as a patient needing a gatekeeper's approval in favor of embracing the skill of picking and choosing surgeons, hospitals, and nursing staff first-hand. Elizabeth felt that she had the skills to decide which hospital was *really* ideal for her, utilizing her technical knowledge to read minute differences in hospital decor as representative of the hospital's attitude toward patients and the level of care offered by its staff.

Here we can see what Kane Race has called a "domain of consumer enunciation," wherein consumption is assumed to confer autonomy or agency.[54] This domain of consumer enunciation is not just a way of speaking; it is a discursive recomposition of the potentialities of the subject—her imaginary geographies, her sense of the world. Mobility here does not simply mean having the economic resources to travel overseas to obtain surgery or hormones elsewhere. It implies the capacity to produce a fantasy of oneself as a consumer of medical procedures and the good life rather than a patient defined by the limitations of publicly available health care and the standards of care. That fantasy of oneself as a different kind of subject, restoring one's lot from the disempowering position of patient to the empowering position of health care consumer, must be sustained to understand accessing GRS overseas as something empowering and "different."

This sense of individualistic entrepreneurialism is so strong that it precedes interpellation into the psychiatric subjectivation framework utilized in gender dysphoria diagnosis and treatment protocols; this is precisely why trans and gender nonconforming patients express such indignation at being pathologized. Both Gemma and Aden resist being placed in a diagnostic framework wherein access to surgery is dependent on the approval of a medical professional. Yet the difference in how they articulate that resistance lies in the fact that Gemma is able to access mobility of many kinds. Her physical mobility is not limited and she has the financial capacity to look elsewhere for surgery. In fact for Gemma, Karen, Emma, and Elizabeth, no matter how they produced the savings necessary to pay for GRS in Thailand or anywhere else, the Monash clinic was always a choice among other choices. The strategies they used to pay for surgery are not insignificant here: Emma saved for many years, while the others sold assets such as houses or took out bank loans. Aden is immobilized in multiple ways: through disability and chronic illness, through the psychiatrist's refusal of access to hormones and surgery, through his lack of economic resources to travel elsewhere or to see different health care providers, and through his lack of financial resources to accrue debt or savings. Disability and obesity diagnoses also produce him as a subject with multiple other relationships to medical protocols, starkly illustrating the point disability studies scholars have long made, that calling for the depathologization of gender dysphoria without depathologizing disability itself only reinforces the boundaries between normal and pathological.[55]

Aden's narration of being "scowled at, looked down upon and scoffed at" for being bisexual, polyamorous, and unemployed also indexes how shame and humiliation are used to pathologize trans and gender nonconforming subjects who refuse to or cannot pass as normative subjects. As I found myself, shame and humiliation are instruments designed to produce compliance. But I also internalized shame; I worried that in posting public criticisms of my psychiatrist, I had failed to be smart in navigating a system I knew would pose difficulties, so perhaps I had no one to blame but myself. Consumer enunciation offers a way to circumvent this shame and self-blame: if one cannot be a proper subject of gender dysphoria diagnosis, one can pass as a productive citizen in an economic sense, able to invest in one's own health. Mobility, economic resources, and (as I show in chapter 6) racial capital enable trans and gender nonconforming subjects in Australia to reject the anachronism of conservative medical authority and embrace their capacity to choose elsewhere, principally in Thailand. As queer and trans of color critique teaches us, gender nonconformity may embody the ruptures and contradictions of capital, but it is also disciplined for reintegration into state and citizenship formations; those bodies that cannot reintegrate continue to be framed as antagonistic and socially disruptive.[56]

Incoherence and Mutation

Most people who access medical care globally enunciate claims on medicine through an entrepreneurialism of the self. Even public health systems interface with their populations in the language of commerce, as consumers of health. Global South nation-states without reliable health care infrastructures rely on nongovernmental aid or informal or criminalized markets, which are another form of consumption. Neoliberal economics and the collapse of welfare state policies mean that most of us are forced into relations of choice, even when our material choices bear little relation to the definition of the word. The opposition between consumer enunciation and patient subjectivation remains, particularly in this context where access to gender transforming technologies is constrained by psychiatry and medicine. However, this contradiction is not necessarily a contradiction at all or, at least, not as far as capital is concerned. In *The Micropolitics of Capital*, Jason Read draws on an article by Eric Alliez and Michael Feher to argue that the differences and dissonances between different social apparatuses constitute subjectivation itself. "Subjection is related to the independence of a subject: as free worker, as responsible citizen, and finally as consumer," Alliez and Feher write. "But this sovereign subjectivity is only actualized by voluntary submission to capitalist conditions of production, consumption and circulation. More specifically, it is in the very crossing of boundaries between sectors that actualizes individuals' freedom while guaranteeing their subjection."[57] Read's commentary follows: "It would be wrong to assume that all these conditions have a uniform effect on the production of subjectivity, that all these causes pile up on top of each other like bricks forming a seamless wall of subjection. . . . The heterogeneity of institutions also produces potential discord. The different institutions cannot but produce divergent and often contradictory messages and effects."[58] We could read this statement as a commentary on how certain forms of mobility between contradictory geopolitical or geocultural zones appear to facilitate a sense of freedom but in fact harness subjects to the weight of being mobile. Alliez and Feher clearly identify the contradictions of capital as constitutive of subjection itself. Thus the key problem here is not that being a patient within state psychiatry or a private consumer of gender reassignment somatechnologies is subject to incoherence or mutation. The key is understanding that incoherence, mutation, and contradiction are central to governmentalities and biopolitics.

Additionally, as I've argued throughout this book, mobility is a form of capital. For those who are able to accrue it, mobility is not merely about geographical travel but about an expanded sense of the world's potentialities and their potentiality as bodies or selves. The imaginaries of autonomy facilitating mobility for trans and gender nonconforming subjects are the same systems that deny mobility to others. While many of the trans women I interviewed and I myself see ourselves as sophisticated, global, and mobile citizens, others, such as Aden, cannot match that sense of mobility with the material capacity to travel internationally. This sense of mobility is racialized. It is also about embodying a form of corporeal citizenship that privileges fitness and physical mobility over chronic illness or disability. We could read Aden's indignation as evincing anger at his treatment but also at not being able to gain access to the comforting affective state of *feeling like* one has mobility, or *feeling like* one has a choice. The dream of escaping restrictive medical regimes by traveling elsewhere and reconstituting oneself as an autonomous consumer is very seductive. It does not, however, change the system that restricts access, and it certainly doesn't change the fact that only those who can afford to spend US$15,000 or more on gender reassignment surgeries may choose that option to begin with.

I want to make clear that this particular form of flight cannot be accessed without economic resources. Given that it relies on an entirely privatized exchange, if this is the extent of mobility as a form of politics, perhaps we need to imagine an exodus that encourages not only autonomy and self-determination but also communality. Or perhaps we should be questioning whether mobility can exemplify a potential politics at all.

Expanding Methodologies

The interdisciplinary scholarship of transnational formations I am performing in this book is indispensable to correct assumptions about equivalence and universality. In a talk at the 2016 Trans*Studies conference on transnational GRS markets, Eric Plemons described how what has become recognized as transgender health care operates in completely different institutional structures in different nations and regions. Transnationally providers have different requirements for treatment, vastly diverging models of health care delivery, divergent clinical capacities and priorities, and different schedules for treatment. Plemons referred to the methodological impasse of collecting reliable data across the diverse nation-states providing different kinds of gender reassignment services. Thus it is impossible for researchers to collect adequate empirical data when one surgery is not like another. Even the same procedure, such as chest reconstruction surgery, looks different depending on where you are. For Dr. Sukit, chest reconstruction is the first stage in a multipart series of surgical procedures and hormone therapy ending in a "real man." Many other surgeons find that chest reconstruction is demanded by people who identify as men, butches, women, trans people, and a huge variety of others. Testosterone therapy may accompany it, or not; genital surgery may follow it, or not. In

Mobile Subjects I've taken this as a given, tracing how patients with the resources for international travel navigate those transnational divergences. But Plemons articulated this as a methodological problem for social scientists who study GRS and trans health care more generally. As he pointed out in his talk, the nonequivalence and radical difference of the social meanings of GRS means that it is impossible to collect adequate empirical data. For Plemons, trans studies scholars and health professionals need reliable data to perform social and medical studies of gender reassignment in order to understand how it can most effectively run.

One criticism of the mode of analysis in which difference becomes a problem hinges on the elision of historical relations of economic production. Transnational instances of GRS come to appear as commensurate through their abstraction as commodities to be consumed. Thus it's important to pay attention to who is centered in an analysis that understands body modifications as services to be consumed on a level playing field. Plemons argued that the expansion of transgender coverage in the United States has resulted in the "second coming" of a holistic gender clinic model that may eventually replace the nonprofit clinic and private surgery model. As health insurance has begun to cover more surgeries, health insurance organizations, teaching hospitals, and universities are launching dedicated transgender clinics to manage every aspect of transgender health.[59] The emergence of these new US clinics may have serious consequences for the Thai GRS industry. In 2016, for example, it appeared that US clients were already dropping out of the Thai market.[60] Plemons expressed cautious optimism about this development. (The conference took place a few months before Donald Trump was elected president, causing uncertainty about US health provision in general.) According to Plemons, health insurance coverage should make gender reassignment surgeries more accessible, while the distribution of surgical skill and practice through local or regional HMOs should also open up access. Under this schema North American consumers of GRS are envisioned to gravitate toward or away from particular markets based on a cost-benefit analysis. This cost-benefit logic is supposed to be the driving force of the industry, whether GRS is accessed through US-based HMOs that cancel out patient cost via the risk assessments of gigantic insurance corporations or in Thailand through an entirely consumer-paid model. But I would argue that the removal of GRS health insurance exclusions is not simply a sign of transgender recognition. Rather, it signals that GRS has become intelligible to US health markets as monetizable: no longer merely the province of individual surgeons but profitable as a model that can be tested, enhanced, and duplicated across the country.

These new avenues of care are also opening up in privatized frameworks. HMOs do not depend on a conception of universal and free health care but are based on their members' enrollment in employer-supplied plans or individual plans with expensive premiums that, even under the Affordable Care Act, remain out of reach for low-income people. Most trans and gender nonconforming people cannot afford basic preventative care, let alone privately funded body modifications. Trans women have one of the highest rates of HIV prevalence (22 percent across five high-income countries, including the United States, according to the conservative Centers for Disease Control). Black trans women have an HIV prevalence rate of 56 percent in the US.[61] Given this fact, universal standards of care for GRS seem less important than tracking the numerous, creative, and different struggles to fight for free health care across the globe and to learn from and join other health care struggles that have created solidarities across disparate communities: campaigns for generic HIV medications; campaigns for access to women's reproductive health; and most especially, campaigns fighting the racialized bio- and necropolitics of risk that tell us communities who die faster and earlier did something to deserve their fates by making visible the violence of nation, democracy, and racial capital.

I also took Plemons to be making an implicit argument for the standardization of trans health care, not just for the benefit of researchers, thus solving the methodological quandaries and making comparative analysis much easier, but for the benefit of trans people who might be better served by universal standards of care. Indeed medical professionals have been attempting just this under the auspices of WPATH, although it seems that such efforts are difficult enough to precipitate the emergence of a number of regional professional associations. The appearances of ANZPATH in 2009, EPATH in 2013, and USPATH in 2016 reflect the growing collaboration of regional trans-focused medical professionals, but also a recognition that global standardization is too contentious to attempt for the time being.

Moreover the idea of universalizing standards of care relies on understanding that health care can exist in an abstracted form separate from the geographical, cultural, and social meanings within which it emerges. As work on racialized and ethnicized understandings of aesthetic surgeries and body modifications shows us, surgical standards of care cannot be universally applicable because understandings of corporeality, faciality, and interiority—not to mention gender—are not universal.[62] Transgender studies needs desperately to retain the complexity of its methodological strategies. While this book uses the transnational as a container to map historical and geographical differences in understandings of gender reassignment (cultural as well as medical), transnational differences are not the only kinds of incommensurabilities that erupt within gender nonconforming communities that practice health or medical care and stymy efforts to collect commensurate forms of data. We can't neglect the differences that pertain within nation-states, states, cities, regions. Transgender health care in, for instance, San Francisco looks radically different when it is practiced in a sex-worker-operated drop-in center, when it's part of an LGBT clinic, when it's part of an HIV prevention clinic, when it happens in a low-income clinic in a historically black neighborhood, and when it happens in a Latinx neighborhood. The protocols and treatment models used in these examples are vastly disparate, not to mention the institutional structures that enable something called "trans health care" to be recognized as a clinical priority. We don't need a turn toward empiricism and collating big data about transgender health across the incommensurate objects of trans health and medicine. Rather we need to calibrate our focus to see the spaces in which *transgender* doesn't even apply as a coherent category, in order to see how practices of bodily transformation might be consistent across some of these different spaces and times, but might also be radically other.

Postscript

Aden stopped posting to his blog in 2010. We lost touch, but got back in touch in 2016. He eventually flew to the far north of Australia after a friend tipped him off about a doctor who might prescribe him hormones. This doctor specializes in HIV prevention and community health and had been a trusted primary care provider for many trans people in Melbourne before moving away. The doctor gave Aden a testosterone prescription. In an email Aden described the suicidal depression he had experienced in the years of waiting for this one thing, a hormone prescription, and how thoughts of suicide lifted permanently on the day he began hormones.

I want to close this chapter by drawing a very brief parallel between the representations of Thai surgeons expressed by the trans women I interviewed and similar representations of US surgeons who practice chest reconstruction surgery for trans men in San Francisco. One of my Melbourne friends, Robot, talked about wanting chest reconstruction surgery for years. Robot had never been on testosterone and didn't intend to be; unlike elsewhere, Australian mental health professionals won't approve candidates for chest reconstruction surgery unless they are permanently taking testosterone. In 2009 Robot could not afford surgery in the United States, nor in 2012 when I revised this chapter the first time. (In 2016 Robot is on a different trajectory and has shelved this plan for the time being.) All the same, for a long time Robot flew to the United States every few years for vacations and to consult surgeons about chest surgery. These surgeons invariably informed Robot that, if the AUS$17,000 for flights, accommodation, and hospital and surgery fees were paid, they were perfectly willing to perform chest reconstruction surgery. The queer and trans fantasy of US exceptionalism is working overtime here: for Robot, the US represents a zone in which trans people are perceived to access more freedom, community, and autonomy than trans people living anywhere else. This is despite the fact that Australia has vastly more accessible welfare and public health care systems.

I have traced the repeated recurrence of such a fantasy of elsewhere throughout this book. At the root of many trans and gender nonconforming people's desire to be mobile is this persistent fantasy: that somewhere else, other trans and gender nonconforming subjects are more free.

THE ROMANCE OF THE AMAZING SCALPEL: RACE, LABOR, AND AFFECT IN THAI GENDER REASSIGNMENT CLINICS

"We All Pay the Same Price"

The Suporn Clinic is a pink-and-white four-story villa on the main highway through Chonburi, a provincial city on the eastern Gulf coast of Thailand, one hour outside Bangkok. A clinic for trans women seeking surgical feminization, it is one of the most impressive buildings in the town. The highway itself spans a smog-filled eight lanes. In this chaotic landscape the Suporn Clinic radiates an unlikely serenity. Inside patients bask in the air-conditioning and check their email on the wi-fi network. After undergoing facial feminization surgery, breast augmentation, or the most complex procedure, genital vaginoplasty, at a local private hospital, patients use this space for consultations with nurses and the surgeon and also as a lounge or a salon. The patients are waited on by a number of Thai attendants. Some are nurses, some are administrative assistants, and some are present to fulfill requests for cushions, water, entertainment, or less tangible services, such as reassurance or affection.

The non-Thai trans women I spoke with who obtained surgery at this clinic described it as a very welcoming place. Although the surgeon's technique is said to be outstanding, patients reported that they pay for more than his surgical skill in creating sensate vaginas and clitorises; they are paying for the entire care package, the term a clinic administrator used. The care package includes full service from the moment one is met at the airport, through lengthy hospital and hotel stays, until one boards the plane to return home, wherever home might be. The service offered, numerous patients told me, is "second to none," even by the high standards of Thai medical travel–oriented hospitals. "We provide the Rolls-Royce treatment here," a clinic manager told me.[1] Extending this analogy, she likened a competing clinic to a BMW and joked that when I visited, perhaps I could spy for her and report back.

This is one of seven or eight gender reassignment clinics in Thailand that service an overwhelmingly foreign clientele, hundreds of patients per year. Most, like the Preecha Aesthetic Institute (PAI) at Piyawate Hospital in Bangkok, are housed within private hospitals with a similarly large non-Thai patient intake. Some surgeons, like Dr. Suporn, work with hospitals but have their own private clinics. Gaining a reputation for managing surgery candidates so well involves careful attention to patient care. During major surgery, a process that involves a considerable and prolonged experience of pain, the practice of care demands attention above all to a patient's comfort.

To offer comfort, of course, is distinct from producing the state of being physically comfortable; one does not guarantee the other. Neither is comfort merely a state that pertains to the corporeal—pillows, climate control, relief of hunger or thirst. It registers an affective disposition, and so does its antonym, discomfort. Comfort may also settle on its intended bearers with more or less success according to the permutations of racialization, gender, sexuality, and ability. Comfort eases our passage as we move through the world; if we have difficulty moving, we experience discomfort. For Sara Ahmed, whiteness is a social and physical orientation that that eases passage through the world for subjects who are white, or whose whiteness is not in dispute. "If whiteness allows bodies to move with comfort through space," Ahmed writes, "and to inhabit the world as if it were home, then these bodies take up more space. Such physical motility becomes the grounds for social mobility."[2] To attend critically to the minute differentiations between comfort and discomfort within the gender clinic then should unfold into more than the mere narration of individual affects. Instead we can explore how the comfort enabled by white subjects' capacity to extend themselves into the world in fact disrupts and constricts the capacity to extend or even simply be, for people of color. As Ahmed observes, drawing on Fanon, "To be black or not white in 'the white world' is to turn back toward oneself, to become an object . . . being diminished as an effect of the bodily extensions of others."[3] Ahmed's use of the term *motility* alerts us to how racialization works at the level of the physical body: it is a form of sociality with corporeal effects.

Not all of the trans women who would talk to me about their sojourns in Thai gender reassignment clinics felt comfortable there. Som, for example, told of her difficulty with the clinic's care after her vaginoplasty, and also of feeling that she could not expect the same service as would be proffered to non-Thai or white patients. Som is Thai and grew up in a poor, rural northern region. She moved away from her village as a teenager, first to Chiang Mai to study, then to Bangkok for work. She eventually met an Australian boyfriend on thailadyboy.com, one of many *kathoey* dating sites around in the 2000s, and he encouraged her to migrate to Australia to live with him. He also paid for her gender reassignment surgeries at the Suporn Clinic. I interviewed Som in an exclusive bayside neighborhood ten months after she'd had surgery. As we sat on a park bench overlooking Sydney Harbor, she initially told me that her experience of reassignment surgery had been excellent. During recovery, she said, she felt like a "princess." Later I mentioned the fact that 95 percent of her surgeon's patients are non-Thai, the majority of them affluent American, British, or European trans women. Thailand is famous for its large population of *sao praphet sorng*, or kathoeys.[4] It seemed remarkable, given this population, that non-Thais constituted the overwhelming majority of patients undergoing gender reassignment surgeries at the most well-known clinics. As Som commented on the apparent disparity of this situation, she revised her previous narrative about the level of care at the clinic:

AREN: When I talked to Dr. ——, he said that most of his patients are *farangs* [foreigners], some from Japan, some from Europe, America, Australia. But not many Thais.[5]

SOM: Because he is very expensive! He put his prices up!

AREN: Many of them put their prices up, I heard. Also Dr. ——?

SOM: Dr. ——, I didn't like. He doesn't even care about the Thais.

AREN: What surgeons do Thai kathoey or ladyboys go to?

SOM: Well, they can do [surgery] in a public hospital, which is quite a reasonable price, and the result might not be . . . not so good. And sometimes I hear from Thai ladyboys and some people, they said that in photos, it looks weird, it's not the same as [*gesturing to herself*].

AREN: Not the same as your surgery?

SOM: No. It looked terrible. Indeed.

AREN: What do you think about this, that the best [clinics] seem to be for farangs, and some surgeons don't seem to care about Thais?

SOM: Dr. ———'s staff [at the clinic] too. When I come to meet them, they will be very nice to foreigners. But they forget about Thais . . . because they think foreigners have lots of money, more than Thai. But we all pay the same price! So we should deserve to have the same service. But we don't have the right to say that.

Other Thai and some Vietnamese people I interviewed shared similar stories. When I visited the PAI in 2006 it was housed in a gleaming, modern section of Bangkok Nursing Hospital (BNH), one of the premier private hospitals in the inner-city Silom neighborhood of Bangkok. Adjacent to the touristy Patpong red-light district and night market, but equally close to other tourist draws like the Lumphini Muay Thai stadium, BNH looked more like a hotel than a hospital. Tastefully decorated in white floor tile and architectural lighting, the PAI consulting rooms resembled the lobby of a day spa. I had come there to interview Dr. Preecha Tiewtranon, the "grandfather" of GRS in Thailand. The clinic manager was a tall young woman named Anh.

After the interview Anh took me to a private ward where I met Emma, one of the clinic's current patients (whom readers will recall from chapter 4). It was three weeks since she'd had vaginoplasty. Aside from a few friends who lived in Bangkok, Emma was alone. Her slight figure made her seem tiny in the hospital bed; she sounded tired and querulous. Because of this it seemed intrusive to introduce myself, but Emma was happy to talk to me. I asked her why she chose Dr. Preecha. He had a friendly reputation, she said, but she chose him mainly because he did not require a deposit for surgery. She was unwilling to pay a deposit to someone in a different country whom she could not meet before committing to surgery.

A little while later Anh came back into the room with pain medication. Emma gave Anh some baht; Anh handed over the medication and left. Then Emma told me she was now questioning whether coming to Thailand for GRS was a good idea. She was alone, in pain, and still unable to walk far without assistance. "I'm very annoyed," she said. "Dr. Preecha is very busy and it's very difficult to get him to come to see me. The nurses don't come to see me. I ring and it takes half an hour for them to come. . . . They told me on the phone that the nurses would take care of me, but where are the nurses?" Like everyone post-vaginoplasty, Emma was on a daily dilation regimen. This process involves inserting a dildo-shaped stent into one's vagina several times a day to maintain its depth and width. While the day spa atmosphere of the clinic's consulting rooms painted a picture of glamorous self-care and aesthetic improvement, behind the scenes life was mundane and arduous, full of instructions on how to prevent postsurgical closure and how to remediate the physical pain and trauma of major surgery.

To place these comments in context, the vast majority of white trans women involved in my project had been scathing about surgical technique in their home nations. Most agreed that the hospital care available in Thailand far surpassed that available in American, Australian, or British private hospitals. Karen obtained GRS in an equally well-resourced hospital in Phuket. She commented that the hospital felt more like a hotel: "[There were] heaps of nurses, everybody always had lots of time. . . . You could ask for something and five minutes later it was in the room." Som's and Emma's stories did not match the overwhelmingly positive narratives I was hearing simultaneously from Americans, Britons, and Australians who attended the same clinics at the same time, underwent the same procedures, and were apparently paying for the same service.

Ahmed appends the lines I cite above on comfort and whiteness with a caveat: "This extension of white motility should not be confused with freedom. To move easily is not to move freely."[6] As I've made clear throughout this book, even white-skinned or affluent trans and gender nonconforming subjects are not guaranteed freedom in the world we live in. The provision of GRS began in Thailand as a way to serve local gender nonconforming people. Over the past twenty years, however, it has transformed into a niche medical travel market targeting affluent citizens of affluent nations, a precursor to the booming medical travel culture across Southeast Asia. Yet the fact that GRS is big business in Thailand does not account for why, in a clinic that is reputed to provide the best care and clearly has the capacity to do so, Som felt that the staff cared more about foreigners than Thais. Neither does it account for why, in a similar situation at a different clinic, Emma felt her needs were not valued. These stories highlight some critical questions: When gender reassignment somatechnologies are freely available to anyone who can meet the financial cost, which trans and gender nonconforming bodies carry more value than others? Within the neoliberal globalization of biomedicine, which racialized subjects constitute the ideal to whom the labors of care and respect are made available, and which subjects fall outside of that sphere of care and respect?

In the first part of this chapter I argue that Thai GRS must be theorized not as a phenomenon but as a market, embedded in the historical and cultural context of Thai genders and sexualities and in the context of Thai medical travel more generally. Building on chapter 4's analysis of clinic marketing strategies, I show how Thai tourist marketing strategies are always already inflected by a Euro-American orientalist discourse, wherein Thailand is imagined as the ultimate space of exotic transformation and the fulfillment of desire. In medical travel marketing, particularly in gender reassignment clinic marketing, this becomes a self-orientalizing strategy. I then turn to non-Thai trans women's accounts of reassignment surgeries in Thailand in interviews and a website photo montage to highlight the pervasiveness of narratives claiming that being present in Thailand somehow facilitates the experience of psychic transformation toward femininity for non-Thai trans women. I ask what situates this feminization as an affective process taking place in an exotic location. What is it about this transformation that specifically interpellates non-Thai trans women? Finally, I argue that to understand the value of racialized bodies, we need to understand the affective labors expended at Thai gender reassignment clinics. The care, nurturing, and transmission of affect to non-Thai trans women patients fulfills a medical function *and* facilitates the self-transformation of those patients into more feminine-feeling subjects. *Affect* can be defined as "bodily capacities to affect and be affected or the augmentation or diminution of a body's capacity to act, engage, and to connect."[7] Affective labor here registers as both embodied emotional work and as a form of biopolitical production, wherein particular practices reproduce the discursive effects of particular forms of subjectivity. The process by which this takes place, I argue, has everything to do with the status of most of the patients as non-Thai and/or Euro-American and with Thailand as both an imagined and a material geocultural space meshing the gendered and sexualized dynamics of global neocolonialism.

Although I refer to GRS in Thailand as medical travel, scholarship on queer tourism offers some useful conceptual tools. Jasbir Puar cautions that queer tourism discourses most often privilege white, middle-class, and affluent queer tourist practices while relegating the specter of the (nonwhite) other to the status of the desired object, encouraging and reproducing "colonial constructions of tourism as a travel adventure into uncharted territory laden with the possibility of taboo sexual encounters, illicit seductions, and dangerous liaisons."[8] This reminder should make us alert to the (neo)colonial constructions floating beneath many tourist discourses. These critical frameworks also informed the development of my research methodology. As I elaborated in chapter 4, my main focus of ethnographic study in Thailand was GRS clinics that provided services to non-Thai foreigners. When it became clear that the seven or eight Thai GRS clinics most popular on English-language resource sites and listservs catered overwhelmingly to non-Thais, I expanded my research to investigate access to surgical modification for Thais—particularly kathoey but also *tom* or trans masculine people. This proved much more difficult, considering my limited Thai-language skills and the fact that surgeons performing GRS for a Thai clientele tend not to advertise as widely online. I was already aware that possibilities for Thais to obtain GRS are constrained. This can be attributed both to the low monetary value of Thai wages in general and to the fact that many kathoey are unable to obtain professional employment. It seemed essential to incorporate an awareness of these inequities into my methodology and, in writing this chapter, to bring the reader's awareness of those inequities into contact with an analysis of what occurs inside the spaces set aside for those gender nonconforming subjects who can afford "Rolls-Royce treatment" in the most luxurious clinics. While these "Rolls-Royce" clinics are a small niche within a much larger local market, however, their operation still warrants analysis.

Gender Reassignment and Medical Travel in Thailand

Access to gender reassignment surgeries in Thailand differs in many ways from the Euro-American context of medicalization and gender dysphoria diagnosis. To understand how, however, we need to explore understandings of gender and sexuality in contemporary Thai society and then to examine how GRS is understood in relation to kathoey identity. Nonmedicalized understandings of body modification coexist uneasily with national debates about Thai modernity in relationship to Asia as a region and in relation to the Global North. But they are also positioned in relation to internal national debates about gender and sexuality, centering on kathoeyness, that are taking place while gender and sexuality terms and categories proliferate—some influenced by English-language terms, and many others not. Gender nonconforming practices were not generally remarked upon in Thailand until the 1930s, when the new democratic Thai state's desire to resist colonial overtures and demonstrate internationally that Thais were civilized resulted in state attempts to enforce binary gender norms through masculine and feminine dress codes.[9] According to Peter Jackson, this biopolitical regulation of gender norms created opportunities to transgress them, effectively producing gender nonconforming subjects.[10] In contemporary times opinions on gender diversity and sexuality in Thailand vary enormously across socioeconomic classes, rural and urban contexts, ethnic subgroups, and generations. Generally, however, Thai social norms do not consider gender nonconforming behavior evidence of a psychiatric condition. The term designating masculine homosexuality (*rak-ruam-phet*) was coined in the 1950s; Jackson argues that understandings of imported Euro-American psychological arguments against homosexuality informed Thai scholarly and medical discourse about homosexuality.[11] He also argues that, contrary to Foucauldian interpretations of Western homosexuality, Thai biomedical discourse emerged after, and in response to, popular media coverage of nonnormative genders and sexualities.[12]

The current most common term to denote cross-gender practices is *kathoey*, which predates Thai terms for same-sex attraction. *Kathoey* appears in Thai vernacular language and in medical texts and covers a wide range of gender nonconforming practices. In some contexts *kathoey* is derogatory; in others it is a self-identifier. It does not specify surgical status nor any body modification. It is sometimes understood as a "third sex" and historically referred to effeminate homosexual men and those assigned male at birth who feel like women.[13] *Kathoey* also once included masculine people assigned female at birth; however, gender nonconforming masculinity is most often popularly referred to as *tom*, a Thai adaptation of *tomboy*.[14] Thai sexuality scholars generally disagree about how Euro-American sexuality and gender formation have influenced Thai culture and vice versa. Rosalind Morris argues that a "traditional" three-sex system in Thai culture coexists with a gradually imperializing "modern" schema in which sexuality and gender are binary, producing four possible positions (male-hetero, male-homo, female-hetero, female-homo).[15] Peter Jackson and Megan Sinnott highlight the multiplication of gender categories that has taken place as non-Thai gender and sexual categories are indigenized. In this interpretation sexual object choice is an extension of gender identification.[16] More recently Dredge Käng's work on Thai genderscapes highlights how understandings of gender and sexuality are influenced by class and location and deployed tactically or resisted according to context.[17]

As Käng's work shows, *kathoey* has both multiplied in meaning over the past ten years and been replaced by other terms. *Sao praphet sorng*, which translates as "second kind of woman," is popular and is considered by some to be more respectful than *kathoey*. The relative absence of medicalization and pathologization has shaped Thai cultural understandings of gender nonconforming embodiment and continues to shape attitudes toward gender reassignment—even by medical practitioners themselves. In the mid-2000s most of the surgeons I interviewed did not regard psychiatric evaluation as a condition for GRS. "Patients in Thailand see the plastic surgeon first, not the psychiatrist, because to them, they are normal people," Dr. Preecha explained in a 2006 interview. "[They say], 'Psychiatrists are for insane crazy people. I am not insane!'" Currently kathoey and sao praphet sorng are not defined within Thai popular discourse by a demand for GRS. Thai news media and popular culture are replete with stories about kathoey and sao praphet sorng who begin taking hormones in adolescence with parental knowledge, if not approval. In Nantiya Sukontapatipark's 2005 study of kathoey and sao praphet sorng subjectivity, only eight out of twenty informants had obtained genital surgery. For Nantiya, kathoeys are far more likely to seek "aesthetic" surgical procedures such as rhinoplasty, breast augmentation, eyelid surgery, and silicon injections than genital reconstruction. In line with broader ideals of modern Thai femininity as taking place at the body's surface, kathoeys value the enhancement of facial or surface beauty more than genitalia. Nantiya argues this is because many kathoeys work in industries like cabaret or sex work, where maintaining physical beauty is necessary to continue working.[18] However, "improving" physical appearance through aesthetic surgery is seen as fashionable and desirable for kathoeys generally. Lara, a contributor to Matzner and Costa's 2007 collection of sao praphet sorng personal narratives, *Male Bodies, Women's Souls*, writes, "If I have a sex-change operation, people will think I am even more strange. . . . I am satisfied with who I am. If I did have surgery, I would have it especially for my face in order to improve my looks. For example, something like nose surgery."[19]

In this context of constantly shifting categories, vernacular, and social knowledge, GRS in Thailand has grown into a large and highly commodified industry. This industry operates as a subset of an equally sprawling and commodified cosmetic or aesthetic surgery market. It is difficult to separate the commodification of cosmetic or aesthetic surgery in Thailand generally (and a concomitant fetishization of particular forms of feminine beauty) from the desires of kathoeys to obtain rhinoplasty, silicon injections, and breast implants. Thus it's important to contextualize the parts of this national industry that cater to Thais before discussing the more recent development of a tourist-oriented GRS market.

During the mid-2000s it seemed that GRS in Thailand was entirely unregulated. This had not always been so and reflected a historical shift from the state-based provision of GRS to the growth of private hospitals and clinics, sometimes called "shop houses." According to Nantiya, GRS was first documented in Thailand in 1972; that year procedures were performed on one trans woman and one trans man. Both cases were covered in newspapers and in an academic article on the "psychology of sex reassignment."[20] After 1972 candidates for GRS were still assessed by psychiatrists, and although surgery was practiced in state-run hospitals, surgery candidates had to pay the entire cost. In the late 1970s and early 1980s, surgeons began to practice GRS in private practice, meaning that kathoeys could obtain GRS without psychiatric assessment. A program at King Chulalongkorn University Hospital still exists, but the others have closed.

Dr. Preecha developed his technique and trained a generation of younger surgeons, many of whom now have their own private clinics. Simultaneously surgical procedures are available at shop houses. These are cheaper private clinics run by surgeons, who often rent rooms in private hospitals to perform surgery. Nantiya's informants generally preferred to obtain surgery in shop houses, which they said "had more facilities than the hospitals, especially the state hospital."[21] Surgeons from the larger cities also visit the rural provinces and perform GRS on multiple patients on one day at a provincial hospital, charging less because of the decreased cost for preparing instruments and hiring anesthetists.[22]

In the mid-1990s non-Thais began traveling to Thailand in larger numbers to seek GRS. A Thai surgeon quoted by Nantiya attributes this to the large number of kathoeys who obtained GRS and then migrated overseas to Europe and North America.[23] Others observe that the explosion of (largely English-language) internet trans culture in the mid-1990s enabled Thai surgeons to advertise more broadly and caused a sharp spike in the number of non-Thais seeking GRS there. According to Dr. Preecha, non-Thai trans women encouraged surgeons to set up websites marketing themselves to a larger client base. (Dr. Preecha's first website was designed by an American patient.) A small number of surgeons gained a reputation outside Thailand and began to attract a large non-Thai customer base. Dr. Suporn reported that in 1996 he was performing around twenty to thirty GRS procedures per year, mainly on Thai patients. By 2006 he was operating on around 220 patients per year and was only performing GRS, breast augmentation, and facial feminization procedures. These 220 patients were almost exclusively non-Thai, traveling from Europe, North America, and other locales outside Asia. Micro-niche marketing targeted at non-Thais has also begun to emerge recently. Another surgeon, Dr. Sanguan Kunaporn, served a mostly Euro-American client base until he began targeting Japanese in 2005, employing a Japanese interpreter and tailoring his marketing to Japanese-language readers. In 2006, he reported, 50 percent of his customer base had traveled from Japan.[24] The explosion of popularity of Thai gender reassignment surgeons among non-Thais also pushed up GRS prices and enabled its rebranding as a luxury service rather than a budget option. One clinic catering mainly to non-Thais raised its price for vaginoplasty from US$2,000 in 2001 to US$15,000 in 2006. Other surgeons followed suit, understanding that non-Thais were willing to pay prices comparable to those found in the United States or Europe for GRS in Thailand. While US$2,000 is still very expensive by Thai standards, the raised prices mean that only very affluent Thais can now afford to obtain surgeries with the five or six surgeons who have international reputations for the best work.

Since they began participating in the medical travel market, GRS surgeons in Thailand have also adapted their protocols to address both national and international anxieties about regulation. In 2009 the Medical Council of Thailand wrote a policy to regulate GRS. Under the new law trans people must consult a psychiatrist, live in their preferred gender for a year, and receive hormone therapy before having GRS.[25] The Thai law addressed an ongoing national concern about a "rash" of teenagers obtaining cheap orchiectomy (castration): the previous year a well-known gay Thai activist, Natee Teerarojjanapongs, had called on the government to prevent clinics from operating on "boys," and the Thai health minister banned nonmedical orchiectomy for a time.[26] While Thailand is often understood as a space where "anything goes," legally and medically, the reality is far more complex. Nonmedicalized understandings of body modification coexist uneasily with national debates about Thai modernity in relationship to Asia as a region and in relation to the Global North, but also internal national debates about gender and sexuality, centering on kathoeyness, that are taking place while gender and sexuality terms and categories proliferate—some of them influenced by English-language terms, but others not. But this does not indicate that a national consensus exists on GRS treatment protocols. Rather the law must be read as responding to Thai national discourses associating kathoeyness with hypermodernity.[27]

This new law offered a double opportunity for Thai GRS surgeons: it helped cement their reputation as modern, reliable, and prestigious, and it also aided in gaining international recognition from Euro-American experts on trans health who had previously ignored (or decried) their existence. However, the law does not appear to be enforced often and is unlikely to be enforced on medical tourists. A further cementing of Thai GRS as internationally recognized happened in February 2014, when WPATH held its twenty-third biannual symposium in Bangkok. For Bangkok to host the international conference for an organization run mainly by North American and European doctors was a coup for Thai surgeons. That Thai surgeons could host and co-organize the 2014 WPATH symposium appears to signal both parties' agreement on basic medical protocols for trans body modification. Anecdotally it appears that WPATH agreed to allow Thailand to host the conference only if Thai GRS surgeons would comply with WPATH protocols; in particular, WPATH requires patients to be assessed by two psychiatrists (which surpasses even the single psychiatric assessment required by the Thai Medical Council).[28] Surgeons have creatively interpreted this and now have GRS patients consult an in-house psychiatrist once they are present at the clinic. In general it seems that flexible surgery protocols still prevail for both Thai and non-Thai trans and gender nonconforming people.

Gender reassignment somatechnologies in Thailand are also framed by the context of global medical travel. The popular medical travel slogan "First World medical treatment at Third World prices" encapsulates the appeal of medical travel: it packages the lower global value of non-North currencies, services, and specialized human labor as a commodity.[29] The popular term *medical tourism* is misleading because it accounts for only those who self-identify as tourists engaged in a leisure experience, not temporary visitors who travel for the sole purpose of obtaining medical or health treatment. Neither does *medical tourism* account for the large expatriate professional communities who may always have accessed a higher quality of medical care than is generally available under state health care systems.

Medical travel to Thailand has exploded since 2000, facilitated by governments eager to find a new source of international revenue in the wake of the 1997 Asian economic crisis. By one estimate the country currently hosts 400,000 medical tourists every year.[30] A different source estimates that more than a million foreign visitors received medical treatment in Thailand in 2006. A number of private hospitals in Bangkok, Phuket, and Chiang Mai cater exclusively to non-Thai patients and Thai elites, the most famous of which is Bumrungrad Hospital, near the popular expatriate neighborhood of Sukhumvit in Bangkok. Dental work (especially laser teeth-whitening) and cosmetic surgery are among the more popular biotechnologies available far more cheaply than in nations with higher-valued currencies. Assisted reproductive technologies are also more freely available in Thailand than in nations that regulate access to in vitro fertilization. As with GRS, niche marketing to address specific populations abounds in other areas of medical travel. For example, Piyawate Hospital in Bangkok caters to Arabic-speaking and Muslim patients.[31] As Ara Wilson points out, expatriate demand for a high standard of medical care in Bangkok has meant that the requisite biomedical infrastructure existed in Thailand prior to the development of a specific medical travel market. Wilson thus theorizes medical travel in Thailand as a "domestically situated, transnational assemblage" that is neither imported from the North nor indigenous.[32] Rather, it redeploys domestic capacities, such as available medical infrastructure, and trades on flexibility and specificity.

Touristic Orientalism and Feminine Transformation

I turn now to consider some of the specific discourses that pervade Thai tourist-marketing strategies and that, I argue, pervade gender reassignment clinics' marketing strategies in particular. Although it is possible to argue that trans people visit Thailand only for the purpose of reassignment surgery and are not tourists, enough of the trans women I interviewed in the course of this project spoke of engaging in tourist practices, such as staying in resorts and visiting cultural sites, to lead me to interpret their subjective relation to Thailand's geography as touristic. As a popular late twentieth-century tourist destination, Thailand has accrued a particularly dense field of the "conflicted and compulsively repetitious stereotypy," to quote Rosalind Morris, that constitutes orientalist discourse.[33] As Edward Said explains, the imagined features of the "Orient" include "romance, exotic beings, haunting memories and landscapes, [and] remarkable experiences."[34] In orientalist discourse Thailand figures as a space of magic, exotic transformation, and the fulfillment of desire. Morris also points to the fantasy of Thailand as a "place of beautiful order and orderly beauty" and, simultaneously, a place where anything goes, whose spaces and people are "responsive to all desire."[35] This fantasy is always racialized and gendered, often iconized in the image of the responsive Thai woman—and, according to Morris, also kathoeys. Here we witness the production of ideal feminine gender through an exoticization of otherness that simultaneously facilitates a moment of self-transformation for the Euro-American subject. Annette Hamilton remarks that this "libidinization" of Thailand is so familiar that it repeats itself in farang discourse everywhere.[36]

Thai tourist marketing strategies reflect this libidinization, even in nonsexual arenas where the tourist promise is more about health than sexuality. A Tourism Authority of Thailand article promoting health tourism expounds upon Thailand's "traditional" assets thus:

> The Kingdom's legendary tradition of superior service and gracious hospitality is working its magic in a new sector. Timeless Thai values and traditions are very much alive in places where it is least expected—in hospitals and clinics around the country. Patients are welcomed as "guests" and made to feel at home in unfamiliar surroundings. The reception is gracious and courteous. Medical staff consistently provide superior service, often surpassing expectations.
>
> Spa operators likewise report that guests are charmed by the traditional *wai*—a courteous greeting gesture that conveys profound respect, infinite warmth, hospitality, and friendliness. Visitors perceive the *wai* to be uniquely and distinctively Thai. The magic is taking hold.[37]

Warmth, hospitality, friendliness, magic, grace, and courtesy: all are stereotypically feminine traits. Even if the Thai individuals meant to embody such attributes are not female and the intended visiting recipients of Thai warmth and grace are not male, this language enshrines a gendered, sexualized, and racialized relationship within the touristic exchange. It comprises part of a strategy Aihwa Ong calls "self-orientalizing." Ong writes that self-orientalization accounts for the fact that "Asian voices are unavoidably inflected by orientalist essentialism that infiltrates all kinds of public exchanges about culture."[38] Self-orientalization involves performing the stereotype of an ethnicity or a nationality to be recognized by the cultural edifice in which the stereotype originates. By framing the Thai medical travel experience as particularly beneficial because of Thai rituals and traditions, the marketing language evokes the stereotype of a Thailand freed from the realities of Bangkok smog, traffic, and political instability.[39] Numerous instances of this strategy can be found in generalized tourist marketing, but as the example above attests, it is particularly apparent in health tourism and medical travel materials.

The marketing strategies Thai GRS clinics use to attract customers follow a similar pattern. When I was interviewing surgeons in Thailand, I found that most were keen to emphasize Thailand's liberal attitudes toward transgender people. When asked what makes Thailand such a popular place for GRS, for example, Dr. Preecha said, "Thailand is a very open and tolerant society. . . . There is no Thai law against the operation." Dr. Sanguan, the proprietor of Phuket Plastic Surgery who, along with Dr. Suporn, is considered by many non-Thai trans women to be one of the best, explained to me that gender reassignment is a successful industry in Thailand because of the surgical technique used and the competitive price, as well as "the hospitality of the people, not only the staff in the hospital but also the Thai people. Very friendly and welcoming! Compromise, high tolerance. I found that a lot of patients of mine say that this is the place they would like to live, if they could choose this. Not only in the hospital, but in the country. They feel safe here when they're walking or shopping."

Often it seemed that surgeons regarded my research as a possible source of English-language publicity for them and emphasized this aspect of Thai culture as they would to potential customers. We might, however, take these positive interpretations with a grain of salt. Most of the gender nonconforming people I have spoken to in Thailand can describe the difficulties of everyday life in detail; in fact many see the West as having a far more liberal and open-minded culture than Thailand. Gay, lesbian, and gender nonconforming people are not overtly criminalized in Thai law, and kathoey, sao praphet sorng, and toms are certainly more visible in Thailand than in North America, Europe, Australia, or New Zealand. Although it may be true that some gender nonconforming Thais are accepted by family and society without the violence, disavowal, and shame that characterize transphobic Euro-American responses to transness, a level of stigma still attaches to gender nonconforming practices in many parts of Thai society. Jackson points out that in Thai films and television series, kathoeys often feature as comic characters or the butt of jokes.[40] Discrimination against gender nonconforming and same-sex-attracted people does exist. Until recently kathoeys were exempted from military service on the basis of mental illness, which was noted on identity documents and made obtaining professional employment difficult.[41] In the same manner that ordinary tourists are encouraged to understand Thai culture generally as timelessly friendly and responsive, Dr. Sanguan's discursive production of Thai culture as universally supportive of gender nonconforming subjects seems designed to resonate with potential clientele—who are coded implicitly as non-Thai.

A brief survey of graphic representations of GRS clinic websites offers another example of self-orientalization in the context of marketing. As I noted in chapter 4, websites and word of mouth constitute the main marketing strategies for Thai GRS surgeons. An explicit connection is made between the "traditional" beauty of feminine Thai bodies and the promises of self-transformation through feminizing physical surgical procedures. The Phuket Plastic Surgery Clinic website banner features the face of a smiling, beautiful Thai woman on a background of white orchids, along with a slideshow of landscape photographs. The GRS section of Hygeia Beauty's website features three glamour shots of equally beautiful women who might be read as kathoey, all with long, coiffed hair, evening dresses, and flawless makeup in the style of the "feminine realness" genre of kathoey beauty pageants. Whether the images of bodies represented here are non-trans women or kathoeys is not as relevant as how they might be read by prospective customers of the clinics. The images fold together ultrafemininity, the destination (Thailand), and surgical transformation in a promise to the non-Thai browsing trans woman that having GRS in Thailand will not only facilitate her transformation into full womanhood but will also transform her into a more beautiful woman.

"Traditional" feminine beauty in Thailand has emerged relatively recently and is a modern discourse that originated more in Thai responses to twentieth-century Euro-American beauty standards and practices than in any "ancient" local Thai culture.[42] Recalling Annette Hamilton's remarks on the libidinization of Thailand as it is represented by Thai women in English-language expat novels, we can read the laughing Thai women on clinic websites as standing in metonymically for Thailand as both an object of desire for non-Thai trans women and the potential vehicle of their own somatic self-transformation. Travel here facilitates somatic and psychic transformation. The key difference is between desire and identification. In the novels Hamilton critiques, the exchange is a heterosexual relationship. Here the exchange is about the non-Thai subject's own feminization, both somatically and psychically.

In exploring how non-Thai trans women relate to marketing discourses associating Thailand metonymically with feminine beauty, I found that many non-Thai trans visitors reflected back the association between traveling to Thailand and self-transformation. As I conducted interviews, I was particularly struck by the descriptions that American, British, and Australian trans women research participants used to frame their journeys to Thailand. Although most were conscious of the urbanized modernity of much of Thailand's actual geography, many talked about their experiences in Thailand as radically distinct from their everyday lives at home. Karen described traveling to Thailand as "a magical experience." Other participants commented that, aside from the novel techniques of Thai surgeons, having GRS in Thailand, this "magical" place, was precisely what marked their surgical experiences as a special rite of passage. When I asked her to identify what made getting GRS in Thailand different from having it in Australia, Gemma asserted that Thai surgeons were more technically skilled at performing GRS than Australian surgeons. When I asked her how she felt overall about traveling to Thailand for GRS, she replied:

> It's something kind of tangible and symbolic, to take a journey [to have GRS]. . . . Do things and see people in a situation outside your normal circumstances. . . . Psychologically, it makes quite a difference to go through a process like that and be outside yourself a bit and come home in a different circumstance, having passed a landmark. With a lot of people who have been over [to Thailand] and have had that same experience, you really notice the feeling that they've done a concrete, tangible thing, you know, and been through quite a symbolic journey. . . . It really does seem to make a difference.

Melanie, a white, middle-aged trans woman from the US Midwest, expressed her feelings about how traveling to Thailand had changed her:

> It kind of imprints on you very deeply. . . . It's such a change, you know. People come here and it's such a changing experience. And you go outside [the hotel] and it's very urban and you're in a different environment. But still, I don't know, it kind of charms you in a way. It makes you start thinking about, you know, spending some more time in Thailand. Really learning more about the country and the culture.

When I asked her to expand on what precisely had charmed her or imprinted on her so deeply, she said, "It's the people. . . . There's just a level of kindness and friendliness that I haven't observed really anywhere else. And if you just even learn just a couple of words in Thai, like 'hello' and 'thank you,' it'll get you a long ways. And [Thai] people, they just, people brighten up, and they want to help." On a previous trip to Thailand, Melanie told me, she had found a painting of a Thai mermaid goddess in a shopping mall near her hotel. The painting, she explained, is "a representation of a goddess of earth—feminine grace [and] beauty." She had liked the painting so much that back home in the United States, she hired a tattooist to reproduce the mermaid goddess on her shoulder, as a marker of what the journey to Thailand meant to her.[43] Melanie's anecdote about her tattoo condenses my argument graphically: for many non-Thai trans women, Thailand symbolizes the potential to transform oneself into (more of) a woman through contact with Thai embodiments and representations of femininity.

As I have argued throughout this book, the geographical journey is almost ubiquitous as a metaphor within English-language trans narratives to narrate transsexual transformation from man into woman or vice versa. The women involved in my project seemed to associate the imagined cultural and spatial milieu of Thailand with femininity (implicitly encoding the West as the masculine part of a heteronormative East/West dyad). Thus Thailand is understood to have a particular transformative power that is specific to trans embodiment. As we saw in *Conundrum*'s orientalist tropes, this in turn hinges on imagining the transformative power of traveling more generally: the alchemical, or magical, properties of journeying to an exotic location. Thus the imagined geography of Thailand combines a set of orientalizing discourses that permit surgical candidates to imagine themselves as becoming more feminine in that space. Just as Melanie's Thai mermaid tattoo marks a moment of personal transformation through the proximity of Thai spirituality and femininity, simply being in "exotic" Thailand marks the experience of not only physical transformation but also psychic transformation: becoming (more of) a woman.

A photo montage produced by one of Dr. Suporn's patients, a trans woman named Rebecca, on an America Online homepage to accompany her account of two trips to Thailand for GRS surgery illustrates precisely this metonymic association between popular Thai iconographies, GRS, and psychic feminization.[44] The Suporn Clinic linked to the montage in a list of patient testimonials until 2012. Rebecca's text reads:

> I had SRS with Dr. Suporn Watanyusakul on January 11, 2005. I had the most wonderful time in Thailand and made friends with some of the most amazing people. . . . If you go to Chonburi leave your inhibitions and worries at the gate. Lose yourself in Thai culture. Enjoy every moment of your experience whether you're heading over for SRS [sex reassignment surgery], FFS [facial feminization surgery],

AM [augmentation mammoplasty] or just visiting! Thailand is a wonderful place. Spend as much time as you can there, you won't regret it.[45]

The montage, which sits at the top of the page and is thus the first thing the reader sees, presents glamour shots of Rebecca after her GRS and FFS, spliced with symbols emblematic of stereotypical Thai culture. Vividly colored shots of tropical blooms, Thailand's most popular botanical commodity, surround the center of the montage, where Rebecca poses with a fan and a spray of cherry blossom in her hair in a dress that gestures toward a cheongsam or a kimono. Surprisingly the outfit looks nothing like a traditional Thai costume or a tourist interpretation thereof; this emphasizes a slippage between the imagined aesthetics of Thai culture (itself collapsing differences within Thai culture) and a generic fantasy of Asian aesthetics. Because it accompanies Rebecca's account of having surgery in Thailand, the montage associates her journey with her feminization, her becoming-woman. The incoherently Asian iconography serves to confirm Rebecca's perception of the power of the exotic to supplement her white-skinned femininity.

To draw attention to the hyperbolic mélange of significations at work in Rebecca's montage is not to dismiss her experience of surgery or of traveling in Thailand as meaningless or insignificant, or to dismiss the medium or the aesthetics she uses to communicate the importance of her trip. Neither do I intend to disregard or discount the personal significance of my informants' experiences. Their affective connection with Thailand as a location is as valid as the sense of connection I experienced there, both as a tourist and a researcher, and in other locations that are not my home. Yet to acknowledge the depth or truth-value of an affective experience is not to naturalize it as somehow existing outside discourse, quarantined from critical consideration.

To return this discussion to questions about the value of particular racialized bodies within the GRS clinic setting, I suggest that a form of subjectivation in which one can metonymically associate traveling to Thailand for GRS with the power to supplement one's femininity already assumes that the subject is non-Thai, non-kathoey, and non-Asian. To imagine Thailand in such precise ways places one within a specifically Euro-American orientalist discourse. A sometimes-resident of Bangkok such as Som, who books into a private hospital and an expensive hotel mostly frequented by non-Thais, would almost certainly experience a very different set of expectations, desires, and affective associations than those expressed in Rebecca's montage or Gemma's and Melanie's accounts.[46] Crucially Som does not see Thailand's culture, landscape, and traditional forms of sociability as exotic. The marketing discourses that targeted specifically non-Thai or Euro-American customers are not designed with her in mind.[47]

Affective Labor in the Clinic

Thus far my argument has been limited to the sphere of symbolic representation: website images, tattoos, photomontages. To relate this to material practices and to ground my analysis in a critique of economies of feminized and racialized transnational labor, I now turn to an analysis of encounters between Thai staff and non-Thai patients in the Suporn Clinic. As I noted earlier, many of the clinic's staff are young non-trans Thai women (and occasionally kathoey) who fulfill various needs for the patients. During a visit to the Suporn Clinic, I had lunch with the English patient-liaison manager and two staff members. I asked about their working conditions, as most of the staff seemed to be on call twenty-four hours a day. Aside from a male driver, all seemed to be women. The consensus among those assembled was that every clinic employee must be friendly, hospitable, and available whenever a patient expresses a need, no matter how trivial, no matter the time. Dr. Suporn's wife, Aoi, who is the clinic's financial administrator, described the working atmosphere as "a big family."[48] She emphasized that being employed at the clinic involved hard work and that an employee who didn't respect the system wouldn't last long.

The patient care manager was a non-trans Thai woman, Mai, who embodied the polite, attractive, and courteous standard of so-called traditional Thai femininity. Mai informed me that because the clinic is so busy, she didn't get to take time off. Sometimes, she said, she was invited to accompany patients on sightseeing trips within Thailand as a guide and assistant, and this gave her a break. Because Mai spoke the most fluent English of all the personal care workers, patients seemed to approach her most often. Throughout the afternoon her cell phone rang constantly with calls from patients. Many of Mai's labors seemed to be mediatory. This involved literal Thai-English translation between patients and staff members, but also the task of translating Thailand itself for the benefit of the patients, as a kind of tour guide, explaining cultural practices, the layout of the town, where to find the best food (Thai, Western, or other), and so on.

Since clinic patients usually spend at least a month after surgery staying in a hotel to convalesce, entertainment activities are very popular. This might involve a trip to the local cinema or a day trip to nearby Pattaya to watch kathoey cabaret shows and shop. The clinic employs a Thai massage specialist, in much the same way as Bangkok hotels and guesthouses employ in-house Thai masseurs. Other activities involve learning about feminine skills; the clinic runs small classes on Thai cookery and makeup application for convalescing patients. Patients can also arrange manicures and pedicures and have their hair cut, colored, and set. To note only these scheduled activities, however, neglects the constant social hum at the clinic, the hotel, and the hospital, all of which involves the attendants aiding the mostly non-Thai, Anglo-European patients in whatever they desire to do. This might include playing with each other's hair, doing each other's nails, or chatting. Mai and other employees were not merely expected to behave in a caring way; they were expected (and saw it as their duty) to make friends and to behave as women friends are expected to do.

These tasks, of course, are affective labor, work that blurs the line between a purely commercial transaction and an exchange of feeling. It involves practices of care, the exchange of affect and work that forms relationships of some kind. Affective labor, or emotional labor, as Arlie Hochschild theorizes it, constitutes a large part of what has been called the feminization of labor.[49] Its presence as a micropolitical practice is intimately related to broader shifts within globalization, migration, and the gendered division of labor.[50] Mai and her fellow workers are part of the global population of what various theorists have termed "third world women workers," "subaltern subjects," or, in Pheng Cheah's theorization of the new international division of reproductive labor, "foreign domestic workers."[51] This is part of what Rey Chow calls the ethnicization of labor, wherein the "ethnic as such stands in modernity as the site of a foreignness that . . . is at once defined by and constitutive of [privileged] society's hierarchized divisions of labor."[52] In being imagined and disciplined to be constantly available, Thai women are placed in the position of the ethnicized worker, naturalizing their subservience as "part of the culture."

Thailand's service industry, on which tourism so heavily relies, is powered mainly by young women who migrate from rural areas to perform various forms of service that blur the boundaries between commercial and noncommercial labor.[53] While these workers are not strictly foreign domestic workers, since they may not migrate transnationally, rural-to-urban migration may be just as significant as transnational migration in marking these workers as other to the metropolitan elites of Bangkok, while also providing the means with which rural migrants can aspire to be modern and socially mobile themselves. For these subjects, domestic work and service-industry work in tourism or hospitality, including sex work, are key industries (as well as textiles and factory work). As Ara Wilson points out, affective labor is a hallmark of many different service industries in Thailand. Forms of caretaking are naturalized within these economies as traditional Thai behaviors, which conceals their function as commodities: "The modes of hospitable engagement found in medical tourism—or sex tourism— are often attributed to Thai culture. The labor involved in gracious caretaking is naturalized in this cultural attribution. Without denying the possibility that structures of feeling or the effects of social hierarchies might produce patterned modes of comportment and interaction, it remains worth considering their commodification."[54]

One of the most important affective labors expected of the Suporn Clinic staff is to pedagogically model femininity for the patients. Through repetition of gendered behaviors, the Thai workers perform a particular, racialized feminine gender that supplements the patients' sense of themselves as women. It is key that the workers may or may not be cisgender. At the Suporn Clinic patients talked about how, some years back, two kathoey Thais ran workshops on makeup application and hair care. Although these two workers were no longer at the Suporn Clinic when I visited, their presence shows that gender nonconforming Thais as well as cisgender women are ethnicized subjects of service labor here. This flies in the face of feminist scholarship on reproductive and affective labor that has focused on cisgender women as the subjects of such labor and opens up a space to inquire about transnational queer or trans chains of care, which I explore in forthcoming work.

The performative gender modeling Mai and other workers do at the Suporn Clinic may or may not be conscious and certainly isn't surprising, given the context. It is also reflective of the generalized orientalization of Thai femininity within tourist cultures. Simultaneously there is something specific to the production of transgender subjectivity happening here. It becomes clearer if we imagine affective labor as biopolitical production, practices that produce and reproduce particular forms of subjectivity. Sandro Mezzadra locates affective labor within Paolo Virno's (among others') theorizations of post-Fordism: "Virno stresses the fact that subjectivity itself—with its most intimate qualities: language, affects, desires, and so on—is 'put to value' in contemporary capitalism. . . . This happens not only with particular jobs or in particular 'sectors' (e.g. in the sector of services), being rather a general characteristic of contemporary living labor. . . . [The] concept of 'biopolitics' itself should be accordingly reworked."[55] Mezzadra's reading of Virno reworks biopolitics in a different direction from Foucault's deployment of the concept to speak about the regulation of populations, as opposed to individuals.[56] It also steers away from a practical definition of affective labor as work that involves the creation of relationships. Mezzadra implies that affective labor is generalized as a feature of post-Fordism. More important for my purposes, he argues that affective labor also plays a role in differentiating subjectivities from each other: "In a situation in which the boundary between friendship and business is being itself blurred (are you building a connection with a certain person because you like him or her, or because he or she can be useful for you?), specific problems arise, which can nurture specific disturbances."[57] This is what I gesture toward when I ask what forms of labor are being performed in a gender clinic in Thailand to produce a particular non-Thai trans feminine subjectivity. As I have argued throughout this chapter, such a biopolitical production of trans feminine subjectivity is made possible through the cultural specificities of Thai gender norms, as understood and circulated in transnational cultural spaces. Further, it is an intersubjective process that occurs principally between feminine Thai subjects (cisgender and gender nonconforming) or their images and non-Thai trans women. Patients attend makeup classes to distract from their discomfort or pain and to pass the time, which flows excruciatingly slowly during recovery. The always already racialized, commodified modeling of feminine-gendered practices unfolds as an inchoate, unobtrusive surplus to the main concern of surgery, but it is central to the care package offered by the clinic.

It is possible to read the scene of the clinic in a number of ways. One way is to return to Jason Read's insight that capital is directly involved in the production of subjectivity: economics and culture are impossible to disentangle, even—and perhaps most especially—in the places we would most like them to be separate. Another way is to regard this intersubjective process as a moment of solidarity between equally dis-enfranchised feminine-identifying subjects under global capitalism. We might also think of it as a moment in which individuals mutu-ally benefit from an economic and social exchange, freely exchanging money for the feeling of being cared for or nurtured, and wages for acts of caring. Alternatively we might regard it as a moment in which affec-tive and biopolitical pedagogies that produce an idealized, imagined femininity conceal the economic dimensions of the exchange. It is dif-ficult to ignore the fact that the trans women who purchase the sur-gical product and its attendant services are by and large affluent, by Thai standards, and white. They have privileged access to consumption practices in ways to which their Thai care workers might only aspire.

I want to steer away, however, from presenting this as a situation in which first world trans people exploit third world care workers. Eco-nomically clinic owners, hospitals, and surgeons benefit most from this exchange. For their part, the Thai workers at various clinics (and in medical travel more generally) might regard their work as of higher status than other forms of care work, offering a chance to learn English and other skills and to be paid relatively higher wages than are avail-able elsewhere. Despite the romanticized vision of Thailand evinced by many of the non-Thai trans women I spoke with, they were also grate-ful to find treatment in a space where their needs were met and where they were valued as human beings, unlike at hospitals in the United States, Europe, and Australia. Additionally we cannot point to Euro-American trans cultures as commodified without acknowledging that more localized kathoey practices of embodied transformation rely just as much on the commodification of trans subjectivity as this GRS clinic catering to non-Thai tourists. However, recalling Som's and Emma's ex-periences of not feeling cared for, it seems evident that the intersubjec-tive practices of affective labor supplementing patients' sense of them-selves as women within the space of gender reassignment clinics relies on a form of racialization that, no matter how pervasive elsewhere, differentiates between the bodies of more and less valuable, more and less ideal trans subjects.

One notable gap in the research for this chapter is detailed accounts of trans men obtaining gender reassignment somatechnologies in Thailand. As I mentioned earlier, during the 2000s only one Thai sur-geon had a large trans masculine clientele: Dr. Sukit Worathamrong at Yanhee International Hospital. Dr. Sukit envisions trans masculine GRS as a multistage process, beginning with chest reconstruction surgery and ending in phalloplasty. While I interviewed Dr. Sukit himself, I was unable to stay in Thailand long enough to conduct comprehensive fieldwork with his trans masculine patients. However, similar themes emerged, which I explore here briefly. Chest reconstruction surgery, metoidioplasty, and phalloplasty are not as widely available in Thailand as vaginoplasty; the global centers for trans masculine surgeries are usually said to be the United States and Belgrade, Serbia, where a team of surgeons has a global reputation for performing phalloplasty and metiodioplasty.[58] Phalloplasty is around five times as expensive as vaginoplasty and can result in extensive complications, resulting in a much lower demand for that procedure. Most of Dr. Sukit's trans masculine clientele travel from other nations within the Asia Pacific. Some trans masculine descriptions of traveling to Thailand reflect a fantasy of that nation as a libidinal space in which one can access self-transformation and desire, predicated on the affective labor of carers and nurses, similar to the accounts of some of my informants. But these fantasies are more often explicitly sexual. To give an example, a Singaporean trans man posted a detailed account of his phalloplasty with Dr. Sukit on an email listserv for Asian and Australian Pacific trans men. Among the details concerning pain medication, comfort, and the process of healing, his email described the Yanhee International Hospital nurses as friendly, beautiful, and flirtatious; they wore real nurses' caps; the mail-girls got around the hospital on roller skates; and he was keen to get out of the hospital so he could show off his newly won manhood to the strippers and go-go dancers in Patpong, Bangkok's red-light district. The writer narrated his surgery by objectifying Thai women who were performing different kinds of care work and by identifying with the stereotype of the male tourist who gets to sample the sexually and racially coded "anything goes" exoticism of Bangkok. Yanhee International Hospital figures in this trans man's imaginary of gender reassignment as a destination wherein he can aspire to recognition as a man, and also as sexually desirable. In this way the racialization of Thai femininity shores up a claim to heterosexual masculinity which, though it is not white, still manages to produce Thai femininity as inferior and sexualized. This brief example shows that racializing imaginaries are not limited to Euro-American trans cultures and that transnational forms of trans masculinity are mediated by heteronormative discourses about proving "real" manhood.[59] These need to be understood in the light of the medicolegal institutions that have produced transsexuality as something that can successfully move past gender indeterminacy and safely maintain gender normativity.

Interrogating Trans Antinormativity

At times readers of this project have questioned whether I am holding "ordinary" trans people accountable for the reproduction of normative gender and sexuality or of colonial relations within transnational medical travel, autobiography, documentary film, and so on. This is emphatically not what I am arguing. It is particularly important to clarify this given the reality that trans people, especially trans women, are repudiated as reproducing and consolidating normative gender, not only by trans-exclusive feminists but by feminists of all kinds for whom a critique of colonialism within trans cultures and centered on trans women is agreeable precisely because it appears to confirm their own surreptitious prejudices. So it is particularly important to identify who or what is being criticized here. Because I point out how whiteness and exoticism pervade Euro-American transgender attitudes to medical travel, some might also read me as reproducing a queer vanguardist dynamic that locates political promise in trans antinormativity. My point is not to hold trans and gender nonconforming people more accountable for being implicated in colonial, imperial, and capitalist modes of production than non-trans people. By attending to how particular trans narratives become legible, we can see clearly how these narratives come to seem inevitable and are institutionalized within gender normative and racializing medical, legal, and social formations. Those forms of legibility are taken up as commodities that have set new markets into motion, along with new forms of reproductive and affective labor, transforming old racial and gendered hierarchies by including trans within them.

Additionally the exoticization of the elsewheres of gender reassignment is not always coterminous with gender normativity. Even if undergoing transition elsewhere conceals gender indeterminacy in a structural sense, the trans subjects who have participated in racializing gender reassignment economies in Casablanca, Thailand, and all the places and times in between have not always folded themselves into gender normativity. Neither would I consider them apolitical. A direct critique of the vision of Thailand as a paradise for transgender surgery candidates appears in ellie june navidson's 2013 zine, *Spiderteeth: Wherein Our Protagonist Flies to Thailand to Get a Brand New Cunt. Spiderteeth* narrates the trip navidson and her partner made to Thailand so that navidson could undergo GRS. The zine has a punk, DIY aesthetic, constructed from cut-and-paste text and images. I discovered its existence via a trans Tumblr weblog and obtained a copy on a small zine "distro," or distribution site. *Spiderteeth*'s form and investments are adjacent to the online weblogs and slideshows I discuss in this chapter, as well as to autobiographical writing, but emerge within a fundamentally different subcultural and political context. Zine-making in the US is heavily influenced by punk, riot grrrl, and the queercore movement of radical queer music, zines, and art. Within punk and riot grrrl zine-making, personal narrative and introspection represent an emergent politics.[60] *Spiderteeth* does echo genres of trans autobiographical disclosure; this is mainly evident in its status as a "perzine," or personal zine, which uses self-disclosure to seek community or mutual aid.[61] But perzines depart from the self-consolidating narratives of more traditional autobiography through a self-reflexiveness about zines' textual and physical impermanence: zine-makers often refuse an understanding of zine content as official or factual.[62] Moreover perzines often use personal narrative as a conduit to articulate indignant observations about injustice.

Not surprisingly, therefore, *Spiderteeth* paints a far less rosy picture of the Suporn Clinic than many of my ethnographic informants. In fact navidson's enraged conclusions about the Suporn Clinic confirm that not all of the trans women who go to Thailand understand themselves as normatively feminine or desire a gender normative femininity:

> When I got to Thailand I had to meet with Dr Suporn's therapist to make sure I was "fit for surgery." . . . I was a freak to him, and frankly to almost everyone working for the Suporn Clinic. There weren't any other explicitly gender non-conforming folks there for surgery. Everyone had a sort of reserved, normative femininity, which helped my punkish high femme to stand out. . . .
>
> Dr Suporn was a hubristic dick. He was way too proud of the vaginas he "created." He repeatedly harped about how pretty they were, and seemed to be taking a strange pleasure in doing the surgery that was

separate from enjoying making folks happy about their bodies—he really wanted to make bodies conform to normative conceptions of gender. There was lots of language at the clinic that implied that a trans woman would only become real upon having surgery—which is gross as hell.

Articulated in the form of a zine, these sentiments do a kind of antipublicity for the Suporn Clinic. Rather than drawing in prospective clientele, they engage in "real talk." Aside from navidson's critical perspective on surgery itself, she writes with vulnerability about not believing that she'd ever have been able to afford vaginoplasty if her middle-class partner had not borrowed money for it, and on the arduous process of recovery and return to "normal life" afterward. Real talk, we should not forget, is discursively constructed and mediated.

However, contrary to my hopes when I heard of the zine, *Spiderteeth* fails to mention how navidson and her partner are engaged in a white touristic practice in Thailand. Thai culture seems of interest to navidson mainly for its "heavily gendered" quality:

Shit here is so HEAVILY GENDERED!
    Labor is completely divided
    Like gender seemed to be a job requirement.

Offended by what she calls the genderedness of the language and divisions of labor in Thailand, navidson finds Thai men particularly crude: "Most women were as sweet as pie and were affirming; Most men were big, mean, scowling jerkfaces who harassed the shit out of my partner and I. Seriously, there were five men who were sweet to us, we counted." Her conclusion: "Men suck." Here navidson appears to evince disillusionment with Thailand as a failed example of potential gender liberation in which normative conceptions of binary gender reign. This vision of Thai culture as entirely subsumed by the gender binary effaces several things: first, that Thailand is home to a huge and diverse gender nonconforming population and, second, that the history of polarized Thai femininity and masculinity emerged from the early twentieth-century modernization project, primarily influenced by the example of European modernity. Once navidson makes this assumption of a Thai gender binary, it becomes foremost; she is unable to parse the "gender normative" scene of the clinic as a scene of strategic performance and gendered labor and is thus unable to understand her own position as the subject who, in failing to successfully be interpellated into that scene, might also be available to forming solidarities with care workers, other trans people who feel similarly about the clinic, and Thai gender nonconforming people. navidson's writing here overcodes the individual performances of reserved femininity modeled by staff and patients at the Suporn Clinic as politically antagonistic, imagining the field as defined by two binary oppositions (reserved femininity/gender nonconforming) that are incompatible and irreconcilable.

In its antinormative demands, *Spiderteeth* thus provokes a question: If resistance to normativity does not always result in political solidarity, how might we locate more capacious and malleable forms of transnational trans politics? Or, as Nick Mitchell writes in a foundational chapter on queer abolitionist politics, this dilemma occasions us to ask "whether, and how, anti-normativity can found a politics that lives beyond oppositionality." For Mitchell, oppositionality doesn't exhaust the political possibilities available; sometimes we must ask how we can "*inhabit* normativity in a way that is corrosive to it."[63] More important, we need a different optic to see others inhabiting normativity in corrosive ways. Mitchell recalls Cathy Cohen's 1997 reminder that the *anti* in anti-normativity does not guarantee "an encompassing challenge to systems of domination and oppression."[64] Cohen herself attributes this failing to a queer politics based on the dichotomy between queer and heterosexual, where all straight people are seen as dominant and controlling. Cohen's broader point is that to insist the dichotomy queer/straight defines allies and adversaries means misrecognizing with communities of color who are policed by, and thus oppositional to, heteronormative state structures but who may not read as queer by a white queer optic. Similarly, we might need to be able to see the Thai clinic workers as illegible, as resistant or corrosive subjects within the genderedness of Thailand, in order for a politics to emerge that imagines solidarity with them.

Nonetheless, navidson's discomfort with the gendered division of caring labor at the Suporn Clinic and in Thailand generally opens toward a different conception of the GRS clinic, one that we would be well advised to imagine along with her. Following from her critique, we can envision a clinic where care is reciprocal, distributed, and detached from gender assignment; where surgical modification and medical intervention do not confer "real" gender confirmation but that we (that is, a general, populationwide "we") readily affirm someone else's stated gender identity whenever we are requested to; and where trans and gender nonconforming people rather than surgeons and medical professionals are the inventors of trans genders.

Envisioning Transnational Trans Solidarities

This chapter began by proposing that gender reassignment clinics in Thailand deploy self-orientalizing images to market surgical services to non-Thai tourists. I argued that a corollary of this process is that some non-Thai trans women who obtain surgery in Thailand narrate their experiences in terms of a magical, transformative (and finally orientalizing) journey that has everything to do with their sense of being gendered subjects. Finally I discussed the affective and micropolitical practices in the clinic scene that facilitate the reproduction of that orientalist narrative. In making this argument I drew attention to the commodification of GRS as a tourist industry in Thailand, consistent with its commodification elsewhere but configured in ways specific to the history of Thai GRS and dominant perspectives on gender nonconforming practices. Most important, I suggested that the biopolitical production of trans subjectivities in this transnational context relies on commodification and forms of labor, the reproduction of gender norms, or racialization, and on simultaneous racializations, gendering, and political economy. Each works through and is inseparable from the other.

It is vital to contextualize the differential value of the racialized patient bodies I reveal in this chapter within an understanding of the low value ascribed to transgender bodies in surgical cultures in general. Access to surgical procedures can often be measured by the difference between what one wishes for and what one bears because it is the only option available. Dominant understandings of surgical reassignment slide between the assumption that surgically modified bodies are always mutilated, abject, and monstrous, and the equally problematic and utopic expectation that GRS renders the trans body whole or properly gendered. Under these circumstances it is helpful to place the micropolitics of GRS in Thailand in the context of ongoing trans political struggles in the region. While I have been writing this book, the Medical Council of Thailand was responding to national anxieties about kathoeyness and in particular unregulated orchiectomies of teenagers by encoding the regulation of GRS into national law. At the same time international interest by WPATH has meant that GRS surgeons are engaging in more exchanges of technical knowledge with surgeons in other countries and becoming recognized as international experts. Simultaneously transgender community members began the Asia-Pacific Transgender Network, which writes policy and does support and awareness work for many different groups in Southeast Asia, Aotearoa, Australia, and the Pacific and is based in Bangkok. And Thai language regarding gender nonconforming practices is changing: in 2010 the Bangkok-based trans celebrity and activist Nok Yollada coined the term *phu-ying kam phet* (trans woman). Nok and her associates deploy what Dredge Käng calls "therapeutic citizenship" by promoting a medical model of transsexuality to advocate for changing sex designations on identity documents and other forms of recognition. Even as a strategic move this has been controversial among Thai trans and kathoey communities. While some argue for more rights based on surgical status or diagnosis, others demand the delisting of gender dysphoria from the World Health Organization's International Classification of Diseases and consciously name themselves kathoey because of its utility as an umbrella term.[65] These new projects and modes of recognition bring with them a whole host of new problems, in particular the export of rights-based logics that assume "transgender" is a universal category, as Aniruddha Dutta and Raina Roy point out in their work on tensions produced by the entry of transgender into gender nonconforming and same-sex-attracted communities in West Bengal.[66] But the emergence of these projects is also a sign that the globe has transformed utterly for transgender and gender nonconforming people—toward more visibility, for good or for bad, and toward a transnational resistance to criminalization, incarceration, and stigmatization largely generated by people in the Global South.

It is essential to engage with the power structures that have made GRS a commodity globally. One of the most important of these is the privatization of health care. Also crucial is dismantling the widely held assumption that gender reassignment surgeries are a choice trans people make, and the opposite but equally pervasive assumption that one cannot be a "real" man or woman, or person, without surgery to make one's genitals congruous with the gender one identifies with. Ideally gender reassignment technologies would be subsidized by the state or free, as all health care should be. But this would not solve the problem that some nations can afford and choose to supply state-funded health care and some cannot. This is the context of global neoliberalism, in which every subjectivity or practice provides another way to extract surplus value. Under these conditions work within national boundaries is insufficient. More trans cross-border solidarity work is needed to trace and cut across these productive or exploitative flows of transnational capital.

VISIONS OF TRANS WORLDING

My major aim in this book has been to analyze transgender and gender nonconforming mobility through a Marxian and critical race framework, understanding mobility as mediated by notions of individualist self-determination, self-transformation, and aspirationalism. I've argued that these concepts are racialized and invested in a biopolitical sorting of trans and gender nonconforming populations into deserving and undeserving recipients of recognition, support, and care. I have also used a transnational feminist and queer lens to examine the historical emergence of gender reassignment itself. In a wide-ranging examination of multiple sites, I've shown how the medical, cultural, and social norms that accumulate around gender reassignment incorporate imperial and, later, liberal multicultural schemas of *home* and *elsewhere*.

The landscape of transnational transgender representation and material life has changed dramatically in the years since I began this book. I'm writing this epilogue in 2017, more than ten years after I began the project. In 2014 Laverne Cox coined the term *transgender tipping point* to signal a radical shift in the public visibility of transgender lives. The effects of the tipping point are everywhere: complex transgender characters now feature in major television shows and Hollywood films, and

new aesthetic modes of representing trans and gender nonconforming lives are being invented. US television shows such as *Orange Is the
New Black*, *Sense8*, and *Transparent* have radically shifted mainstream
media's attitudes to production of representations of gender nonconforming people: trans communities have pressed producers and show
runners to involve trans writers, directors, and actors in their shows.
Debates about trans recognition are part of both the mainstream media
and social media landscape and are even sometimes name-checked
(whether positively or negatively) as the singular issue of the "identity
politics" era. Meanwhile the question of whether this public visibility
has translated to material forms of justice remains hotly debated.[1]

Plus ça change, plus c'est la même chose. While the new aesthetics of
transness challenges gender normativity, the racial and colonial politics
of trans representation continue to reproduce themselves. The Netflix
television show *Sense8* is a prime example. Created by the Wachowski
sisters, who both came out as trans after long careers as Hollywood directors, *Sense8* features a trans woman as a lead character, blogger and
hacker Nomi Marks, played by a white trans woman (Jamie Clayton).
As many critics have commented, *Sense8* presents the exigencies of
trans life not as exceptional or freakish but as part of the complex fabric of Nomi's character and the ongoing plot about sensates, a group of
people located in different parts of the world who are telepathically and
telekinetically connected. *Sense8* is motored by a queer Spinozist vision
that asks what bodies can do, rather than determining their capacities
in advance. This vision has assimilated the lessons of affect theory and
science and technology studies via trans and queer studies: *Sense8*
imagines telepathic connection not merely as "reading thoughts" but
as the intensity of autonomic response, activated and reproduced by
subgenetic codes and manifested through feelings. In this universe
all bodies are always already trans-ed or queered. *Sense8* is also global
to the extent that the action unfolds in eight different locations (San
Francisco is only one of these). In the opening credits color-saturated
shots of global cities with the light trails of traffic flash up, mimicking
the time-space compression of globalization—London, San Francisco,
Seoul, Berlin, Mumbai, Nairobi, Mexico City. This globalized worldview
positions its viewers as global citizens surfing on a wave of sensate diversity, capable of submersively accessing how the "other" feels, tastes,
smells, thinks, and, most important, emotes. Sensate networking is
simultaneous, multiuser, haptic, and happens in surround rather than

mono or stereo. Moreover *Sense8* fantasizes that the asymmetries of global capitalism can be equalized through individuals connecting, in a process that transcends the particularities of their culture. Sexuality and gender are often framed as the vehicles for this transcendence: the sensates' embodied connections allow each one to temporarily exceed the limitations of their own gendered bodies. As we learn in *Sense8*'s subplot, the sensates are a different species, *Homo sensorium*, which in its biological capacity for intersubjectivity poses a fundamental threat to the alienated individualism of human existence and contemporary geopolitics. This vision presents a radically different idea of trans. As Cáel Keegan points out, the show's tagline, "I am a we," evokes gender identity as processual and multiplicitous.[2] Rather than understanding the trajectory of transness as a one-way trip with a preordained destination, or even as a departure-and-return-home narrative, *Sense8* presents transness as plural, decentralized, and endlessly mobile.

Sense8's representation of transness as mobile, multiplicitous, and processual rather than having a beginning and an end corresponds with Jasbir Puar's argument in her 2015 essay "Bodies with New Organs" that biomedical models of passing and wholeness are no longer the privileged discourse through which transness is intelligible. Instead exceptional trans subjects must be able to perform "piecing": selectively recombining parts of ourselves as needed in order to flexibly capitalize on the value attributed to differentiated fragments.[3] Piecing produces a new normativity in which trans bodies must be able to demonstrate the capacity to mobilize, to regenerate through biomedical technologies, and in so doing to embody exceptional futurity, extracting uninterrupted value *through* mobility and flexibility. In proposing piecing as an addition to trans normativities premised on passing, Puar deftly illustrates how the biomedical narrative of transsexuality as culminating in *womanhood* or *manhood* has become less consequential to contemporary trans cultures and communities in the US, while the body modifications once labeled as transsexual are now being practiced with or without trans identity. But this is not necessarily cause for celebration. The project of endless modification—aesthetic, embodied, both and neither—requires and exemplifies distinction and neoliberal social mobility. Under these terms piecing may appear to be transgressive, but it constitutes transness as a market value and a commodified process.[4] The lesson is that inhabiting the mobility and flexibility of *trans* itself is not possible for everyone, nor is universal inclusion the goal. Racialized and biopolitical status as valuable or disposable still dictates who can be perceived to access or fulfill the promise of trans piecing. As I've shown, this differential positioning and inhabiting of bodies is a key problem of mobility in all its forms.

Unsurprisingly *Sense8*'s treatment of race and geopolitics tends to confirm these problems with trans piecing and with fantasies of mobility more generally. Multiple critics have observed that at least in its first season, the show presented life outside the US in cultural stereotypes: Lito in Mexico City acts "overdramatically" in telenovelas; the Mumbai character Kala is a sexually repressed medical researcher who dances in Bollywood numbers; Capheus in Nairobi has problems involving HIV medication and armed gangs; Sun in Korea is a corporate businesswoman and a martial arts expert. Despite the supposed transcendence of culture through connection, these individuals are introduced and marked through cultural tropes. As Claire Light pointed out in a blog post on the first season, the Wachowskis' vision of global "sharing" of otherness is most desirable to those who inhabit a monolingual and imperial cultural environment: the show's producers and its main audience in the United States.[5]

By inventing an aesthetics of transness as flexible and intersubjective, *Sense8* attempts to write a trans vision of what has become known in affect theory as "worlding": the generative capacity to navigate the world, to be acted upon, and to act in the world. But worlding has other genealogies. In an essay on the erasure of race in literature, David Eng assigns two meanings to this term. The first meaning is the worlding of historicism, in which "certain creatures and things are brought into the time and space of European modernity (worlded) while others are consigned to wait, excluded and concealed." Here Eng invokes Chakrabarty's critique of a historicism in which the temporal flow toward modernity is inevitable, disciplining time and space into political and economic logics and consigning racial others to the "waiting-room of history." This version of worlding is violently racializing: racial others are excised as unable to inhabit modernity at all or produced as permanently not-yet-ready. Yet as Eng observes, more than waiting takes place in this waiting-room. In fact, the occupants of the waiting-room push on the space and invent temporalities that refuse the suspension of waiting: to put it another way, "they are *living* within these waiting-rooms."[6] Eng locates an opening in the argument that if modernity is constructed through binary oppositions—"public and private, work and home, labor and affect, and productive and reproductive labor"—a second form of worlding emerges in the interstices of these oppositions. A portal opened up in the waiting-room, as it were. Eng describes this portal as a "site of affective density" that is distinct from, even as it resides within, the times and spaces of modernity.[7] This site of affective density makes space for alternative ways of knowing, being, and becoming, what he calls queer worldings.

Read in relation to the racializing techniques of modernity that emplace and fix colonial subjects in the "waiting-room of history" while advancing others into modernity, *Sense8* can also be read as a queer and trans articulation of colonial worlding. While trans subjects might themselves experience medical waiting-rooms as traumatic and obstructive, white queer and trans subjects benefit most from aesthetic internationalism. This global perspective marks the presence of a modernity that reproduces colonial moves, even as it bills itself as queer, trans, and transgressive. For example, with the exception of Will, the Chicago police officer, *Sense8*'s white characters tend to transgress sexual and social norms. Nomi is the San Francisco lesbian trans woman with hacker credentials; Icelandic Riley is an electronic dance music DJ with bleached hair; German Wolfgang parties in the wild underground clubs of Berlin. Telepathic and telekinetic contact with the other sensates causes the nonwhite sensates to begin transgressing the limitations of their environments: Lito finally comes out as gay; Kala admits to her desire for men other than her husband. We never discover how the sensates deal with the linguistic translation, let alone the racial and cultural differences that mark them as individuals. As Moya Bailey wrote in a roundtable on *Sense8* in 2017, "Are we to assume that the sensate cluster members are all anti-racist, queer, and trans positive prior to understanding themselves as mentally linked?"[8] The sensate orgies in season 1 were celebrated as evidence of the show's queerness. However, they did not include Sun, Kala, or Capheus: evidence of how mainstream queer representation is limited by racial orders of who is understood to be sexy or sexual at all, whose sexuality can be seen, and simultaneously consolidating a postracial fantasy that everyone is really the same at heart (and in bed).[9] This is typical of US sexual exceptionalism, where a radical sexual agenda rides on the back of a consolidation of racial norms.

As much as anything within the show, a speech Lana Wachowski delivered at the Trans 100 Gala in Chicago in 2015 illustrates the dangers of

Sense8's vision of worlding. The speech began with Wachowski discussing her visit to Mumbai to film *Sense8*. In Mumbai, she recalled, people would stare at her fuchsia-colored dreadlocks: "I am used to people staring, I am used to taking pictures, pointing. But it was wild to be followed by circles of people wanting to touch it, wanting me to hold their babies." At first Wachowski could not understand why people were staring at her: "I was surrounded by so much difference, surrounded by so much diversity, the bright beautiful colors of their clothes, the patterns, the textures, the wild variety of spices and the breadth of their art." Surrounded by all this difference, Wachowski arrives at the punchline of her tale: "I realized that the hundred men that are following me, staring at me across the street, they all had the identical [short] haircut." The audience guffaws, Wachowski smiles, and she makes her point that conformity to tradition, or normality, is both limiting and antithetical to her progressive, individualist, and trans-friendly worldview. Wachowski's epiphany swings from one stereotype to another: she revises her original orientalist vision of Indianness as a diversity of color and variety to the perception that Indians are tradition-bound, consolidating a vision of Asian conformity to tradition. This, she implies, is the opposite of her own American queerness, which she clearly considers endlessly creative, courageous, and exceptional. This move requires willful ignorance of the quite conventional white appropriation and consumption of dreadlocks in North America, in which African and African American hair trends are removed from their context in black political traditions; as Kobena Mercer argues, dreadlock styles "sought to liberate the materiality of black hair from the burdens bequeathed by racist ideology."[10] In the process Wachowski also resecures the borders of modernity and places herself at the center of the scene. In the context of her remarks, *Sense8* reads not as an attempt to represent and connect with the real material diversity of the world. Instead it invents a trans worlding wherein transcending the incommensurable differences and structural asymmetries of global capitalism can be accomplished by consuming the exotic diversity of globality, while devaluing the human bearers of that diversity as conformist and conservative. Wachowski's comment calls us back to Jan Morris's opinions of Casablanca, in which everything is exotic but also disappointingly mundane. Even as *Sense8* pushes US audiences to acknowledge the possibilities of planetary species-being rather than nationalism, its vision of globalized species-being relies on representations of racial others as fundamentalist, identitarian, and sectarian, for example the Hindu nationalists who attack Kala's neoliberal capitalist father-in-law in season 1 and in season 2 send Kala's husband bomb threats. While the show and its vision of processual and multiplicitous gender trajectories are speculative and exciting, it also indicates that the institutional power of transgender whiteness is not waning but consolidating itself.

Decolonizing Zombies and Divas

What narratives issue from Eng's vision of queer worlding, what he describes as the portal that makes space for decolonial subjectivity inside or outside the waiting-room of history? Where are the templates for the alternative ways of knowing, being, and becoming that resist the many white trans colonial narratives I've critiqued in this book? These are not to be located in primetime television shows, nor in the genres of autobiography and documentary I examined. One place to locate them is in scholarship that speaks back to the whiteness of the standard transsexual narrative and of the historiographies, aesthetic frames, and visual languages that marginalize or exclude racialized gender nonconforming bodies, and that writes the times and spaces of trans of color life, being, and politics.[11] Other bodies of scholarship illuminate alternative questions and methods, invoking radically different theories of race, migration, diaspora, and gender identity or nonidentity. Much of this work draws on decolonization as an epistemology that interrogates settler colonialism and the complications of comparative racialization, histories of different forms of mobility, and the complicated meanings *colonization* has in different geographical spaces. Decolonization has multiple meanings here: in the context of queer indigenous studies it might mean a literal call to repatriate indigenous land and life and to undo the gendered and sexual violences of settler colonialism.[12] In yet another context, decolonizing work might take place through the refusal and/or speaking back to orientalization or exoticism. The most exciting work from my perspective seeks to dismantle hierarchies of knowledge production rather than encoding trans subjects (piecing, passing, or something else entirely) as the proper objects of an academic gaze.[13]

To conclude this epilogue I look to film and interdisciplinary art to illustrate some of the possibilities of this work. In particular I examine two gender nonconforming artists working across different media, Jai

Arun Ravine and Tannia Tanwarin Sukkhapisit. Both work in a transnational Thai context, and their artistic work speaks back to colonial and exoticist discourses of knowledge about Thai subjects and Thai gender nonconforming embodiment in particular by invoking different kinds of subjectivity, among them zombies and divas. Ravine's and Tanwarin's bodies of work indicate that alternative ways of knowing, being, and becoming within queer and trans of color rewritings of the human might take shape precisely by drawing attention to the labor (affective, corporeal, feminized, and otherwise) of inhabiting that subjectivity.[14] Both artists work with aesthetic duration to complicate representations of Thai gender nonconforming embodiment. Both engage with the background or ground of tourist imperialism, the imperialism of language, and the imperialism of politics (whether in relation to transnational or national Thai settings). The labor of embodiment and somatic experience itself may offer the key to generating conversations beyond the recuperations of piecing or the trap of passing.

Self-described as a "mixed-race, mixed-gender" artist, Ravine is of Thai and white descent and grew up in West Virginia. Ravine's 2011 short film, *Tom/Trans/Thai*, opens with footage of a road in rural northern Thailand. Cicadas whir loudly on the soundtrack. In jeans, a purple T-shirt, and flip-flops, Ravine walks into the frame and squats down. "I'm trying to find myself here," subtitles read. As the camera peers down the road to the left, text appears: "In one direction is a Thai girl." And as the camera peers in the opposite direction, the text reads, "In the other, a *farang* boy." From a distance we see Ravine standing on the road, their body spiraling into a choreography that moves them out of the directional plane of right and left and into a series of slow, deliberate, lateral steps. In the next shot we see the road from the perspective of a dirt track: "I'm here, at the intersection of tom, trans, and Thai."

Tom/Trans/Thai is part of a years-long engagement with dance, film, poetry, scholarly writing, and performance that engages the decolonization of whiteness in relation to trans and queer identity as well as trans of color cultural representation. The film was made during an artist's residency near Chiang Mai; Ravine's aim for the film was to translate interviews conducted with Thai toms and Thai trans men into embodied movement. Moving out of the realm of explicit representation and naming, Ravine writes, allowed them to use contemporary dance to "translat[e] what I know and feel intuitively as our truths into a text that can be communicated and analyzed conceptually."[15] By using corporeal movement as its principal form of communication or translation, Ravine also shows how geographical movement cannot be analyzed without reference to the body: to the body's capacity to be read radically differently in different spaces, and to how bodies exceed and disrupt the production of official knowledges such as anthropology, popular culture, and biomedicine. These official knowledges are diverse and not always what we might expect. In one shot we see a paperback copy of Megan Sinnott's book *Toms and Dees: Transgender Identity and Female Same-Sex Relationships in Thailand* propped up against a bamboo plant, followed by shots of the Thai-language tom popular culture magazine *Tom Act* propped against the same plant.[16] Through a doorway we see a shot of a binder (commonly used by trans masculine people to bind their chests) hung on a coat-hanger, then a syringe, needle, and alcohol pads used to inject testosterone all pegged to a washing line outside.

The official knowledges Ravine engages with include popular culture stereotypes about trans and gender nonconforming communities in Thailand, specifically the phobic myth of trans feminine beauty that congeals around the figure of the kathoey. Ravine's poem "Backpackers 2: White Goes East" from *The Romance of Siam: A Pocket Guide* (2016) directs a blistering laser lens at the forms of touristic orientalism that circulate around Thailand and Thainess, focusing in particular on gender and sexuality. I quote it at length:

> When you say Thailand is tolerant of gender variance, you're referring to the "ladyboy" you almost had sex with who turned into a zombie and threw an arsenal of coconut bombs at your head until you went into a coma. You were airlifted in a special issue Orchid helicopter operated by Thai Airways. When you came to, you got a massage ("that kind" of massage) and sat at a table with a tablecloth and silverware in a restaurant catering to White expats and served by zombies.[17]

The "you" here refers to the English-speaking or white subject addressed by mainstream pocket guides to Thailand like *Lonely Planet* and numerous internet forums, which provide advice, warnings, and etiquette instruction. We might on first reading imagine that the "you" is a cisgender, heterosexual white male, the kind of tourist who would visit Thailand intending to frequent brothels, anxious that a Thai sex worker or date may turn out to be *sao praphet sorng*. The disgust at this possibility evinced by male tourists is akin to the disgust of the taxi driver in *Bubot Niyar* upon seeing Sally and the other Paper Dolls. But the statement "You say Thailand is tolerant of gender variance" implicates a much larger population, some of them undoubtedly gay, lesbian, queer, and/or trans, who, like Gemma in chapter 5, understand Thailand as a liberatory space providing political inspiration for the supposedly less-progressive transphobic Global North. This population would probably consider themselves positively disposed toward transness and think of themselves as "ethical" tourists. However, the Global North's fantasy of Thailand as a liberatory space for trans and gender nonconforming people likewise imagines white subjects as saviors. The next stanza cements this reading, revealing how the fantasy of a Euro-American knowledge about "authentic" Thailand and Thainess also incorporates orientalist desire:

> You think "ladyboys" are so articulate and earnest and innocent, you want to take them out to restaurants to teach them how to use forks and knives, you want to take them home and make them cook with Lite Coconut Milk from Trader Joe's, because the real kind makes you fat. You make them give you massages every afternoon at 3, you make them put tiny little orchids in your cocktails. "Devastating" and "beautiful" are adjectives used to describe orchids and the second kind of woman who finally learns how to be a boxer and defend herself on the street.[18]

Ravine here understands the white gaze as fundamentally embedded in civilizational discourses (e.g., "teach them how to use forks and knives") and objectifying in its emplacement of sao prophet sorng as analogous to flowers.

The "you" in the poem experiences all the stereotypical fantasies voiced by visitors to Thailand, including sexual service. However, the surrealism of the poem amplifies a subtext of danger and threat, which eventually becomes explicit and insurgent: rather than the woman being revealed as trans, the "ladyboy" is revealed to be a zombie throwing an "arsenal of coconut bombs." Instead of being trapped as a foil for transphobic and racialized tourist anxieties, the Thai gender nonconforming figure reconfigures the boundaries between life and death as a zombie and fights back. The apparently lifeless commodities that function as markers of cosmopolitan consumption of Thainess become weaponized in decolonial struggle.

At other times insurrection might materialize in a performance of what looks like docility. *I'm Fine* (*Sa-bai-dee-kha!*, 2008) is a short experimental film in which Tanwarin Sukkhapisit locks herself in a large cage underneath the Democracy Monument in Bangkok. Tanwarin is a Thai transgender independent filmmaker and the director of *Insects in the Backyard* and *It Gets Better*, both of which received international critical acclaim. I include a discussion of *I'm Fine* because it offers another important rejoinder to the absence and/or captured presence of gender nonconforming subjectivity, not within a US trans of color cultural and political milieu but from within Thai and Southeast Asian cinema. *I'm Fine* is three minutes long. As it opens, we hear traffic noises and see a figure—Tanwarin—sitting in a cage with her legs crossed and hands folded. She is wearing a red dress with a pleated shawl over one shoulder, with impeccable makeup and glossy red lipstick. The columns of the Democracy Monument are visible in the background, and in the foreground, superimposed over Tanwarin's body, are the horizontal and vertical bars of the cage. In these establishing shots Tanwarin remains motionless, assuming the position of a statue or monument herself. Cars, trucks, and tuk-tuks race by on the busy road in the background; some shots are filmed in time lapse to accentuate Tanwarin's relative stillness against the speed of the traffic. Shutter sounds and flashes on Tanwarin's face indicate that someone is taking her photograph. Then we see her face. She is impassive and stares into the distance as if posing for a photo. After the credits, people off-camera address her in Thai (I use English translations here): "Are you uncomfortable over here?" "The weather's so hot!" To all of these questions, Tanwarin smiles politely, shakes her head, and replies, "I am fine." One shot shows us the padlock to the cage with the key in it, but no one unlocks it. Off-camera someone asks, "Do you want us to unlock and release you?" "No, thank you," Tanwarin replies. "I'm so fine in here." Sweat drips down her nose and she wipes it off. "Why are you so fine?" the same person asks. "Because I am a Thai citizen," Tanwarin replies. She continues to smile and pose. The final shot features a torn Thai national flag waving aimlessly in the breeze as the end credits roll and the drone of the traffic continues.

Seen in the light of the previous decade of political crisis in Thailand (which resulted in a military coup in 2008, the year *I'm Fine* was made), the film can be read as a commentary on Thai politics. Numerous pro-democracy protests have taken place at the Democracy Monument; it is also the site of at least three massacres of student protestors. Tanwarin's red dress recalls the red shirts of supporters of the neoliberal and corrupt prime minister at the time, Thaksin Shinawatra. Although this particular moment did not result in a state response, Tanwarin's 2010 feature film *Insects in the Backyard* was banned by the Thai Ministry of Culture because of its depiction of a kathoey parent, which, as Arnika Fuhrmann observes, challenged Thai heteronormative familial nationalism.[19] *Sabai dee kha*, meaning "Everything's fine" or "I am fine," is emblematic of the global stereotype of Thai temperament as relaxed and friendly. (The *kha* genders the speaker as feminine; masculine speakers would say *Sabai dee krap*.)

By locking herself in a cage in such a public place, Tanwarin might be understood as performing a form of what Lauren Berlant calls Diva Citizenship: "when a person stages a dramatic coup in a public sphere in which she does not have privilege."[20] The tattered flag at the end of *I'm Fine* supports this reading: in relation to the flag, the person in the cage embodies Thai citizens who are oppressed by an authoritarian regime. But where Berlant's theory and examples of Diva Citizenship rely on intensity—"flashing up"—Tanwarin's aesthetic performance in *I'm Fine* sidesteps explicit political speech. As Nguyen Tan Hoang points out, it is unclear what is happening in *I'm Fine*: it could be a public protest, but it could just as easily be product marketing or a fashion shoot. Viewers do not know how long Tanwarin has spent in the cage, or if and when she is released or releases herself. As Nguyen observes, the indeterminacy of the film mirrors a contradiction between the visual images of Tanwarin perspiring freely in her confinement and her cheerful insistence that she is fine. Nguyen argues that this performs a doubleness he names *wer* aesthetics. In Thai, *wer* is a Thai translation of the English word "over," and Nguyen theorizes it as a form of "over-aesthetics," adjacent to camp but singular in articulating an aesthetic position that is "over something yet simultaneously invested in it." Tanwarin appears to be modeling good citizenship through her speech, while the words "I am fine" are clearly meant to be ironic. Beyond this irony, though, lies a complicit enjoyment. Tanwarin's performance of impeccable femme adornment appears not only to be oppressive but pleasurable.

If we remember the Democracy Monument's proximity to Khao San Road and the historic Old City neighborhood (Rattanakosin), one of Bangkok's largest tourist areas, Tanwarin's critique extends beyond the Thai nation to a transnational imaginary. In that context the film can be read as a comment on transnational orientalism in Thailand. After all, Thai tourism and service industries are supposed to function as congenially and courteously as ever even during extended political crises. By focusing on the exertion of holding a pose throughout a hot day while one is on display, Tanwarin draws attention to the invisible labor fundamental to the femme technologies of adornment expected of Thai feminine subjects (kathoey and women). In this reading Tanwarin's presence in the cage materializes how transnational capital has continued to extract value in Thailand through the service and hospitality industries, and polite Thai femininity in particular, during a succession of corrupt "democratic" governments, military juntas, and rigged elections. Tanwarin restages the orientalized stereotype performatively, mimicking it and turning it against itself to reveal a form of aesthetic agency within corporeal immobility and the project's durational resolve.

It may seem odd that I end this book about transgender mobility by discussing a film that features someone locked in a cage, literally immobile. But this is by design. Considered in relation to the representations of mobility I've analyzed in *Mobile Subjects*, Tanwarin's performance of immobility reminds us that the mobility experienced by some trans and gender nonconforming subjects (whether passing or piecing) depends on the literal or epistemological immobility of others. Eng points out that while the colonial waiting-room of history may seem empty, it's the lens we use to define what is "empty" or "full," deserted or lively that matters. It's also about the kinds of mobility we frame as important, the major mobilities that accrue value and narrative such as often occlude minor mobilities that are imperceptible to the optic of racialized capitalism, states, and institutions. In a new project I move away from the major or privileged narrative of trans and gender nonconforming mobility to look at minor mobilities: rhythms of movement that may look like restless perpetual motion or stuckness but are replete with liveliness and wild and directed impulses. We just need the right field of vision to perceive their power.

NOTES

Introduction

1 *Transsexual and Transgender Road Map.*
2 Amin, "Temporality," 220, quoting Freeman, *Time Binds*, 3.
3 Horak, "Trans on YouTube," 580.
4 Salah, "'Time Isn't after Us,'" 17.
5 Clare, "Gawping, Gaping, Staring," 260.
6 See Christine Hogan, "Man Who Became Woman Wants to Be a Man Again," *Sydney Morning Herald*, August 21, 2003, http://www.smh.com.au/articles/2003 /08/30/1062194756832.html; Jill Stark, "Sex Change Clinic 'Got It Wrong,'" *Sydney Morning Herald*, May 31, 2009, http://www.smh.com.au/national /sexchange-clinic-got-it-wrong-20090530-br3u.html.
7 An informed consent approach means that medical practitioners give patients comprehensive, reliable information so patients may decide on a particular treatment. Harm-reduction approaches refer to social policies addressing criminalized behavior such as drug use and sex work. Broadly, a harm-reduction approach focuses on reducing the harms or risks associated with behaviors in relation to drug use: needle exchanges, injecting rooms, and so on. In transgender health harm reduction refers to making body modification technologies more available in the context of regulated health services, reducing the risks associated with black market or privatized body modification.
8 I use *obtain* in an active sense here, as a process that trans people must initiate and work at.

9   Monash Gender Dysphoria Clinic opened in 1975, was attached to a local public hospital, and was run by a multidisciplinary team including psychiatrists, a surgeon, endocrinologists, and speech therapists. In the 1990s it became an independent entity managed by the Department of Health and Human Services. See Damodaran and Kennedy, "The Monash Gender Dysphoria Clinic." For a critical perspective see Sinnott, "Best Practice Models for the Assessment, Treatment and Care of Transgender People and People with Transsexualism," 21.

10 The exception is the state of South Australia, which has legislation governing change of gender marker and medical treatment for transition, and has a gender dysphoria health service modeled on the Monash Clinic.

11 A few private practice psychiatrists across Australia are willing to provide gender dysphoria diagnoses, but they are expensive and only locatable through word of mouth.

12 Letter reprinted in the *Australian Good Tranny Guide*, a guide to health, legal, and support services for trans people in Australia. After a 2007 internal review and a change of leadership, a new flyer appeared in which mention of true transsexuality was removed.

13 Benjamin, *The Transsexual Phenomenon*, 45.

14 Benjamin, *The Transsexual Phenomenon*, 54. For an excellent critique of Benjamin on these grounds, see Irving, "Normalized Transgressions."

15 The Monash clinic's mention of true transsexuality was removed in 2007, after the clinic underwent internal review (and after Dr. K. had stepped down as director).

16 The HBIGDA Standards of Care document had comparatively progressive treatment protocols at the time. The model of primary and secondary transsexuality became unfashionable as early as 1975, as sexology and psychiatry moved toward a theory of gender dysphoria or gender identity disorder. Everyone reading the Monash letter was aware of this fact, including patients, gender clinic psychiatrists, and general practitioners who referred patients to the clinic. The two-year period "living full time in the chosen gender role" mentioned in the flyer reflects a far more conservative protocol than HBIGDA advised at the time. Beginning with Harry Benjamin, medical professionals required a trial period in which transgender people live full time in their "preferred" gender prior to surgery to ascertain whether they could function socially and maintain employment and to prove that other people besides the therapist knew of the person's transition. The HBIGDA Standards of Care refer to this as the Real Life Experience. However, from HBIGDA's earliest version of the Standards of Care, this trial period has always been one year prior to genital surgery, not two.

17 Weston, "Get Thee to a Big City."

18 In *Provincializing Europe*, Dipesh Chakrabarty critiques the progressivist historical narrative through which the colonized Global South is understood to

have arrived at modernity late, while European modernity is understood as primary, universal, and inevitable.

19 For example, it is impossible to apply the theoretical insights of postcolonial theory everywhere outside the Euro-American metropole both because Europeans did not colonize some nation-states and because colonialism and imperialism work differently in different locations.

20 Clare, "Body Shame, Body Pride."

21 In 2006 Paisley Currah writes, "Taking the legal structures as they find them, not as they ought to be, transgender rights advocates have pursued reformist goals" ("Gender Pluralisms under the Transgender Umbrella," 6–7).

22 Spade, *Normal Life*, 1.

23 See Serano, *Whipping Girl*.

24 Valentine, *Imagining Transgender*, 32.

25 Valentine, *Imagining Transgender*, 108.

26 Valentine, *Imagining Transgender*, 45.

27 This follows Judith Butler's theory of gender performativity in *Gender Trouble* and *Bodies That Matter*.

28 Stryker, "Call for Papers."

29 Grant et al., *Injustice at Every Turn*.

30 See the special issue on medical travel in *Medical Anthropology: Cross-Cultural Studies in Health and Illness* 2, no. 4 (2010).

31 See for example Plemons, "Anatomical Authorities"; Plemons, "Description of Sex Difference as Prescription for Sex Change"; Enteen, "Transitioning Online."

32 See Spade, *Normal Life*, 5.

33 See Derrida, *Archive Fever*. Ann Cvetkovich's idea of a "queer archive," constituted of ephemeral objects and informalized subcultural memories, also influences my thinking here (*An Archive of Feelings*, 23).

34 Crawford, "Following You."

35 For the phrase *traveling cultures* I am indebted to Clifford, "Travelling Cultures."

36 Marcus, "Ethnography in/of the World System," 109.

37 Rajan, *Biocapital*, 31.

38 My use of "sex/gender/sexuality" is deliberate here and references Gayle Rubin's theorization of the sex/gender system, as well as later anthropological theories including Sinnott, who coined the term *gendered sexualities* to refer to systems in which sexual orientation is understood to be an extension of gender identity rather than independent of it. See Rubin, "The Traffic in Women"; Sinnott, *Toms and Dees*, 28.

39 See Clarke, "Thoughts on Biomedicalization and Its Transnational Travels," 393.

40 Simpson, *Trafficking Subjects*, xxv.

41 On mobility studies, see Hannam et al., "Mobilities, Immobilities and Moorings." On hybridity, see Bhabha, *The Location of Culture*. On traveling cultures, see Clifford, *Routes*; Appadurai, *Modernity at Large*.

42 Kaplan, *Questions of Travel*, 2.

43 Schick, *The Erotic Margin*, 33.

44 Puar, "Circuits of Queer Mobility," 113.

45 See Halberstam, *In a Queer Time and Place*.

46 On the butch/FTM borderlands, see Halberstam and Hale, "Butch/FTM Border Wars"; Halberstam, "Transgender Butch"; Hale, "Consuming the Living, Dis(re)membering the Dead in the Butch/FTM Borderlands."

47 Prosser, "Exceptional Locations," 103.

48 Salamon, *Assuming a Body*, 173.

49 Cotten, introduction, 2. See also Bhanji, "Trans/Scriptions."

50 Here I draw on Spade's summation of neoliberal policies in *Normal Life*, 49–50.

51 I follow Louis Althusser here in defining historical materialism as "the Marxist science of the development of social formations" (*For Marx*, 251). The works I cite here are a provisional and incomplete list, but offer a thumbnail sketch of these traditions: Althusser and Balibar, *Reading Capital*; Lezra, *Depositions*; Virno, *A Grammar of the Multitude*; Read, *The Micro-Politics of Capital*.

52 I follow Jason Read's reading of real subsumption in *The Micro-Politics of Capital* here. Read's interpretation remains connected to Foucault and offers a route to theorizing racially, gendered, and sexually differentiated subjectivity and labor. Thus social practices and/or consumption processes in contemporary post-Fordist social formations can be understood as forms of immaterial labor in themselves. The concept of immaterial labor has been taken up in useful ways through an engagement with affect, intimacy, and gendered and sexual labor. See Marx, *Grundrisse*, 670–712; Lotringer and Marazzi, *Autonomia*; Virno, "Notes on the General Intellect"; Read, *The Micro-Politics of Capital*, particularly chapter 3, "The Real Subsumption of Subjectivity by Capital."

53 Ward, "Gender Labor."

54 Ferguson, *Aberrations in Black*, 11. Ferguson focuses on the black trans sex worker in particular to illustrate historical materialism's inability to comprehend nonheteronormativity. Pointing to how Marx understands sex workers as the pathological sign of capitalist social relations, Ferguson instead asks how this imbrication of queerness and capital might critique capital rather than merely embody the dehumanization of labor. While this reading models an indispensable critical relation to historical materialism, it is particularly useful for transgender theorizing. Traditional anticapitalist critiques, from trans-exclusive radical feminism to antipsychiatry, have depicted trans people as dupes or victims of the commercial body modification industry and thus symbolic of capital's worst excesses. For example, Dwight Billings and Thomas Urban frame surgical and hormonal treatment for gender dysphoria as the "illusions of consumerism"; according to them, "transsexuals are in danger of becoming surgical junkies as they strive for an idealized sexuality [*sic*] via surgical commodities" ("The Socio-Medical Construction of Transsexualism," 276–77). See also Szasz, *Sex by Prescription*, 74–89; Jeffreys, *Beauty and Misogyny*, 29; Raymond, *The Transsexual Empire*, 184.

55 Spivak unsettles the terms by which the autonomists understood immaterial labor as a historical opening to the end of work by asking for whom work "ends." She points out that instead of "ending," manual labor and factory production have been outsourced to the Global South. See "Scattered Speculations on the Question of Value," 80.

56 Aizura, "Affective Vulnerability and Transgender Exceptionalism," 126.

57 Reddy, *Freedom with Violence*.

58 Haritaworn and Snorton, "Transsexual Necropolitics," 73.

59 Haritaworn and Snorton, "Transsexual Necropolitics," 72.

60 Shakhsari, "Killing Me Softly with Your Rights," 94.

61 Gopinath, *Impossible Desires*, 3. See also Manalansan, *Global Divas*.

62 Grewal and Kaplan, *Scattered Hegemonies*, 667.

63 Altman, "On Global Queering."

64 See the forum on Altman's "On Global Queering" in the *Australian Humanities Review* 2 (1996), especially Martin, "Fran Martin Responds to Dennis Altman." See also Manalansan, *Global Divas*; Martin et al., *AsiaPacifiQueer*.

65 Instructive texts rethinking modernities within queer transnational studies include Benedicto, *Under Bright Lights*; Wilson, *The Intimate Economies of Bangkok*; Boellstorff, *The Gay Archipelago*.

Chapter 1. The Persistence of Trans Travel Narratives

1 For an overview of these events, see Stryker, *Transgender History*, 135–44.

2 Feinberg, *Transgender Warriors*, 21.

3 See commentary on *Transgender Warriors* in Towle and Morgan, "Romancing the Transgender Native," 481–83, 487. Consistent with Feinberg's expressed preference, I use the gender neutral pronouns *ze* and *hir* to refer to Feinberg.

4 Feinberg, *Transgender Warriors*, 7.

5 Stryker, "Christine Jorgensen's Atom Bomb," 100.

6 Love, *Feeling Backward*, 31. Other recent work on desire, queer temporality, and history includes Arondekar, *For the Record*; Dinshaw et al., "Theorizing Queer Temporalities"; Freeman, *Time Binds*.

7 See, for example, Jason Cromwell's chapter on the Oregon physician Alan Hart, "Passing Women and Female-Bodied Men." See also Stryker's "Transgender History, Homonormativity, and Disciplinarity." Other debates focus on the risks of claiming figures as transgender at all, for instance Valentine's critique of historical reclamation in *Imagining Transgender*.

8 Love, *Feeling Backward*, 31.

9 See Spade, "Mutilating Gender," 318.

10 Prosser, *Second Skins*, 89.

11 Prosser, *Second Skins*, 90.

12 Thompson and Sewell, *What Took You So Long?*; Ashley and Fallowell, *April Ashley's Odyssey*; Griggs, *Journal of a Sex Change*.

13 Prosser, *Second Skins*, 90.

14 Prosser, *Second Skins*, 97.

15 Salamon, *Assuming a Body*, 39–40.

16 Salamon, *Assuming a Body*, 98.

17 In considering Jorgensen's story as an archive, I am indebted to scholars working on queer archival practices, among them Cvetkovich, *An Archive of Feelings*, and Halberstam, *In a Queer Time and Place*.

18 Gunther, "'Trans'-forming Corporate America."

19 Joanne Herman, "Transgender? You're Fired!," July 29, 2006, *The Advocate*, accessed December 11, 2015, http://www.advocate.com/politics/commentary /2006/07/28/transgender-youre-fired.

20 University College London, "Transgender Issues."

21 Women and Equality Unit, *Gender Reassignment*, 14.

22 Walworth, "Managing Transsexual Transition in the Workplace."

23 Center for Gender Sanity, "Gender Sanity Strategies for Managing Transition."

24 There is much more of a critique to be made of employment resources for trans people than is possible here.

25 Garber, *Vested Interests*, 17.

26 Prosser critiques both authors in chapter 1 of *Second Skins*; see also Namaste, *Invisible Lives*, 9–43.

27 Butler defines the heterosexual matrix as "that grid of cultural intelligibility through which [heterosexual] bodies, genders, and desires are naturalized" (*Gender Trouble*, 151n6).

28 Spade, "Mutilating Gender," 321.

29 Grant et al., *National Transgender Discrimination Survey Report on Health and Health Care*.

30 Here I follow Jodi Melamed's definition of neoliberal citizenship in *Represent and Destroy*, 40.

31 On journey narratives more generally, see Islam, *The Ethics of Travel*; Robertson et al., *Travelers' Tales*; and Mary Louise Pratt's classic postcolonial critique of travel writing, *Imperial Eyes*.

32 On the imagined community of nationalism, see Anderson, *Imagined Communities*.

33 Bhanji, "Trans/Scriptions," 167, quoting Ahmed, *Strange Encounters*, 89.

34 De Certeau, *The Practice of Everyday Life*, 218, 219.

35 See Aizura, "Of Borders and Homes"; Bhanji, "Trans/Scriptions."

36 Bhanji, "Trans/Scriptions," 170.

37 Foucault, "Nietzsche, Genealogy, History," 81.

38 Meyerowitz, *How Sex Changed*, 28.

39 Meyerowitz, *How Sex Changed*, 28.

40 Meyerowitz, *How Sex Changed*, 17. See Lind, *Autobiography of an Androgyne*, 196.

41 See Meyerowitz, *How Sex Changed*, 19. On the history of Hirschfeld's research into gender variance, see Hirschfeld, *Transvestites*; Hekma, "A Female Soul in a Male Body"; Bullough, "Transsexualism in History"; Fausto-Sterling, *Sexing the Body*.

42 Meyerowitz, *How Sex Changed*, 34.

43 See Meyerowitz, *How Sex Changed*; Denny, "Black Telephones, White Refrigerators"; Stryker, "Christine Jorgensen's Atom Bomb."

44 Denny, "Black Telephones, White Refrigerators," 36.

45 Meyerowitz notes in *How Sex Changed* that Vern Bullough, a friend of Jorgensen's, confirmed this suggestion that Jorgensen had informed the press herself (62, 300n32). See Denny, "Black Telephones, White Refrigerators," 41–42.

46 Jorgensen, *Christine Jorgenson*, 183.

47 The *American Weekly* images are archived at http://www.christinejorgensen .org, accessed December 11, 2015.

48 Prosser, *Second Skins*, 124; Prosser, "Exceptional Locations," 98.

49 Martino, *Emergence*, 40.

50 Meyerowitz, "Sex Change and the Popular Press," 175–76.

51 See Meyerowitz, "Sex Change and the Popular Press," for a full account.

52 See archived images of the *American Weekly* features at http://web.archive .org; personal communication, Susan Stryker, January 2009.

53 Docter, *Becoming a Woman*.

54 An exception might be made for Roberta Cowell, an English trans woman who transitioned around 1954 and who was feted as the first *English* transsexual. See Meyerowitz, *How Sex Changed*, 83–84.

55 Meyerowitz, *How Sex Changed*, 73, 67.

56 Jorgensen, *Christine Jorgenson*, 55–56.

57 Jorgensen, *Christine Jorgenson*, 195.

58 Jorgensen, *Christine Jorgenson*, 122.

59 It might be assumed that the traditional American self-invention narrative was accessible only to men, thus making Jorgensen an outlier as a woman celebrated for fulfilling the narrative. However, women were marketed equally compelling self-reinvention narratives in the form of consumption, in particular fashion and beauty products. See for example Felski, *The Gender of Modernity*, 62; Cardon, *Fashion and Fiction*; Haiken, *Venus Envy*.

60 Tocqueville, *Democracy in America*, 514.

61 Foucault, "What Is Enlightenment?," 41.

62 On the history of cosmetic surgery, see Gilman, *Making the Body Beautiful*; Haiken, *Venus Envy*.

63 Meyerowitz, *How Sex Changed*, 73.

64 Benjamin, *The Transsexual Phenomenon*, quoted in Irving, "Normalized Transgressions," 49.

65 Irving, "Normalized Transgressions," 49.

66 Simpson, *Trafficking Subjects*, xxv–vi.

67 I'm grateful to Cathy Hannabach for helping me make this point explicit.

68 Chakrabarty, *Provincializing Europe*, 6, 46.

69 Meyerowitz, *How Sex Changed*, 34.

70 Meyerowitz, *How Sex Changed*, 69–70.

71 Stryker, "Christine Jorgensen's Atom Bomb," 101, 102. Stryker quotes Baudrillard (*Symbolic Exchange and Death*, 20), and I reproduce this quote here.

72 Stryker, "Christine Jorgensen's Atom Bomb," 102.

73 Another critique of Baudrillard's equation of transsexuality with postmodernity is Felski's "Fin de Siècle, Fin de Sexe."

74 Stryker, "Christine Jorgensen's Atom Bomb," 108.

75 Denny, "Black Telephones, White Refrigerators," 39, 42.

76 Jesse Bayker's (personal communication, 2013) research on the centrality of head and body hair cutting, shaping, and decoration to gender nonconforming historical figures in the 1850s–90s is a great example of different somatic technologies used to transform the body before surgery and before hormone therapy.

77 Hayward, "Lessons from a Starfish," 255.

78 The theoretical currents I allude to here are large and messy. On autonomist Marxist epochal breaks, see Hardt and Negri, *Empire* and *Multitude*, as well as Virno and Hardt, *Radical Thought in Italy*. On posthumanist Deleuzian affect and media, see Thacker, *Biomedia*; Massumi, *Parables of the Virtual* and *What Animals Teach Us about Politics*. See also the oeuvre of speculative realism and object-oriented ontology: Bogost, *Alien Phenomenology*; Bryant, *The Democracy of Objects*; Bryant et al., *The Speculative Turn*. In developing this critique I'm indebted to an illuminating dialogue with Jordy Rosenberg apropos of their essay "The Molecularization of Sexuality," which makes a far more comprehensive critique of this body of theory on similar grounds.

79 See Raymond, *The Transsexual Empire*; Hausman, *Changing Sex*; Billings and Urban, "The Socio-Legal Construction of Transsexualism"; the famed antipsychiatry theorist Thomas Szasz's review of *The Transsexual Empire*, "Male and Female Created He Them."

80 Stryker, "Call for Papers."

81 Roen, "Transgender Theory and Embodiment"; Stryker, "*We Who Are Sexy*."

82 Other interrogations of settler colonialism and gender and sexuality include Driskill et al., *Queer Indigenous Studies*; Morgensen, *Spaces between Us*; Rifkin, *When Did Indians Become Straight?*; Justice et al., "Sexuality, Nationality, Indigeneity."

83 See Aizura et al., "Decolonizing Transgender."

Chapter 2. On Location

The epigraph is from Spivak, "Poststructuralism, Marginality, Postcolonialism and Value," 201.

1 Docter, *Becoming a Woman*, 199. Burou was also the inventor of a new vaginoplasty method, folding up the skin of the penis to line the neovagina with erotically sensitive tissue. See Conway, "Vaginoplasty."

2 Foerster, "On the History of Transsexuals in France," 21.

3 Prosser, "Exceptional Locations," 98; Meyerowitz, *How Sex Changed*, 188–89; Ashley and Fallowell, *April Ashley's Odyssey*, 77–96.

4 Meyerowitz, *How Sex Changed*, 120–25.

5 Prosser and Stone both point out the orientalism of transsexual accounts of journeys to Casablanca. See Prosser, "Exceptional Locations," 99; Stone, "The Empire Strikes Back," 281.

6 Prosser, "Exceptional Locations," 92.

7 Pratt, *Imperial Eyes*, 4.

8 De Certeau, "Ethno-Graphy."

9 Pozner, "Gender Immigrant."

10 Foucault, *History of Sexuality*, 65.

11 Meyerowitz, *How Sex Changed*, 35–36.

12 Morris, *Conundrum*; Martino, *Emergence*; Richards and Ames, *Second Serve*; Cossey, *My Story*; Ashley and Fallowell, *April Ashley's Odyssey*.

13 A list of trans autobiographies was compiled by Dallas Denny in 2012 and published online. See Denny, "A Comprehensive List of Trans Autobiographies."

14 See also Taste This Collective, *Boys Like Her*.

15 Prosser, "Exceptional Locations," 89. It is difficult to tell whether Prosser originally theorized that "stable" subject position as ontological or foundational. He later questioned his prior equation of the "Real" of transsexuality with ontological realness. See Prosser, "A Palinode on the Transsexual Real."

16 This is partially because no single destination became popular for trans men to access gender reassignment surgeries. However, as places of subcultural and community significance, some locations have been central in some transsexual men's autobiographies. In Max Wolf Valerio's *The Testosterone Files: My Social and Hormonal Transition from Female to Male*, San Francisco functions as a queer subcultural urban space in which the author comes of age as a lesbian *and* transitions to male.

17 Plummer, *Telling Sexual Stories*, 54–55.

18 On transcendental subjects, see Foucault, "Truth and Power," 117.

19 Hausman, *Changing Sex*, 143, 156. Hausman does not entertain the possibility that trans readers might actively disidentify with the "hegemonic" transsexual narrative and/or utilize that hegemonic narrative as a point of friction with which to initiate a different account.

20 Prosser, *Second Skins*, 116.

21 Jose Esteban Muñoz theorizes disidentification as partial identifications by marginalized subjects with majoritarian spheres (*Disidentifications*, 4).

22 Halperin, *Saint Foucault*, 45.

23 See Butler, *Gender Trouble*, 17.

24 Scott, "The Evidence of Experience," 777.

25 Massey, *Space, Place, and Gender*, 148.

26 Massey, *Space, Place, and Gender*, 149.

27 See for example Grewal, *Home and Harem*; Clifford, *Routes*; Kaplan, *Questions of Travel*; MacCannell, *The Tourist*; Simpson, *Trafficking Subjects*; Pratt, *Imperial Eyes*.

28 Clifford, *Routes*, 35.

29 Grewal, *Home and Harem*, 2.

30 Simpson, *Trafficking Subjects*, xxiii.

31 Kaplan, *Questions of Travel*, 3–4.

32 Melamed, *Represent and Destroy*, 31–32.

33 Turner and Ash, *The Golden Hordes*, 156.

34 Pennell, *Morocco*, 236.

35 See Wolanen, *Writing Tangier in the Postcolonial Transition*.

36 Gender reassignment surgery was very difficult to obtain in the United States and Europe in the 1950s and 1960s. According to Meyerowitz, much legal debate took place in the United States over the legality of gender reassignment operations, and doctors were generally unwilling to perform them (*How Sex Changed*, 120–21). In the 1960s Mexico was regarded as another possible destination for American trans people to obtain surgery. See, for example, Canary Conn's account of GRS in *Canary*.

37 Morris, *Conundrum*, 1, 40, 92, 101.

38 Morris, *Conundrum*, 118, 111.

39 Morris, *Conundrum*, 119.

40 Morris, *Conundrum*, 119, 123, 126.

41 Ashley and Fallowell, *April Ashley's Odyssey*, 82.

42 Prosser, "Exceptional Locations," 100.

43 Holland and Huggan, *Tourists with Typewriters*, 119.

44 Kabbani, *Imperial Fictions*, 45.

45 Holland and Huggan, *Tourists with Typewriters*, 119.

46 Morris, *Conundrum*, 41.

47 See also a reading of Kinglake in Kabbani, *Imperial Fictions*, 9.

48 Edward Said points out that popular British writing contended in a more "pronounced and harder" way with West Asia and North Africa precisely because of its interest in sustaining access to its primary imperial project: India (*Orientalism*, 192).

49 Kinglake, *Eothen*, 54. See Said's remarks on Kinglake (*Orientalism*, 193–94) and Kabbani's critique (*Imperial Fictions*, 9–11).

50 Said, *Orientalism*, 193–94.

51 Kabbani, *Imperial Fictions*, 11.

52 Rancière, "Discovering New Worlds," 33.

53 Kabbani, *Imperial Fictions*, 11.

54 Morris, *Conundrum*, 86, 87–88.

55 I am grateful to Annie Hill for suggesting this formulation.

56 Morris, *Conundrum*, 88.

57 Rosaldo, *Culture and Truth*, 68.

58 Hall, "Black Diaspora Artists in Britain," 17.

59 Grewal, *Home and Harem*, 4.

60 Morris, *Conundrum*, 80, 79, 112.

61 It is tempting to assert that this vision of mobility as a given also marks Morris's history as an upper-class British man: the form of mobility she engages in is also a masculine privilege. This is no doubt true. However, making such a reading opens this critique to the claim that Morris's socialization as male defines her identity. This reading would imply that all trans people are defined by the gender they are assigned at birth. Such a biologically essentialist view of trans women fails to acknowledge that they are also subject to social and institutional discrimination on the basis of their femininity and/or womanhood.

62 Melamed, *Represent and Destroy*, 27.

63 McCloskey, *Crossing*, 127.

64 McCloskey, *Crossing*, xi.

65 McCloskey, *Crossing*, xii, emphasis in original.

66 McCloskey, *Crossing*, xii.

67 McCloskey, *Crossing*, xii.

68 McCloskey, *Crossing*, 89.

69 McCloskey, *Crossing*, 122.

70 McCloskey, *Crossing*, 140.

71 Boylan, *She's Not There*, 111, 112–13.

72 Boylan, *She's Not There*, 113.

73 Boylan, *She's Not There*, 114.

74 Bigler, *American Conversations*, 117.

75 hooks, "Eating the Other," 21, 25.

76 Ang, *On Not Speaking Chinese*, 195.

77 Cheng, *The Melancholy of Race*, 11, 9, 12.

78 Jacobson, *Roots Too*. Jacobson additionally points out that white ethnic revival discourse can be found in progressive discourse. Its most potent appropriations have been staged by the political right in the service of delegitimizing black struggle: "The pervasive conceit of the nation of immigrants . . . blunted the charges of the Civil Rights and Black Power movements and eased the conscience of a nation that had just barely begun to reckon with the harshest contours of its history forged in white supremacism" (9).

79 Jacobson, *Roots Too*, 9.

80 For instance, the entire catalog of US-based Topside Press, which publishes transgender fiction and poetry; Tolbert and Peterson, *Troubling the Line*; see also *TSQ Transgender Studies Quarterly* 1, no. 4 (2014) on transgender cultural production.

81 In *Anachronism and Its Others* (68–70), Valerie Rohy incisively critiques "gay is the new black" in a chapter about racial melancholic incorporation of blackness in Willa Cather's novel *Sapphira and the Slave Girl*. Although we arrive at racial melancholia by different routes, Rohy's analysis has been formative for my argument.

82 Sexton, "People-of-Color-Blindness," 42.

83 Bassichis and Spade, "Queer Politics and Anti-Blackness," 203.

84 See Gehi, "Gender (In)security" and "Struggles from the Margins."

85 Jennifer Finney Boylan, "Longing for the Day When Chelsea Manning and I Both Seem Boring," *Washington Post*, August 22, 2013, accessed January 17, 2016, http://www.washingtonpost.com/lifestyle/style/longing-for-the-day -when-chelsea-manning-and-i-both-seem-boring/2013/08/22/7bf52c42-0b5d -11e3-b87c-476db8ac34cd_story.html.

Chapter 3. Documentary and the Trans Migration Plot

1 In referring to the Paper Dolls as overseas contract workers, I follow Neferti Tadiar. She uses the term to highlight the continuities between overseas contract work and the Philippine state's adoption of private subcontracting (*Fantasy-Production*, 301n2).

2 The introductory titles in *Bubot Niyar* claim that Israel introduced more overseas foreign workers after shutting out Palestinian workers at the beginning of the 2001 Second Intifada, initiating a labor shortage. However, Israel has relied on overseas foreign workers to replace Palestinian workers since the early 1990s. See Gross, "Thinking Is in the Grey Area." Notes provided courtesy of the author.

3 See for example Butler, "Gender Is Burning," in *Bodies That Matter*, 121–40; Sullivan, *A Critical Introduction to Queer Theory*, 81–99; Phelan, *Unmarked*, 93–111.

4 See for example Muñoz, who calls *Paris Is Burning* "a highly sensationalized rendering of Latino and black transvestite and transsexual communities." *Disidentifications*, 162.

5 hooks, *Black Looks*, 151.

6 hooks, "Is Paris Burning?," 61. While hooks's disappointing critique of the film's ballgoers as aspiring unselfconsciously to the whiteness and capitalist wealth they perform onstage should be disregarded, her warning to attend to power relations in queer documentary stands.

7 By "Global South" I refer to regions and nation-states with histories of colonialism or postcolonial neo-imperialism in the form of development, debt, and structural adjustment. While the binary terminology of Global North/Global South is insufficient to describe the unevenness of colonial imperialism and neoliberal capitalism, I continue to use it here because any alternative terms are just as flawed.

8 *Les travestis pleurent aussi* was not commercially released on DVD at the time of writing, but it is now on YouTube: http://www.youtube.com/watch?v =INoKo5geY7A.

9 Kaplan, *Questions of Travel*, 3.

10 Halberstam, *In a Queer Time and Place*, 36–37.

11 See Johnson et al., "Queering the Middle."

12 See for example Florida, *The Rise of the Creative Class*. See also Karen Tongson's critique of Florida in *Relocations*, 204–5.

13 Haritaworn et al., introduction, 17. In *Safe Space*, Christina Hanhardt also critiques discourses marking gay and lesbian gentrifiers as willing to take "risks" while marking spaces inhabited by people of color as dangerous.

14 Grewal and Kaplan, "Global Identities," 669.

15 Grewal and Kaplan, "Global Identities," 670.

16 Luibhéid and Cantú, *Queer Migrations*, xxv.

17 Power, "US Leadership to Advance Equality for LGBT People Abroad."

18 See Spade, "Under the Cover of Gay Rights," 87.

19 Puar, *Terrorist Assemblages*.

20 On pinkwashing see Maya Mikdashi, "Gay Rights as Human Rights: Pinkwashing Israel," *Jadaliyya*, December 16, 2011, http://www.jadaliyya.com/pages/index/3560/gay-rights-as-human-rights_pinkwashing-homonationa; Darwich and Maikey, "The Road from Antipinkwashing Activism to the Decolonization of Palestine"; Franke, "Dating the State."

21 Bacchetta and Haritaworn, "There Are Many Transatlantics."

22 Shakhsari, "Killing Me Softly with Your Rights."

23 Gopinath, *Impossible Desires*, 10.

24 Eng, "Transnational Adoption and Queer Diasporas," 303.

25 Reading Mohinder Kaur Bhamra's Giddha song "Don't Come to England Girlfriend," Gopinath notes that Indian factory and sweatshop workers are often recruited by their friends and relatives. Home life and capital intersect; there is nothing outside of them (*Impossible Desires*, 49–52).

26 Chow, *The Protestant Ethnic and the Spirit of Capitalism*, 33–34; Wallerstein, "The Ideological Tensions of Capitalism," 34.

27 Luibhéid, "Introduction," xi.

28 Mitropoulos, "Proliferating Limits." Drawing on Mitropoulos, Brett Neilson and Sandro Mezzadra in *Border as Method* refer to this shifting terrain as the multiplication of labor.

29 On the transformation of skilled worker categories, see Neilson and Mezzadra, "Border as Method." On the shifting terrain framing definitions of *refugee* and *asylum-seeker*, see Mitropoulos, "A Spectre Is Haunting Left Nationalism," 24.

30 Aizura, "Affective Vulnerability and Transgender Exceptionalism" and "Transnational Transgender Rights and Immigration Law."

31 Papadopoulos et al., *Escape Routes*, 162.

32 For instance, see Halberstam's analysis of the transgender gaze in *In a Queer Time and Place*; Leung, "Unsung Heroes"; Kheshti, "Cross-Dressing and Gender (Tres)Passing."

33 See Straayer, "Transgender Mirrors," 145.

34 Milliken, "*Unheimlich* Maneuvers," 48.

35 An important exception is Eve Oishi's comparison of *Paris Is Burning* and Wu Tsang's *Wildness* (2011) in "Reading Realness."

36 Sullivan, *A Critical Introduction to Queer Theory*, 94–97.

37 Trinh, "The Totalizing Quest of Meaning," 96.

38 Harper, "'The Subversive Edge,'" 101. The point about racial and economic conditions is made by Nyong'o in "After the Ball."

39 Cameron, "When Strangers Bring Cameras," 426.

40 Cameron, "When Strangers Bring Cameras," 426.

41 Raimondo, "The Queer Intimacy of Global Vision," 116, 117.

42 See Spade, "Under the Cover of Gay Rights"; Greyson, "Pinkface."

43 Crawford, "Transgender without Organs?," 138.

44 Aizura, "Trans Feminine Value," 133–37.

45 Manalansan, "Queering the Chain of Care Paradigm"; Manalansan, "Queer Intersections"; Manalansan, "Servicing the World."

46 Film synopsis, accessed January 20, 2018, http://tomerheymann.com/film/paper-dolls/synopsis.

47 Kevin Thomas, "'Dolls' Living on Israel's Margins," *LA Times*, October 6, 2006, accessed February 1, 2016, http://articles.latimes.com/2006/oct/06/entertainment/et-paper6.

48 Cohen, *Soldiers, Rebels, and Drifters*, 158.

49 Schulman, "A Documentary Guide to Brand Israel and the Art of Pinkwashing."

50 Consistent with how others in the film refer to Jan, I use male pronouns here.

51 Sally returned to the Philippines before finding a job in the United Arab Emirates. In 2009 she was found dead in an alley in Sharjah. I've written elsewhere about the politics of her death, as well as a different perspective on *Bubot Niyar*. See Aizura, "Trans Feminine Value."

52 Hage, *White Nation*, 93.

53 See Hage, *White Nation*; Berlant, *The Queen of America Goes to Washington City*, particularly chapter 5 on diva citizenship.

54 See Kuntsman, *Figurations of Violence and Belonging*; Lavie, *Wrapped in the Flag of Israel*.

55 Cohen makes precisely this point (*Soldiers, Rebels, and Drifters*, 158).

56 Aeyal Gross, "Thinking Is in the Grey Area," also draws attention to how the Paper Dolls' drag performances reflect a desire to reclaim Israeli nationality for themselves. They often perform Israeli songs, such as when Sally does a very flirtatious, sexualized rendition of "Havah Nagilah" for Shirazi's entourage. Chiqui has the Israeli flag on his apartment wall. While this reading is convincing, *Bubot Niyar*'s total elision of settler colonialism in the Occupied Territories, or any mention of how the Paper Dolls understand the Palestine-Israel conflict, makes this reading difficult to sustain.

57 Benedicto, *Under Bright Lights*, 74.

58 Tan, "From Bakla to Gay"; Garcia, *Philippine Gay Culture*. See also Cannell, *Power and Intimacy in the Christian Philippines*; Johnson, *Beauty and Power*.

59 Manalansan, *Global Divas*, ix.

60 Manalansan, *Global Divas*, 21.

61 Benedicto, *Under Bright Lights*, 79.

62 A transgender mirror scene is a stereotype of trans representation (textual and visual) and presents the transgender subject staring at herself in a mirror. Prosser writes that mirrors are a "key trope for how the subject figures his/her transsexuality," staging a "split gendered subject" ("No Place Like Home," 497).

63 Berlant, "Nearly Utopian, Nearly Normal," 279.

64 Lewis, "Thinking Figurations Otherwise."

65 Kulick, Travestí, 6. The generalizing positivism of these accounts illustrates one of the problems with cross-cultural analyses of gender nonconforming life outside the Global North.

66 Berkins, "Travestis."

67 Rees-Roberts, "Down and Out," 145.

68 See for example Parreñas, Illicit Flirtations; Ditmore, "In Calcutta, Sex Workers Organize"; Bernstein, "Bounded Authenticity and the Commerce of Sex"; Hoang, "Economies of Emotion, Familiarity, Fantasy, and Desire."

69 See for instance Spade's work in Normal Life; Conrad, Against Equality; Stanley, "Introduction"; Bassichis et al., "Building an Abolitionist Trans Movement with Everything We've Got."

70 Chow, The Protestant Ethnic and the Spirit of Capitalism, 33–34.

Interlude

1 Grewal and Kaplan, "Global Identities," 667.

Chapter 4. Transnational Entrepreneurialisms

1 According to Dr. Preecha's estimates in a 2006 interview, fewer than 1 percent of the Preecha Aesthetic Institute patients were Thai. The Suporn Clinic's manager noted in an interview that the vast majority of Dr. Suporn's patients are non-Thai. Ninety-five percent of the Phuket Plastic Surgery Center's clientele are non-Thai clientele. I follow Thai etiquette in referring to Thai surgeons by their first names.

2 In Transgender Nation, Gordene Mackenzie writes, "A large number of transsexuals not approved for surgery by gender clinics or not wanting to follow guidelines, can easily obtain sex-reassignment surgery in other countries" (17). Similarly Dhejne et al. frame accessing surgery overseas as reflecting "a wish to speed up the process or avoid the evaluation process" ("An Analysis of All Applications for Sex Reassignment Surgery in Sweden, 1960–2010," 1543). In Transsexual and Other Disorders of Gender Identity, James Barrett, director of the UK's Charing Cross Gender Identity Clinic, does not refer to patients accessing GRS overseas except in two cases. Barrett describes one person assigned male at birth who sees the WPATH criteria as an unrealistic hurdle and obtains GRS "abroad" but immediately regrets it and is suicidal (63). In another case Barrett describes "hormone treatment without change of role" after

a patient receives chest surgery overseas. In his opinion the patient does not present as masculine and is thus not a "correct" case of transsexualism (122).

3 See Aizura, "Feminine Transformations" and "The Romance of the Amazing Scalpel."

4 I use the term *medical travel* rather than *medical tourism* to index the fact that tourism activities per se are often not involved in this form of travel. See Kangas, "Therapeutic Itineraries in a Global World"; Whittaker, "Pleasure and Pain."

5 Ochoa, *Queen for a Day*, 173–74, 175.

6 See Deborah Lupton's discussion of medical dominance in *Medicine as Culture*, 114.

7 Hanssmann, "Passing Torches?," 126.

8 I define domains of consumer enunciation at length later in this chapter. See Race, "Recreational States."

9 Foucault, *The Birth of Biopolitics*, 226.

10 Gordon, "The Soul of the Citizen," 300. Focusing on the individual elides how social and kinship units might also be thought of as entrepreneurial. Mitropoulos draws attention to Becker's own preoccupation with household economics to observe that the family unit is as central to neoliberalism as the individual entrepreneur and to interrogate how Foucault elides race, gender, and sexuality in positing an abstracted conception of individuality (*Contract and Contagion*, 149).

11 Brown, "Neo-Liberalism and the End of Liberal Democracy," 4, 5.

12 Clarke et al., "Biomedicalization," 162, 182.

13 Lewis, "DIY Selves?"

14 On challenges to medical authority, see Halpern, "Medical Authority and the Culture of Rights"; Murphy, *Seizing the Means of Reproduction*; Nelson, *More Than Medicine*.

15 Shim, *Heart Sick*, 108–9.

16 Comprehensive histories of these programs have yet to be written, but for an overview see Meyerowitz, *How Sex Changed*, 222–24 (including the footnotes).

17 The Erickson Educational Foundation subsidized the Johns Hopkins Program from its beginning, according to Meyerowitz (*How Sex Changed*, 219).

18 See Szasz, *Sex by Prescription*; Billings and Urban, "The Socio-Medical Construction of Transsexualism."

19 Meyerowitz, *How Sex Changed*, 271.

20 Meyerowitz, *How Sex Changed*, 273.

21 Medical costs rose from 3.2 percent annually in 1960 to 7.9 percent annually in 1970. Meanwhile national health expenditure rose from US$142 per capita in 1960 to US$336 per capita in 1970. In 1974, during the energy crisis and recession, the inflation rate for medical services was 12.1 percent. See Starr, *The Social Transformation of American Medicine*, 384, 406.

22 Starr, *The Social Transformation of American Medicine*, 387.

23 National Center for Transgender Equality, "Medicare and Transgender People."

24 For instance, HIV prevention providers at the Tom Waddell Health Center in San Francisco began the first US transgender clinic of this kind in 1993, using a harm-reduction protocol and basing the clinic in the Tenderloin neighborhood.

25 See Edmonds, "The Poor Have the Right to Be Beautiful," 372.

26 Facial surgeries are common in Thailand among women, men, and gender nonconforming subjects: *kathoeys, sao prophet sorng,* and people who self-identify as transgender or transsexual. Facial surgeries are racialized to bring faces into conformation with whiteness, although the version of whiteness is not about Europeanness as much as classed and racialized distinctions within Asia. See Aizura, "Where Health and Beauty Meet."

27 Barrett, "Referrals," in *Transsexual and Other Disorders of Gender Identity,* 9.

28 Denny, "The Clarke Institute of Psychiatry." The Clarke Institute clinic is now the CAMH Gender Identity Clinic, and as of 2015 is still the only place to access state-funded GRS in Ontario.

29 Ma, "A Systems Approach to the Social Difficulties of Transsexuals in Hong Kong," 71.

30 The legality of transsexuality in Iran has been covered with some surprise in the Western media; it appeared inconsistent that this could take place in an Islamic state that criminalizes homosexuality. An analysis of this perceived incongruence is not my concern here.

31 Najmabadi, *Professing Selves,* 48, 145, 165.

32 Canada also has a state-based and largely centralized health system in which trans health care is generally far more conservative than in the United States. See Irving and Raj, *Trans Activism in Canada.*

33 In South African parlance *coloured* is an official racial category that categorizes the multiracial communities of the Western Cape region and indexes people descended from indigenous groups, white settlers, West African slaves, Malay indentured laborers, and others. Politically contested, colouredness has a fraught ideological history in South Africa and is considered to be a cultural identity distinct from African; it is used as a self-identification as well as a biopolitical classification. See Adhikari, *Not White Enough, Not Black Enough.*

34 Swarr, *Sex in Transition,* 90, 96.

35 Swarr, *Sex in Transition,* 100, 75, 51.

36 Here, however, I would challenge Swarr's comparison of South Africa and Iran. Swarr quotes Najmabadi at length while pointing to the film *Be Like Others,* arguing that "matching sex and gender proves more acceptable than same-sex sexuality" (*Sex in Transition,* 105). This is misleading, as Najmabadi's more recent work has complicated the scene of access to gender reassignment in Iran, addressing Islamophobic fears about coercive gender reassignment.

37 Aizura, "Of Borders and Homes," 299–300.

38 Bode, "Aussie Battler in Crisis?"

39 On arrival in Australia, immigrants had to pass a dictation test modeled on the "natal formula" used to restrict immigration in South Africa: they had to write

out fifty words in a European language chosen by the immigration officer. Officers would choose Gaelic, Hungarian, Swedish, or any language that immigrants clearly could not speak to deny them entry. See Jupp, *The Australian People*, 46.

40 See Povinelli, *The Cunning of Recognition*, 18.

41 On lesbians' and single women's access to assisted reproductive technologies in Australia, see Dempsey, "Active Fathers, Natural Families and Children's Origins." On intersex treatment, see Jones et al., *Intersex*.

42 Nurse practitioners in Australia were awarded the power to diagnose and prescribe medicine in 2010; culturally, trained doctors are seen as the first port of call for an illness or health condition, unlike in the United States.

43 Walker and Sobocinska, "Introduction," 4.

44 Sharma quotes a sex tourism brochure that states, "Thailand is a world of extremes, and the possibilities are endless. Anything goes in this exotic country—especially when it comes to girls." While these stereotypes most often refer to sex tourism, other goods and services are understood in the same light (*Tourism and Development*, 170). I complicate and expand on this understanding of an exotic "anything goes" atmosphere in Thailand at length in chapter 5.

45 While I generally refer to the clinicians using initials here, Elizabeth explicitly instructed me to name this provider.

46 See Couch et al., *Tranznation*. In a chapter on health care use the authors note, "The process of assessing whether someone met a transgender or transsexual standard that qualified them for hormone treatment or surgery was experienced as a degrading experience for some participants. They felt interrogated, exposed, and humiliated by 'insensitive questions' about their bodies and could feel like their lives were being 'ripped to pieces by [their] psychiatrist'" (35). The report also noted that some participants were reluctant to use particular health services because the presence of gatekeeping medical professionals would limit the participants' autonomy.

47 Spade, "Mutilating Gender," 319.

48 Metzl, *The Protest Psychosis*; Roberts, *Fatal Invention*. On medical experimentation in Australia, see Kowal, "Disturbing Pasts and Promising Futures."

49 These photographs are usually unidentified. The Suporn Clinic reproduces these photographs with the consent of patients, who often add their own testimonials. While readers may assume this disempowers patients, many patients evince pride in their postsurgical appearance and share photographs in online forums, email listservs, and websites designed to help others select a surgeon.

50 See also the website of the Phuket Plastic Surgery.

51 Interview, Brisbane, July 30, 2006.

52 Interview, Sydney, February 19, 2007.

53 Interview, Melbourne, January 30, 2007.

54 Race, "Recreational States."

55 Clare, "Body Shame, Body Pride"; Puar, "Bodies with New Organs."

56 See Ferguson, *Aberrations in Black*, 17.

57 Alliez and Feher, "The Luster of Capital," 345.

58 Read, *The Micro-Politics of Capital*, 143.

59 For example, Kaiser Permanente started the Gender Pathways Clinic in San Francisco in 2015. According to its website, the Gender Pathways Clinic "provides culturally competent care to transgender and gender-expansive patients. Gender Pathways is a unique place for Kaiser Permanente members to receive integrated care in a comfortable, supportive setting." Kaiser has another clinic in the East Bay Area as well as one in Portland, Oregon.

60 Jillana Enteen, personal communication, September 7, 2016.

61 Centers for Disease Control, "HIV among Transgender People."

62 See for example Kaw, "Medicalization of Racial Features"; Aizura, "Where Health and Beauty Meet."

Chapter 5. Thai Gender Reassignment Clinics

1 The manager asked to remain anonymous.

2 Ahmed, *Queer Phenomenology*, 136.

3 Ahmed, *Queer Phenomenology*, 139.

4 In this chapter I use a number of Thai terms to speak about Thai gender variant identities and practices. *Kathoey* can refer to male-to-female transgender or transsexual categories, but historically it has many different connotations, including male homosexuality, a third sex or gender (*phet-thi-sam*), and cross-dressers who are assigned male or female at birth. *Ladyboy* is a Thai coinage of English words to mean *kathoey*. *Sao praphet sorng* is a Thai term meaning "second type of woman." It is preferred by many gender variant Thais over *kathoey*. See Jackson, "Performative Genders, Perverse Desires."

5 The Thai word *farang* generally refers to white non-Thais rather than foreign visitors from other regions in Asia or other nonwhite, non-Thai people.

6 Ahmed, *Queer Phenomenology*, 136.

7 Clough, introduction, 2.

8 Puar, "Circuits of Queer Mobility," 113.

9 See Penny Van Esterik's account of beauty pageants as a way to institutionalize gender norms in *Materializing Thailand*, 140.

10 Jackson, "Performative Genders, Perverse Desires."

11 Jackson, "Thai Research on Male Homosexuality and Transgenderism and the Cultural Limits of Foucaultian Analysis," 54. See also Jackson and Sullivan, *Lady Boys, Tom Boys, Rent Boys*, 10–11.

12 Jackson, "Performative Genders, Perverse Desires."

13 Jackson, "Kathoey >< Gay >< Man," 170.

14 On toms, see Sinnott, *Toms and Dees*.

15 Morris, "Three Sexes and Four Sexualities."

16 See Jackson, "Kathoey ><Gay >< Man"; Sinnott, *Toms and Dees*.

17 Käng, "Kathoey 'In Trend,'" 476.

18 Sukontapatipark, "Relationship between Modern Medical Technology and Gender Identity in Thailand," 99, 95.

19 Costa and Matzner, *Male Bodies, Women's Souls*, 63.

20 Sukontapatipark, "Relationship between Modern Medical Technology and Gender Identity in Thailand," 63.

21 Sukontapatipark, "Relationship between Modern Medical Technology and Gender Identity in Thailand," 99.

22 Personal communication, Prempreeda Pramoj na Ayutthaya, January 17, 2008.

23 Sukontapatipark, "Relationship between Modern Medical Technology and Gender Identity in Thailand," 73.

24 Not coincidentally this happened at around the same time (2004) that Japan introduced new laws allowing trans people to change their gender markers on identity documents and to have GRS legally. See McLelland and Dasgupta, *Genders, Transgenders, and Sexualities in Japan*; Mitsuhashi, "The Transgender World in Contemporary Japan."

25 See the Thai Medical Council's announcement "Regarding Guidelines for Persons Manifesting Confusion concerning Their Sexual Identity or Desiring Treatment by Undergoing a Sex Change Operation," published on the Thai Law Forum website, November 17, 2009, http://www.thailawforum.com /Guidelines-sex-change-operations.html. The Thai news media covered the story, as did the international LGBT press. See Pongphon Sarnsmak, "New Sex Change Regulations from Nov. 29," *The Nation*, September 12, 2009, accessed June 12, 2014, http://www.nationmultimedia.com/2009/09/12/national /national_30112040.php.

26 "Thailand Temporarily Bans Castration Done for Nonmedical Reasons," *The Advocate*, April 3, 2008, http://www.advocate.com/health/health-news/2008 /04/03/thailand-temporarily-bans-castration-nonmedical-reasons.

27 See Käng, "Kathoey 'In Trend.'"

28 Personal communication, Jillana Enteen, September 8, 2016.

29 "Medical Tourism for Saudi Vacationers in Focus," *Arab News*, August 3, 2006, http://www.arabnews.com/?page=1&section=0&article=85985&d=3&m =8&.

30 Bookman and Bookman, *Medical Tourism in Developing Countries*, 3.

31 According to the *New York Times*, 125,000 Arab patients sought medical treatment at Bumrungrad Hospital in 2011. Sara Hamdan, "Thailand Profits from Health Care to Arab Patients," *New York Times*, February 8, 2012, accessed September 12, 2016, http://www.nytimes.com/2012/02/09/world/middleeast /09iht-m09-gulf-medical.html.

32 Wilson, "Medical Tourism in Thailand," 119.

33 Morris, "Educating Desire," 61.

34 Said, *Orientalism*, 63.

35 Morris, "Educating Desire," 61.

36 Hamilton, "Primal Dream," 145. See also Manderson, "Parables of Imperialism and Fantasies of the Exotic."

37 Tourism Authority of Thailand e-magazine.

38 Ong, *Flexible Citizenship*, 81.

39 Doubtless this is one specific Thai tourism marketing strategy among many.

40 Jackson, "Tolerant but Unaccepting."

41 Sanders, "The Rainbow Lobby."

42 Van Esterik, "The Politics of Beauty in Thailand," 203.

43 I explore the significance of this tattoo in more depth in Aizura, "Feminine Transformations."

44 See Rebecca, "Rebecca's Life on Mars." Unfortunately the entire AOL Hometown site was removed in December 2008, so the text and image I use here are from my own archive.

45 Rebecca, "Rebecca's Life on Mars."

46 Similar orientalizing tropes can be located within Japanese and Korean trans women's accounts of GRS in Thailand, suggesting that Thailand represents an exotic but devalued location for populations within the Asian region as well.

47 Som's and Emma's experiences push us past centering white European and Americans here; it is equally instructive to think about how different kinds of Asian trans-feminine subjects might find themselves reflected in marketing material, and psychically identify or disidentify with the self-orientalizing discourses I examined above. These might lead us to an examination of different racial hierarchies within Asia, premised on the privileging of lighter skin and national ideologies of superiority in relation to other Asian nations (for example Japan).

48 This situation seems consistent with more generalized labor relations in Thailand, particularly the ideological power of *bun khun* reciprocity, or family obligations, taking place between employers and employees. See Mills, *Thai Women in the Global Labor Force*, 122–24.

49 Hochschild, *The Managed Heart*, 138; Cheah, "Biopower and the New International Division of Reproductive Labor," 94.

50 Cheah, "Biopower and the New International Division of Reproductive Labor," 94.

51 On third world women workers, see Mohanty, "Women Workers and Capitalist Scripts," 3–29. On the subaltern see Spivak, "Can the Subaltern Speak?" On foreign domestic workers, see Cheah, "Biopower and the New International Division of Reproductive Labor."

52 Chow, *The Protestant Ethnic*, 34.

53 Wilson, *The Intimate Economies of Bangkok*, 84.

54 Wilson, *The Intimate Economies of Bangkok*, 8.

55 Mezzadra, "Taking Care." Mezzadra cites Virno, *Il Ricordo del Presente*, 122–30.

56 On biopolitics, see Foucault, *The History of Sexuality*, 137–41; Foucault, *Security, Territory, Population*.

57 Mezzadra, "Taking Care," 1.

58 On Belgrade as a center for trans masculine surgeries see Djordjevic et al., "Metoidioplasty as a Single Stage Sex Reassignment Surgery in Female Transsexuals."

59 See also Aizura, "Of Borders and Homes," for an account of trans masculinity, nationalism, and gender normativity.

60 See Alison Piepmeier's discussion of zines and "first-person singular feminism" in *Girl Zines*, 121.

61 Regales, "My Identity Is Fluid as Fuck," 90.

62 Poletti, *Intimate Ephemera*, 57.

63 Mitchell et al., "Critical Theory, Queer Resistance, and the Ends of Capture," 271.

64 Cohen, "Punks, Bulldaggers, and Welfare Queens," 440.

65 Käng, "Kathoey 'In Trend,'" 487.

66 Dutta and Roy, "Decolonizing Transgender in India"; Dutta, "Legible Identities and Legitimate Citizens."

Epilogue

1 For an analysis of trans visibility in the era of identity politics, see Aizura, introduction to "Unrecognizable," particularly 607–8.

2 Cáel Keegan, "Tongues without Bodies," 607.

3 Puar coins the term *piecing* from disability studies, reorienting David Mitchell and Sharon Snyder's observation that "we are now perpetual members of an audience encouraged to experience our bodies in pieces—as fractured terrains where the 'bad' parts of ourselves are multiple." See "Disability as Multitude," 190–91.

4 Puar, "Bodies with New Organs," 54.

5 Light, "Sense8 and the Failure of Global Imagination."

6 Povinelli, *Economies of Abandonment*, 77.

7 Eng, "The End(s) of Race," 1485, 1488.

8 Bailey et al., "*Sense8* Roundtable," 82.

9 Lothian, "Sense 8 and Utopian Connectivity," 95.

10 Mercer, "Black Hair Style Politics," 108.

11 There are many scholars to name here, and the archive of scholarship I cite is necessarily brief. See for example cárdenas, "Shifting Futures"; Haritaworn, *Queer Lovers and Hateful Others*; Snorton, *Black on Both Sides*; Ellison et al., "The Issue of Blackness"; Dutta, "Legible Identities and Legitimate Citizens."

12 Tuck and Yang, "Decolonization Is Not a Metaphor," 1; Driskill et al., introduction, 4.

13 Eric A. Stanley, in Boellstorff et al., "Decolonizing Transgender," 425.

14 I refer to Thai persons by their first name in keeping with Thai etiquette.

15 Ravine, "Toms and Zees," 396.

16 Sinnott's *Toms and Dees* is widely regarded as the first book to feature masculine gender nonconforming Thai practices, although it understands them largely in a framework of lesbianism rather than transness.

17 Ravine, *Romance of Siam*, 16.

18 Ravine, *Romance of Siam*, 17.

19 Fuhrmann, *Ghostly Desires*, 125.

20 Berlant, *The Queen of America Goes to Washington City*, 223.

BIBLIOGRAPHY

Adhikari, Mohamed. *Not White Enough, Not Black Enough: Racial Identity in the South African Coloured Community*. Athens: Ohio University Press, 2005.

The Aggressives. Directed by Daniel Peddle. Image Entertainment, 2006.

Ahmed, Sara. *Queer Phenomenology: Orientations, Objects, Others*. Durham, NC: Duke University Press, 2007.

Ahmed, Sara. *Strange Encounters: Embodied Others in Post-Coloniality*. London: Routledge, 2000.

Aizura, Aren Z. "Affective Vulnerability and Transgender Exceptionalism: Norma Ureiro in *Transgression*." In *Trans Studies: The Challenge to Hetero/Homo Normativities*, edited by Yolanda Martínez-San Miguel and Sarah Tobias, 122–39. New Brunswick, NJ: Rutgers University Press, 2016.

Aizura, Aren Z. "Feminine Transformations: Gender Reassignment Surgical Tourism in Thailand." *Medical Anthropology* 29, no. 4 (2010): 424–33.

Aizura, Aren Z. Introduction to "Unrecognizable: On Trans Recognition in 2017." *South Atlantic Quarterly* 116, no. 3 (2016): 606–11.

Aizura, Aren Z. "Of Borders and Homes: The Imaginary Community of (Trans) sexual Citizenship." *Inter-Asia Cultural Studies* 7, no. 2 (2006): 289–309.

Aizura, Aren Z. "The Romance of the Amazing Scalpel: 'Race,' Labour and Affect in Thai Gender Reassignment Clinics." In *Queer Bangkok: 21st Century Markets, Media, and Rights*, edited by Peter A. Jackson, 142–62. Hong Kong: Hong Kong University Press, 2011.

Aizura, Aren Z. "Trans Feminine Value: Racialised Others and the Limits of Necropolitics." In *Queer Necropolitics*, edited by Jin Haritaworn, Adi Kuntsman, and Silvia Posocco, 129–48. Oxford: Routledge, 2014.

Aizura, Aren Z. "Transnational Transgender Rights and Immigration Law." In *Transfeminist Perspectives in and beyond Transgender and Gender Studies*, edited by A. Finn Enke, 133–51. Philadelphia: Temple University Press, 2012.

Aizura, Aren Z. "Where Health and Beauty Meet: Femininity and Racialization in Thai Cosmetic Surgery Clinics." *Asian Studies Review* 33, no. 3 (2009): 303–17.

Aizura, Aren Z., Trystan Cotten, Carsten Balzer/Carla LaGata, Marcia Ochoa, and Salvador Vidal-Ortiz, eds. "Decolonizing Transgender." Special issue, *TSQ: Transgender Studies Quarterly* 1, no. 3 (2014).

Alliez, Eric, and Michael Feher. "The Luster of Capital." Translated by Alyson Waters. *Zone* 1–2 (1986): 315–59.

Althusser, Louis. *For Marx*. Translated by Ben Brewster. London: Verso, 1993.

Althusser, Louis, and Étienne Balibar. *Reading Capital*. Translated by Ben Brewster. London: New Left Books, 1975.

Altman, Dennis. "On Global Queering." *Australian Humanities Review* 2 (1996). http://www.australianhumanitiesreview.org/archive/Issue-July-1996/altman.html.

Ames, Jonathan. *Sexual Metamorphosis: An Anthology of Transsexual Memoirs*. New York: Vintage, 2005.

Amin, Kadji. "Temporality." *TSQ: Transgender Studies Quarterly* 1, nos. 1–2 (2014): 219–22.

Anderson, Benedict. *Imagined Communities: Reflections on the Origin and Spread of Nationalism*. New York: Verso, 1999.

Ang, Ien. *On Not Speaking Chinese: Living between Asia and the West*. New York: Routledge, 2001.

Appadurai, Arjun. *Modernity at Large: Cultural Dimensions of Globalization*. Minneapolis: University of Minnesota Press, 1996.

Arondekar, Anjali. *For the Record: On Sexuality and the Colonial Archive in India*. Durham, NC: Duke University Press, 2009.

Ashley, April, with Duncan Fallowell. *April Ashley's Odyssey*. London: Cape, 1982.

Australian Good Tranny Guide. 2002. National Library of Australia Archives. Accessed January 20, 2018. http://pandora.nla.gov.au/pan/24770/20020529-0000/www.tgfolk.net/sites/gtg/monash_intro.html.

Bacchetta, Paola, and Jin Haritaworn. "There Are Many Transatlantics: Homonationalism, Homotransnationalism and Feminist-Queer-Trans of Color Theories and Practices." In *Transatlantic Conversations: Feminism as Traveling Theory*, edited by Kathy Davis and Mary Evans, 127–44. Aldershot, UK: Ashgate, 2011.

Bailey, Moya, micha cárdenas, Laura Horak, Lokeilani Kaimana, Cáel M. Keegan, Genevieve Newman, Roxanne Samer, and Raffi Sarkissian. "*Sense8* Roundtable." *Spectator* 37, no. 2 (2017): 37–88.

Barrett, James, ed. *Transsexual and Other Disorders of Gender Identity: A Guide to Practical Management*. Oxford: Radcliffe, 2007.

Bassichis, Morgan, Alexander Lee, and Dean Spade. "Building an Abolition-ist Trans Movement with Everything We've Got." In *The Transgender Studies Reader 2*, edited by Susan Stryker and Aren Z. Aizura, 653–67. New York: Rout-ledge, 2013.

Bassichis, Morgan, and Dean Spade. "Queer Politics and Anti-Blackness." In *Queer Necropolitics*, edited by Jin Haritaworn, Adi Kuntsman, and Silvia Posocco, 191–210. Oxford: Routledge, 2014.

Baudrillard, Jean. *Symbolic Exchange and Death*. Translated by Iain Hamilton Grant. London: Sage, 1993.

Benedicto, Bobby. *Under Bright Lights: Gay Manila and the Global Scene*. Minneapo-lis: University of Minnesota Press, 2014.

Benjamin, Harry. *The Transsexual Phenomenon: A Scientific Report on Transsexualism and Sex Conversion in the Human Male and Female*. New York: Julian Press, 1966.

Ben-Moshe, Liat, Che Gossett, Nick Mitchell, and Eric A. Stanley. "Critical The-ory, Queer Resistance, and the Ends of Capture." In *Death and Other Penalties: Philosophy in a Time of Mass Incarceration*, edited by Geoffrey Adelsberg, Lisa Guenther, and Scott Zeman, 266–96. New York: Fordham University Press, 2015.

Berkins, Lohana. "Travestis: Una identidad política." *e-Misférica: Performance and Politics in the Americas* 4, no. 2 (2007). http://hemisphericinstitute.org/journal /4.2/eng/en42_pf_berkins.html.

Berlant, Lauren. "Nearly Utopian, Nearly Normal: Post-Fordist Affect in *La Promesse* and *Rosetta*." *Public Culture* 19, no. 2 (2007): 273–301.

Berlant, Lauren. *The Queen of America Goes to Washington City: Essays on Sex and Citizenship*. Durham, NC: Duke University Press, 1997.

Bernstein, Elizabeth. "Bounded Authenticity and the Commerce of Sex." In *In-timate Labors: Cultures, Technologies, and the Politics of Care*, edited by Rhacel Salazar Parreñas and Eileen Boris, 148–65. Stanford: Stanford University Press, 2010.

Bhabha, Homi. *The Location of Culture*. New York: Routledge, 2004.

Bhanji, Nael. "Trans/Scriptions: Homing Desires, (Trans)Sexual Citizenship and Racialized Bodies." In *Transgender Migrations: The Bodies, Borders, and Politics of Transition*, edited by Trystan Cotten, 157–75. New York: Routledge, 2012.

"Big Fat Stupid Doctors." *Fat Sexy Gender*. April 17, 2008. http://fatsexygender .blogspot.com/2008/04/big-fat-stupid-doctors.html.

Bigler, Ellen. *American Conversations: Puerto Ricans, White Ethnics, and Multicultur-alism*. Philadelphia: Temple University Press, 1999.

Billings, Dwight D., and Thomas Urban. "The Socio-Legal Construction of Trans-sexualism: An Interpretation and Critique." *Social Problems* 29, no. 3 (1982): 266–82.

Billings, Dwight D., and Thomas Urban. "The Socio-Medical Construction of Transsexualism: An Interpretation and Critique." In *Blending Gender: Social Aspects of Cross-Dressing and Sex-Changing*, edited by Richard Ekins and Dave King, 99–117. London: Routledge, 1996.

Bode, Katherine. "Aussie Battler in Crisis? Shifting Constructions of White Australian Masculinity and National Identity." *ACRAWSA Journal* 2, no. 1 (2006). https://acrawsa.org.au/wp-content/uploads/2017/12/CRAWS-Vol-2-No-1-2006.pdf.

Boellstorff, Tom. *The Gay Archipelago: Sexuality and Nation in Indonesia*. Princeton, NJ: Princeton University Press, 2005.

Boellstorff, Tom, Mauro Cabral, micha cárdenas, Trystan Cotten, Eric A. Stanley, Kalaniopua Young, and Aren Z. Aizura. "Decolonizing Transgender: A Roundtable Discussion." *TSQ: Transgender Studies Quarterly* 1, no. 3 (2014): 419–39.

Bogost, Ian. *Alien Phenomenology, or, What It's Like to Be a Thing*. Minneapolis: University of Minnesota Press, 2012.

Bookman, Karla R., and Milica Bookman. *Medical Tourism in Developing Countries*. New York: Palgrave Macmillan, 2007.

Bornstein, Kate. *Gender Outlaw: On Men, Women, and the Rest of Us*. New York: Routledge, 1994.

Boylan, Jennifer Finney. *She's Not There: A Life in Two Genders*. New York: Broadway Books, 2003.

Brown, Wendy. "Neo-Liberalism and the End of Liberal Democracy." *Theory and Event* 7, no. 1 (2003). https://muse.jhu.edu/article/48659.

Bryant, Levi R. *The Democracy of Objects*. Ann Arbor, MI: Open University Press, 2011. http://openhumanitiespress.org/democracy-of-objects.html.

Bryant, Levi, Nick Srnicek, and Graham Harman, eds. *The Speculative Turn: Continental Materialism and Realism*. Melbourne: re.press, 2011.

Bullough, Vern L. "Transsexualism in History." *Archives of Sexual Behaviour* 4, no. 5 (1975): 561–71.

Butler, Judith. *Bodies That Matter: On the Discursive Limits of Sex*. New York: Routledge, 1993.

Butler, Judith. *Gender Trouble: Feminism and the Subversion of Identity*. New York: Routledge, 1990.

Cameron, Ardis. "When Strangers Bring Cameras: The Poetics and Politics of Othered Places." *American Quarterly* 54, no. 3 (2002): 411–35.

Cannell, Fenella. *Power and Intimacy in the Christian Philippines*. Cambridge: Cambridge University Press, 1999.

cárdenas, micha. "Shifting Futures: Digital Trans of Color Praxis." *Ada: A Journal of Gender, New Media, and Technology* 6 (2015). doi:10.7264/N3WH2N8D.

Cardon, Lauren S. *Fashion and Fiction: Self-Transformation in Twentieth-Century American Literature*. Charlottesville: University of Virginia Press, 2016.

Carter, Julian B., David J. Getsy, and Trish Saleh, eds. "Trans Cultural Production." Special issue, *TSQ: Transgender Studies Quarterly* 1, no. 4 (2014).

Center for Gender Sanity. "Gender Sanity Strategies for Managing Transition (Advice for Employers)." N.d. Accessed December 11, 2015. http://www.gendersanity.com/strategies.html.

Centers for Disease Control and Prevention. "HIV among Transgender People." N.d. Accessed February 21, 2017. https://www.cdc.gov/hiv/group/gender/trans gender.

Chakrabarty, Dipesh. *Provincializing Europe: Postcolonial Thought and Historical Difference*. Princeton, NJ: Princeton University Press, 2000.

Cheah, Pheng. "Biopower and the New International Division of Reproductive Labor." *boundary 2: An International Journal of Literature and Culture* 34, no. 1 (2007): 79–113.

Cheng, Anne Anlin. *The Melancholy of Race: Psychoanalysis, Assimilation, and Hidden Grief*. Oxford: Oxford University Press, 2001.

Chow, Rey. *The Protestant Ethnic and the Spirit of Capitalism*. New York: Columbia University Press, 2002.

The Christine Jorgensen Story. Directed by Irving Rapper. Edward Small Productions, 1970.

Clare, Eli. "Body Shame, Body Pride: Lessons from the Disability Rights Movement." In *The Transgender Studies Reader 2*, edited by Susan Stryker and Aren Z. Aizura, 261–65. New York: Routledge, 2013.

Clare, Eli. "Gawking, Gaping, Staring." *GLQ: A Journal of Lesbian and Gay Studies* 9, nos. 1–2 (2003): 257–61.

Clarke, Adele. "Thoughts on Biomedicalization and Its Transnational Travels." In *Biomedicalization: Technoscience, Health, and Illness in the U.S.*, edited by Adele E. Clarke, Laura Mamo, Jennifer Ruth Fosket, Jennifer R. Fishman, and Janet K. Shim, 380–406. Durham, NC: Duke University Press, 2010.

Clarke, Adele E., Janet K. Shim, Laura Mamo, Jennifer Ruth Fosket, and Jennifer R. Fishman. "Biomedicalization: Technoscientific Transformations in Health, Illness, and Medicine." *American Sociological Review* 68, no. 2 (2003): 161–94.

Clifford, James. *Routes: Travel and Translation in the Late Twentieth Century*. Cambridge, MA: Harvard University Press, 1997.

Clifford, James. "Travelling Cultures." In *Cultural Studies*, edited by Lawrence Grossberg, Cary Nelson, and Paula Treichler, 96–116. New York: Routledge, 1992.

Clough, Patricia Tinecito. Introduction to *The Affective Turn: Theorizing the Social*, edited by Patricia Tinecito Clough and Jean Halley, 1–33. Durham, NC: Duke University Press, 2007.

Coccinelle. *Coccinelle*. Paris: Filipaci, 1997.

Cohen, Cathy J. "Punks, Bulldaggers, and Welfare Queens: The Radical Potential of Queer Politics?" *GLQ: A Journal of Lesbian and Gay Studies* 3, no. 4 (1997): 437–65.

Cohen, Niv. *Soldiers, Rebels, and Drifters: Gay Representation in Israeli Cinema*. Detroit: Wayne State University Press, 2011.

Conn, Canary. *Canary: The Story of a Transsexual*. New York: Bantam Books, 1974.

Conrad, Ryan, ed. *Against Equality: Queer Revolution, Not Mere Inclusion*. Oakland, CA: AK Press, 2014.

Conway, Lynn. "Vaginoplasty: Male to Female Sex Reassignment Surgery." Artificial Intelligence Lab, University of Michigan, 2000. http://ai.eecs.umich.edu/people/conway/TS/SRS.html.

Cossey, Caroline. My Story. London: Faber and Faber, 1991.

Costa, LeeRay M., and Andrew Matzner. Male Bodies, Women's Souls: Personal Narratives of Thailand's Transgendered Youth. London: Haworth Press, 2007.

Cotten, Trystan T., ed. "Introduction: Migration and Morphing." In Transgender Migrations: The Bodies, Borders, and Politics of Transition, edited by Trystan T. Cotten, 1–7. New York: Routledge, 2012.

Couch, Murray, Marian Pitts, Hunter Mulcare, Samantha Croy, Anne Mitchell, and Sunil Patel. Tranznation: A Report on the Health and Wellbeing of Transgender People in Australia and New Zealand. Melbourne: Australian Research Centre for Sex, Health and Society, 2007.

Crawford, Kate. "Following You: Disciplines of Listening in Social Media." Continuum: Journal of Media and Cultural Studies 23, no. 4 (2009): 525–35.

Crawford, Lucas. "Transgender without Organs? Mobilizing a Geo-Affective Theory of Gender Modification." WSQ: Women's Studies Quarterly 36, nos. 3–4 (2008): 127–43.

Cromwell, Jason. "Passing Women and Female-Bodied Men: (Re)claiming FTM History." In Reclaiming Genders: Transsexual Grammars at the Fin de Siècle, edited by Kate More and Stephen Whittle, 34–61. London: Cassell, 1999.

Cromwell, Jason. Transmen and FTMs: Identities, Bodies, Genders, and Sexualities. Urbana: University of Illinois Press, 1999.

Currah, Paisley. "Gender Pluralisms under the Transgender Umbrella." In Transgender Rights, edited by Paisley Currah, Richard M. Juang, and Shannon Prince Minter, 3–31. Minneapolis: University of Minnesota Press, 2006.

Cvetkovich, Ann. An Archive of Feelings: Trauma, Sexuality, and Lesbian Public Cultures. Durham, NC: Duke University Press, 2003.

Damodaran, Saji S., and Trudy Kennedy. "The Monash Gender Dysphoria Clinic: Opportunities and Challenges." Australasian Psychiatry 8, no. 4 (2000): 355–57.

Darwich, Lynn, and Haneen Maikey. "The Road from Antipinkwashing Activism to the Decolonization of Palestine." WSQ: Women's Studies Quarterly 42, nos. 3–4 (2014): 281–85.

de Certeau, Michel. "Ethno-Graphy: Speech, or the Space of the Other: Jean de Léry." In The Writing of History, 209–43. Translated by Tom Conley. New York: Columbia University Press, 1988.

de Certeau, Michel. The Practice of Everyday Life. Translated by Stephen Rendall. Berkeley: University of California Press, 1988.

Dempsey, Deborah. "Active Fathers, Natural Families and Children's Origins: Dominant Themes in the Australian Political Debate over Eligibility for Assisted Reproductive Technology." Australian Journal of Emerging Technologies and Society 4, no. 1 (2006): 28–44. http://pandora.nla.gov.au/pan/36357/20061123-0000/www.swin.edu.au/sbs/ajets/journal/V4N1/pdf/V4N1-3-dempsey.pdf.

Denny, Dallas. "Black Telephones, White Refrigerators: Rethinking Christine Jorgensen." In *Current Concepts in Transgender Identity*, edited by Dallas Denny, 35–44. New York: Garland, 1998.

Denny, Dallas. "The Clarke Institute of Psychiatry: Canada's Shame." *Transgender Forum*, April 13, 1998. http://dallasdenny.com/Writing/2013/08/15/the-clarke -institute-of-psychiatry-canadas-shame-1999.

Denny, Dallas. "A Comprehensive List of Trans Autobiographies." *TGForum. com*, September 17, 2012. http://www.tgforum.com/wordpress/index.php/a -comprehensive-list-of-trans-autobiographies.

Derrida, Jacques. *Archive Fever: A Freudian Impression.* Translated by Eric Prenowitz. Chicago: University of Chicago Press, 1998.

Derrida, Jacques. *Of Grammatology.* Translated by Gayatri Chakravorty Spivak. Baltimore: Johns Hopkins University Press, 1998.

Devor, Aaron. *FTM: Female-to-Male Transsexuals in Society.* Bloomington: University of Indiana Press, 1997.

Dhejne, Cecilia, Katarina Öberg, Stefan Arver, and Mikael Landén. "An Analysis of All Applications for Sex Reassignment Surgery in Sweden, 1960–2010: Prevalence, Incidence, and Regrets." *Archives of Sexual Behavior* 43, no. 8 (2014): 1535–45.

Dinshaw, Carolyn, Lee Edelman, Roderick A. Ferguson, Carla Freccero, Elizabeth Freeman, Judith Halberstam, Annamarie Jagose, Christopher S. Nealon, and Tan Hoang Nguyen. "Theorizing Queer Temporalities: A Roundtable Discussion." *GLQ: A Journal of Lesbian and Gay Studies* 13, nos. 2–3 (2007): 177–95.

Ditmore, Melissa. "In Calcutta, Sex Workers Organize." In *The Affective Turn*, edited by Patricia Ticineto Clough and Jean Halley, 170–87. Durham, NC: Duke University Press, 2007.

Djordjevic, Miroslav L., Dusan Stanojevic, Marta Bizic, Vladimir Kojovic, Marko Majstorovic, Svetlana Vujovic, Alexandar Milosevic, Gradimir Korac, and Sava V. Perovic. "Metoidioplasty as a Single Stage Sex Reassignment Surgery in Female Transsexuals: Belgrade Experience." *Journal of Sexual Medicine* 6, no. 5 (2009): 1306–13.

Docter, Richard F. *Becoming a Woman: A Biography of Christine Jorgensen.* New York: Haworth Press, 2008.

Driskill, Qwo-Li, Chris Finley, Brian Joseph Gilley, and Scott Lauria Morgensen, eds. Introduction to *Queer Indigenous Studies: Critical Interventions in Theory, Politics, and Literature*, edited by Qwo-Li Driskill, Chris Finley, Brian Joseph Gilley, and Scott Lauria Morgensen, 1–28. Tucson: University of Arizona Press, 2011.

Dutta, Aniruddha. "Legible Identities and Legitimate Citizens: The Globalization of Transgender and Subjects of HIV-AIDS Prevention in Eastern India." *International Feminist Journal of Politics* 15, no. 4 (2013): 494–514.

Dutta, Aniruddha, and Raina Roy. "Decolonizing Transgender in India: Some Reflections." *TSQ: Transgender Studies Quarterly* 1, no. 3 (2014): 320–37.

Edmonds, Alexander. "The Poor Have the Right to Be Beautiful: Cosmetic Surgery in Neoliberal Brazil." *Journal of the Royal Anthropological Institute* 13, no. 2 (2007): 363–81.

Elbe, Lili. *Man into Woman: An Authentic Record of a Change of Sex.* Boston: Beacon Library, 1933.

Ellis, Havelock, and John Addington Symonds. *Sexual Inversion: A Critical Edition.* Edited by Ivan Crozier. New York: Palgrave Macmillan, 2008.

Ellison, Treva, Kai M. Green, Matt Richardson, and C. Riley Snorton, eds. "We Got Issues: Toward a Black Trans*/Studies." *TSQ: Transgender Studies Quarterly* 4, no. 2 (2016): 162–69.

Eng, David L. "The End(s) of Race." *PMLA* 123, no. 5 (2016): 1479–93.

Eng, David L. *The Feeling of Kinship: Queer Liberalism and the Racialization of Intimacy.* Durham, NC: Duke University Press, 2010.

Eng, David L. "Transnational Adoption and Queer Diasporas." In *The Routledge Queer Studies Reader*, edited by Donald E. Hall, Annemarie Jagose, Andrea Bebell, and Susan Potter, 301–23. New York: Routledge, 2012.

Enteen, Jillana B. "Transitioning Online: Cosmetic Surgery Tourism in Thailand." *Television and New Media* 15, no. 3 (2014): 238–49.

Fausto-Sterling, Anne. *Sexing the Body: Gender Politics and the Construction of Sexuality.* New York: Basic Books, 2000.

Feinberg, Leslie. *Transgender Warriors: Making History from Joan of Arc to Dennis Rodman.* New York: Beacon, 1996.

Felski, Rita. "Fin de Siècle, Fin de Sexe: Transsexuality and the Death of History." In *Doing Time: Feminist Theory and Postmodern Culture*, 137–53. New York: New York University Press, 2000.

Felski, Rita. *The Gender of Modernity.* Cambridge, MA: Harvard University Press, 2009.

Ferguson, Roderick A. *Aberrations in Black: Towards a Queer of Color Critique.* Minneapolis: University of Minnesota Press, 2003.

Film synopsis. *Heymann Films.* N.d. Accessed January 20, 2018. http://tomer heymann.com/film/paper-dolls/synopsis.

Florida, Richard. *The Rise of the Creative Class and How It's Transforming Work, Leisure, Community, and Everyday Life.* New York: Basic Books, 2002.

Foerster, Maxime. "On the History of Transsexuals in France." In *Transgender Experience: Place, Ethnicity, and Visibility*, edited by Chantal Zabus and David Coad, 19–30. London: Routledge, 2013.

Foucault, Michel. *The Birth of Biopolitics: Lectures at the Collège de France, 1978–1979.* Edited by Michel Senellart. Translated by Graham Burchell. New York: Palgrave Macmillan, 2008.

Foucault, Michel. *The History of Sexuality, Volume I: An Introduction.* Translated by Robert Hurley. New York: Vintage, 1990.

Foucault, Michel. "Nietzsche, Genealogy, History." In *Language, Counter-Memory, Practice: Selected Essays and Interviews.* Edited by Donald F. Bouchard, 139–64. New York: Pantheon, 1980.

Foucault, Michel. *Security, Territory, Population: Lectures at the Collège de France 1977–78.* Translated by Graham Burchell. London: Palgrave Macmillan, 2007.

Foucault, Michel. "Truth and Power." In *Power/Knowledge: Selected Interviews and Other Writings, 1972–1977,* edited by Colin Gordon, 109–33. Translated by Colin Gordon, Leo Marshall, John Mepham, and Kate Soper. New York: Pantheon, 1980.

Foucault, Michel. "What Is Enlightenment?" In *The Foucault Reader,* edited by Paul Rabinow, 32–50. New York: Pantheon Books, 1984.

Franke, Katherine. "Dating the State: The Moral Hazards of Winning Gay Rights." *Columbia Human Rights Law Review* 49, no. 1 (2012): 1–46.

Freeman, Elizabeth. *Time Binds: Queer Temporalities, Queer Histories.* Durham, NC: Duke University Press, 2010.

Fuhrmann, Arnika. *Ghostly Desires: Queer Sexuality and Vernacular Buddhism in Contemporary Thai Cinema.* Durham, NC: Duke University Press, 2016.

Funny Kinda Guy. Directed by Travis Reeves. Sprocketeers, 2005.

Garber, Marjorie. *Vested Interests: Cross-Dressing and Cultural Anxiety.* New York: Routledge, 1992.

Garcia, J. Neil C. *Philippine Gay Culture: Binabae to Bakla, Silahis to MSM.* Quezon City: University of the Philippines Press, 2008.

Gehi, Pooja. "Gendered (In)security: Migration and Criminalization in the Security State." *Harvard Journal of Law and Gender* 35, no. 2 (2012): 357–98.

Gehi, Pooja. "Struggles from the Margins: Anti-Immigrant Legislation and the Impact on Low-Income Transgender People of Color." *Women's Rights Law Report* 30 (2009): 315–29.

"Gender Pathways Clinic." Kaiser Permanente. 2017. https://thrive.kaiserpermanente .org/care-near-you/northern-california/sanfrancisco/departments/gender -pathways-clinic.

Gender Redesigner. Directed by Johnny Bergmann. Outcast Films, 2007.

Gilman, Sander L. *Making the Body Beautiful: A Cultural History of Aesthetic Surgery.* Princeton, NJ: Princeton University Press, 1999.

Gopinath, Gayatri. *Impossible Desires: Queer Diasporas and South Asian Public Cultures.* Durham, NC: Duke University Press, 2005.

Gordon, Colin. "The Soul of the Citizen: Max Weber and Michel Foucault on Rationality and Government." In *Max Weber, Rationality and Modernity,* edited by Scott Lash and Sam Whimster, 293–316. London: Routledge, 1987.

Grant, Jaime M., Lisa A. Mottet, and Justin Tanis. *Injustice at Every Turn: A Report of the National Transgender Discrimination Survey.* Washington, DC: National Center for Transgender Equality and National Gay and Lesbian Task Force, 2011. http://www.thetaskforce.org/static_html/downloads/reports/reports /ntds_full.pdf.

Grant, Jaime M., Lisa A. Mottet, and Justin Tanis, with Jody L. Herman, Jack Harrison, and Mara Keisling. *National Transgender Discrimination Survey Report on Health and Health Care.* Washington, DC: National Gay and Lesbian Task Force and National Center for Transgender Equality, 2010. http://www

.thetaskforce.org/static_html/downloads/resources_and_tools/ntds_report
_on_health.pdf.

Grewal, Inderpal. *Home and Harem: Nation, Gender, Empire, and the Cultures of Travel*. Durham, NC: Duke University Press, 1996.

Grewal, Inderpal, and Caren Kaplan. "Global Identities: Theorizing Transnational Studies of Sexuality." *GLQ: A Journal of Lesbian and Gay Studies* 7, no. 4 (2001): 663–79.

Grewal, Inderpal, and Caren Kaplan. *Scattered Hegemonies: Postmodernity and Transnational Feminist Practice*. Minneapolis: University of Minnesota Press, 2002.

Greyson, John. "Pinkface." *Camera Obscura* 27, no. 2 (2012): 145–53.

Griggs, Claudine. *Journal of a Sex Change: Passage through Trinidad*. Oxford: Berg, 2004.

Gross, Aeyal. "Thinking Is in the Grey Area: Gender, Family, Home and Diaspora in the Paper Dolls." Paper delivered at Transsomatechnics Conference, Vancouver, Canada, May 2008.

Gunther, Mark. "'Trans'-forming Corporate America." *Fortune*, August 27, 2007. http://archive.fortune.com/2007/07/23/magazines/fortune/transgender _workplace.fortune/index.htm.

Hage, Ghassan. *White Nation: Fantasies of White Supremacy in a Multicultural Society*. New York: Routledge, 2000.

Haiken, Elizabeth. *Venus Envy: A History of Cosmetic Surgery in America*. Baltimore: Johns Hopkins University Press, 1999.

Halberstam, Jack. *In a Queer Time and Place: Transgender Bodies, Subcultural Lives*. New York: New York University Press, 2005.

Halberstam, Jack. "Transgender Butch: Butch/FTM Border Wars and the Masculine Continuum." *GLQ: A Journal of Lesbian and Gay Studies* 4, no. 2 (1998): 287–310.

Halberstam, Jack, and C. Jacob Hale. "Butch/FTM Border Wars: A Note on Collaboration." *GLQ: A Journal of Lesbian and Gay Studies* 4, no. 2 (1998): 283–85.

Hale, C. Jacob. "Consuming the Living, Dis(re)membering the Dead in the Butch/FTM Borderlands." *GLQ: A Journal of Lesbian and Gay Studies* 4, no. 2 (1998): 311–48.

Hall, Stuart. "Black Diaspora Artists in Britain: Three 'Moments' in Post-war History." *History Workshop Journal* 61, no. 1 (2006): 1–24.

Halperin, David. *Saint Foucault: Towards a Gay Hagiography*. New York: Oxford University Press, 1995.

Halpern, Sydney A. "Medical Authority and the Culture of Rights." *Journal of Health Politics, Policy and Law* 29, nos. 4–5 (2004): 835–52.

Hamilton, Annette. "Primal Dream: Masculinism, Sun, and Salvation in Thailand's Sex Trade." In *Sites of Desire, Economies of Pleasure: Sexualities in Asia and the Pacific*, edited by Lenore Manderson and Margaret Jolly, 145–65. Chicago: University of Chicago Press, 1997.

Hanhardt, Christina. *Safe Space: Gay Neighborhood History and the Politics of Violence*. Durham, NC: Duke University Press, 2013.

Hannam, Kevin, Mimi Sheller, and John Urry. "Mobilities, Immobilities and Moorings." *Mobilities* 1, no. 1 (2006): 1–22.

Hanssmann, Christoph. "Passing Torches? Feminist Inquiries and Trans-Health Politics and Practices." *TSQ: Transgender Studies Quarterly* 3, nos. 1–2 (2016): 120–36.

Hardt, Michael, and Antonio Negri. *Empire*. Cambridge, MA: Harvard University Press, 2000.

Hardt, Michael, and Antonio Negri. *Multitude: War and Democracy in the Age of Empire*. New York: Penguin, 2004.

Haritaworn, Jin. *Queer Lovers and Hateful Others: Regenerating Violent Times and Places*. London: Pluto Press, 2015.

Haritaworn, Jin, Adi Kuntsman, and Silvia Posocco. Introduction to *Queer Necropolitics*, edited by Jin Haritaworn, Adi Kuntsman, and Silvia Posocco, 1–25. Oxford: Routledge, 2011.

Haritaworn, Jin, and C. Riley Snorton. "Transsexual Necropolitics." In *The Transgender Studies Reader 2*, edited by Susan Stryker and Aren Z. Aizura, 66–76. New York: Routledge, 2006.

Harper, Phillip Brian. "'The Subversive Edge': Paris Is Burning, Social Critique, and the Limits of Subjective Agency." *Diacritics* 24, nos. 2–3 (1994): 90–103.

Hausman, Bernice L. *Changing Sex: Transsexualism, Technology, and the Idea of Gender*. Durham, NC: Duke University Press, 1995.

Hayward, Eva. "Lessons from a Starfish." In *Queering the Non/Human*, edited by Noreen Giffney and Myra J. Hird, 249–64. London: Ashgate, 2008.

Hekma, Gert. "A Female Soul in a Male Body: Sexual Inversion as Gender Inversion in Nineteenth-Century Sexology." In *Third Sex, Third Gender: Beyond Sexual Dimorphism in Culture and History*, edited by Gilbert Herdt, 213–40. New York: Zone, 1994.

Hirschfeld, Magnus. *Transvestites: The Erotic Drive to Cross-Dress*. Translated by Michael Lombardi-Nash. New York: Prometheus, 1991.

Hoang, Kimberly Kay. "Economies of Emotion, Familiarity, Fantasy, and Desire: Emotional Labor in Ho Chi Minh's Sex Industry." In *Intimate Labors: Cultures, Technologies, and the Politics of Care*, edited by Eileen Boris and Rhacel Salazar Parreñas, 166–82. Stanford: Stanford University Press, 2010.

Hochschild, Arlie. *The Managed Heart: Commercialization of Human Feeling*. 2nd ed. Berkeley: University of California Press, 2003.

Holland, Patrick, and Graham Huggan. *Tourists with Typewriters: Critical Reflections on Contemporary Travel Writing*. Ann Arbor: University of Michigan Press, 2000.

hooks, bell. "Eating the Other: Desire and Resistance." In *Black Looks: Race and Representation*, 21–39. Boston: South End Press, 1992.

hooks, bell. "Is Paris Burning?" *Z Magazine*, June 1991.

Horak, Laura. "Trans on YouTube: Intimacy, Visibility, Temporality." *Transgender Studies Reader* 1, no. 4 (2014): 572–85.

Hygeia Beauty. "Sex Reassignment Surgery: Sex Change." *Destination Beauty by Hygeia Healthcare*. N.d. Accessed May 23, 2008. https://web.archive.org/web /20090620092454/http://www.hygeiabeauty.com/sex-change.html.

Irving, Dan. "Normalized Transgressions: Legitimizing the Transsexual Body as Productive." *Radical History Review*, 2008, no. 100 (2008): 38–59.

Irving, Dan, and Rupert Raj, eds. *Trans Activism in Canada: A Reader*. Toronto: Canadian Scholars' Press, 2014.

Islam, Syed Manzurul. *The Ethics of Travel: From Marco Polo to Kafka*. Manchester, UK: Manchester University Press, 1996.

Jackson, Peter A. "Kathoey >< Gay >< Man: The Historical Emergence of Gay Male Identity in Thailand." In *Sites of Desire/Economies of Pleasure: Sexualities in Asia and the Pacific*, edited by Lenore Manderson and Margaret Jolly, 166–90. Chicago: University of Chicago Press, 1997.

Jackson, Peter A. "Performative Genders, Perverse Desires: A Bio-History of Thailand's Same-Sex and Transgender Cultures." *Intersections: Gender, History and Culture in the Asian Context* 9 (2003). http://intersections.anu.edu.au/issue9 /jackson.html.

Jackson, Peter A. "Thai Research on Male Homosexuality and Transgenderism and the Cultural Limits of Foucaultian Analysis." *Journal of the History of Homosexuality* 8, no. 1 (1997): 52–85.

Jackson, Peter A. "Tolerant but Unaccepting: The Myth of a Thai 'Gay Paradise.'" In *Genders and Sexualities in Modern Thailand*, edited by Peter A. Jackson and Nerida Cook, 226–42. Chiang Mai, Thailand: Silkworm Books, 1999.

Jackson, Peter A., and Gerard Sullivan, eds., *Lady Boys, Tom Boys, Rent Boys: Male and Female Homosexualities in Contemporary Thailand*. Binghamton, NY: Haworth Press, 1999.

Jacobson, Matthew Frye. *Roots Too: White Ethnic Revival in Post–Civil Rights America*. Cambridge, MA: Harvard University Press, 2009.

Jeffreys, Sheila. *Beauty and Misogyny: Harmful Cultural Practices in the West*. London: Routledge, 2005.

Johnson, Colin, Mary Gray, Scott Herring, E. Patrick Johnson, and Karen Tongson, eds. "Queering the Middle." Special issue, *GLQ: A Journal of Lesbian and Gay Studies* 20, nos. 1–2 (2014).

Johnson, Mark. *Beauty and Power: Transgendering and Cultural Transformation in the Southern Philippines*. London: Bloomsbury Academic, 1997.

Jones, Tiffany, Bonnie Hart, Morgan Carpenter, Gavi Ansara, William Leonard, and Jayne Lucke. *Intersex: Stories and Statistics from Australia*. Cambridge, UK: Open Book Publishers, 2016. https://interactadvocates.org/wp-content /uploads/2016/01/Intersex-Stories-Statistics-Australia.pdf.

Jorgensen, Christine. *Christine Jorgensen: A Personal Autobiography*. New York: Bantam, 1968.

Jupp, James, ed. *The Australian People: An Encyclopedia of the Nation, Its People and Their Origins*. Cambridge: Cambridge University Press, 2001.

Justice, Daniel Heath, Mark Rifkin, and Bethany Schneider, eds. "Sexuality, Nationality, Indigeneity." Special issue, *GLQ: A Journal of Gay and Lesbian Studies* 16, nos. 1–2 (2010).

Kabbani, Rana. *Imperial Fictions: Europe's Myths of Orient*. London: Pandora Books, 1994.

Käng, Dredge Byung'chu. "Kathoey 'In Trend': Emergent Genderscapes, National Anxieties and the Re-Signification of Male-Bodied Effeminacy in Thailand." *Asian Studies Review* 36, no. 4 (2012): 475–94.

Kangas, Beth. "Therapeutic Itineraries in a Global World: Yemenis and Their Search for Biomedical Treatment Abroad." *Medical Anthropology* 21, no. 1 (2002): 35–78.

Kaplan, Caren. *Questions of Travel: Postmodern Discourses of Displacement*. Durham, NC: Duke University Press, 1996.

Kaw, Eugenia. "Medicalization of Racial Features: Asian American Women and Cosmetic Surgery." *Medical Anthropology Quarterly* 7, no. 1 (1993): 74–89.

Keegan, Cáel M. "Tongues without Bodies: The Wachowskis' *Sense8*." *TSQ: Transgender Studies Quarterly* 3, nos. 3–4 (2016): 605–10.

Kheshti, Roshanak. "Cross-Dressing and Gender (Tres)passing: The Transgender Move as a Site of Agential Potential in the New Iranian Cinema." *Hypatia* 24, no. 3 (2009): 158–77.

Kinglake, Alexander William. *Eothen*. London: J. M. Dent and Sons, 1928.

Kowal, Emma. "Disturbing Pasts and Promising Futures: The Politics of Indigenous Medical Research in Australia." In *Biomapping Indigenous Peoples: Towards an Understanding of the Issues*, edited by Susanne Berthier-Foglar, Sheila Collingwood-Whittick, and Sandrine Tolazzi, 329–48. Amsterdam: Rodopi, 2012.

Krafft-Ebing, Richard von. *Psychopathia Sexualis: A Medico-Legal Study*. Translated by Charles Gilbert Chaddock. Philadelphia: F. A. Davis, 1894.

Kulick, Don. *Travestí: Sex, Gender, and Culture among Brazilian Transgendered Prostitutes*. Chicago: University of Chicago Press, 1998.

Kuntsman, Adi. *Figurations of Violence and Belonging: Queerness, Migranthood and Nationalism in Cyberspace and Beyond*. Oxford: Peter Lang, 2009.

Lavie, Smadar. *Wrapped in the Flag of Israel: Mizrahi Single Mothers and Bureaucratic Torture*. New York: Berghahn Books, 2014.

Les travestis pleurent aussi. Directed by Sebastiano D'Ayala Valva. Sebastiano D'Ayala Valva, 2007.

Leung, Helen Hok-Sze. "Unsung Heroes: Reading Transgender Subjectivities in Hong Kong Action Cinema." In *The Transgender Studies Reader*, edited by Susan Stryker and Stephen Whittle, 685–97. New York: Routledge, 2006.

Lewis, Tania. "DIY Selves? Reflexivity and Habitus in Young People's Use of the Internet for Health Information." *European Journal of Cultural Studies* 9, no. 4 (2006): 461–79.

Lewis, Vek. "Thinking Figurations Otherwise: Reframing Dominant Knowledges of Sex and Gender Variance in Latin America." In *The Transgender Studies Reader 2*, edited by Susan Stryker and Aren Z. Aizura, 66–76. New York: Routledge, 2006.

Lezra, Jacques, ed. *Depositions: Althusser, Balibar, Macherey, and the Labor of Reading*. New Haven, CT: Yale University Press, 1995.

Light, Claire. "*Sense8* and the Failure of Global Imagination." *Nerds of Color* (blog), June 10, 2015. http://thenerdsofcolor.org/2015/06/10/sense8-and-the-failure -of-global-imagination.

Lind, Earl. *Autobiography of an Androgyne*. New York: Medico-Legal Journal, 1918.

Lothian, Alexis. "*Sense8* and Utopian Connectivity." *Science Fiction Film and Television* 9, no. 1 (2016): 93–95.

Lotringer, Sylvére, and Christian Marazzi, eds. *Autonomia: Post-Political Politics*. Los Angeles: Semiotext(e), 2007.

Love, Heather. *Feeling Backward: Loss and the Politics of Queer History*. Cambridge, MA: Harvard University Press, 2007.

Luibhéid, Eithne. "Introduction: Queering Migration and Citizenship." In *Queer Migrations: Sexuality, U.S. Citizenship, and Border Crossings*, edited by Eithne Luibhéid and Lionel Cantú Jr., ix–xlvi. Minneapolis: University of Minnesota Press, 2005.

Luibhéid, Eithne, and Lionel Cantú Jr., eds. *Queer Migrations: Sexuality, U.S. Citizenship, and Border Crossings*. Minneapolis: University of Minnesota Press, 2005.

Lupton, Deborah. *Medicine as Culture: Illness, Disease, and the Body*. London: Sage, 2012.

Ma, Joyce L. C. "A Systems Approach to the Social Difficulties of Transsexuals in Hong Kong." *Journal of Family Therapy* 19, no. 1 (1997): 71–88.

MacCannell, Dean. *The Tourist: A New Theory of the Leisure Class*. New York: Schocken, 1989.

MacKenzie, Gordene Olga. *Transgender Nation*. Bowling Green, OH: Bowling Green State University Popular Press, 1994.

Manalansan, Martin F., IV. *Global Divas: Filipino Gay Men in the Diaspora*. Durham, NC: Duke University Press, 2003.

Manalansan, Martin F., IV. "Queering the Chain of Care Paradigm." *S&F Online* 6, no. 3 (2008). http://sfonline.barnard.edu/immigration/manalansan _01.htm.

Manalansan, Martin F., IV. "Queer Intersections: Sexuality and Gender in Migration Studies." *International Migration Review* 40, no. 1 (2006): 224–49.

Manalansan, Martin F., IV. "Servicing the World: Flexible Filipinos and the Unsecured Life." In *Political Emotions*, edited by Janet Staiger, Ann Cvetkovich, and Ann Reynolds, 215–28. New York: Routledge, 2010.

Manalansan, Martin F., IV, Chantal Nadeau, Richard T. Rodriguez, and Siobhan B. Somerville. "Queering the Middle: Race, Region, and a Queer Midwest." *GLQ: A Journal of Lesbian and Gay Studies* 20, nos. 1–2 (2014): 1–12.

Manderson, Lenore. "Parables of Imperialism and Fantasies of the Exotic: Western Representations of Thailand—Place and Sex." In *Sites of Desire, Economies of Pleasure: Sexualities in Asia and the Pacific*, edited by Lenore Manderson and Margaret Jolly, 123–44. Chicago: University of Chicago Press, 1997.

Marcus, George E. "Ethnography in/of the World System: The Emergence of Multi-Sited Ethnography." *Annual Review of Anthropology* 24, no. 1 (1995): 95–117.

Martin, Fran. "Fran Martin Responds to Dennis Altman." *Australian Humanities Review* 2 (1996). http://www.australianhumanitiesreview.org/emuse /Globalqueering/martin.html.

Martin, Fran, Peter A. Jackson, Mark McLelland, and Audrey Yue, eds. *AsiaPacifiQueer: Rethinking Genders and Sexualities*. Urbana: University of Illinois Press, 2008.

Martino, Mario. *Emergence: A Transsexual Autobiography*. London: Crown, 1977.

Massey, Doreen. "A Global Sense of Place." *Marxism Today* 38 (1991): 24–29.

Massey, Doreen. *Space, Place, and Gender*. Minneapolis: University of Minnesota Press, 1994.

Massumi, Brian. *Parables of the Virtual: Movement, Affect, Sensation*. Durham, NC: Duke University Press, 2002.

Massumi, Brian. *What Animals Teach Us about Politics*. Durham, NC: Duke University Press, 2014.

Marx, Karl. *Grundrisse: Foundations of the Critique of Political Economy*. Translated by Martin Nicolaus. London: Penguin, 1993.

McCloskey, Deirdre N. *Crossing: A Memoir*. Chicago: University of Chicago Press, 1999.

McLelland, Mark, and Romit Dasgupta, eds. *Genders, Transgenders and Sexualities in Japan*. London: Routledge, 2005.

Melamed, Jodi. *Represent and Destroy: Rationalizing Violence in the New Racial Capitalism*. Minneapolis: University of Minnesota Press, 2011.

Mercer, Kobena. "Black Hair Style Politics." In *Welcome to the Jungle: New Positions in Black Cultural Studies*, 97–130. New York: Routledge, 1994.

Metzl, Jonathan M. *The Protest Psychosis: How Schizophrenia Became a Black Disease*. Boston: Beacon Press, 2009.

Meyerowitz, Joanne. *How Sex Changed: A History of Transsexuality in the United States*. Cambridge, MA: Harvard University Press, 2002.

Meyerowitz, Joanne. "Sex Change and the Popular Press: Historical Notes on Transsexuality in the United States, 1930–1955." *GLQ: A Journal of Lesbian and Gay Studies* 4, no. 2 (1998): 159–87.

Mezzadra, Sandro. "Taking Care: Migration and the Political Economy of Affective Labor." Talk given at Goldsmiths University of London—Center for the Study of Invention and Social Process, London, March 2005. https://caringlabor.files .wordpress.com/2010/12/mezzadra_taking_care.pdf.

Mezzadra, Sandro, and Brett Neilson. *Border as Method, or, the Multiplication of Labor*. Durham, NC: Duke University Press, 2013.

Milliken, Christie. "*Unheimlich* Maneuvers: The Genres and Genders of Transsexual Documentary." *Velvet Light Trap* 41 (1998): 47–61.

Mills, Mary Beth. *Thai Women in the Global Labor Force: Consuming Desires, Contested Selves*. New Brunswick, NJ: Rutgers University Press, 1999.

Miranda, Deborah A. "Extermination of the *Joyas*: Gendercide in Spanish California." *GLQ: A Journal of Lesbian and Gay Studies* 16, nos. 1–2 (2010): 253–84.

Mitchell, David, and Sharon Snyder. "Disability as Multitude: Re-working Non-Productive Labor." *Journal of Literary and Cultural Disability Studies* 4, no. 2 (2010): 179–93.

Mitropoulos, Angela. *Contract and Contagion: From Biopolitics to Oikonomia*. Brooklyn, NY: Minor Compositions, 2012.

Mitropoulos, Angela. "Proliferating Limits: Capitalist Dynamics, Oikonomia and Border Technologies." *sometim3s.com*, January 24, 2012. http://sometim3s .com/2012/01/24/proliferating-limits.

Mitropoulos, Angela. "A Spectre Is Haunting Left Nationalism." *Arena Magazine*, October 1, 2003.

Mitsuhashi, Junko. "The Transgender World in Contemporary Japan: The Male to Female Cross-Dressers' Community in Shinjuku." Translated by Kazumi Hasegawa. *Inter-Asia Cultural Studies* 7, no. 2 (2006): 202–27.

Mohanty, Chandra Talpade. "Women Workers and Capitalist Scripts: Ideologies of Domination, Common Interests, and the Politics of Solidarity." In *Feminist Genealogies, Colonial Legacies, Democratic Futures*, edited by M. Jacqui Alexander and Chandra Talpade Mohanty, 3–29. New York: Routledge, 1997.

Morgensen, Scott Lauria. *Spaces between Us: Queer Settler Colonialism and Indigenous Decolonization*. Minneapolis: University of Minnesota Press, 2011.

Morris, Jan. *Conundrum*. London: Faber and Faber, 2002.

Morris, Rosalind C. "Educating Desire: Thailand, Transnationalism, and Transgression." *Social Text*, nos. 52–53 (1997): 53–79.

Morris, Rosalind C. "Three Sexes and Four Sexualities: Redressing the Discourses on Gender and Sexuality in Contemporary Thailand." *positions* 2, no. 1 (1994): 15–43.

Muñoz, José Esteban. *Disidentifications: Queers of Color and the Performance of Politics*. Minneapolis: University of Minnesota Press, 1999.

Murphy, Michelle. *Seizing the Means of Reproduction: Entanglements of Feminism, Health, and Technoscience*. Durham, NC: Duke University Press, 2012.

My Prairie Home. Directed by Chelsea McMullan. National Film Board of Canada, 2014.

Najmabadi, Afsaneh. *Professing Selves: Transsexuality and Same-Sex Desire in Contemporary Iran*. Durham, NC: Duke University Press, 2013.

Namaste, Vivian K. *Invisible Lives: The Erasure of Transsexual and Transgendered People*. Chicago: University of Chicago Press, 2000.

National Center for Transgender Equality. "Medicare and Transgender People." May 2014. https://transequality.org/sites/default/files/docs/kyr/MedicareAnd TransPeople.pdf.

Neilson, Brett, and Sandro Mezzadra. "Border as Method, or, the Multiplication of Labor." *European Institute for Progressive Cultural Policies*. March 2008. http://eipcp.net/transversal/0608/mezzadraneilson/en.

Neilson, Brett, and Sandro Mezzadra. *Border as Method, or, the Multiplication of Labor*. Durham, NC: Duke University Press, 2013.

Nelson, Jennifer. *More Than Medicine: A History of the Feminist Women's Health Movement*. New York: New York University Press, 2015.

Nestle, Joan, Clare Howell, and Riki Wilchins, eds. *GenderQueer: Voices from Beyond the Sexual Binary*. Los Angeles: Alyson Books, 2002.

Nguyen, Tan Hoang. "Wer Aesthetics in Contemporary Thai Cinema." *Camera Obscura* 97, 33, no. 1 (2018): 139–69.

Nyong'o, Tavia. "After the Ball." *Bully Bloggers*, July 7, 2015. https://bullybloggers.wordpress.com/2015/07/08/after-the-ball.

Ochoa, Marcia. *Queen for a Day: Transformistas, Beauty Queens, and the Performance of Femininity in Venezuela*. Durham, NC: Duke University Press, 2014.

Oishi, Eve. "Reading Realness: *Paris Is Burning*, *Wildness*, and Queer and Transgender Documentary Practice." In *A Companion to Contemporary Documentary Film*, edited by Alexandra Juhasz and Alisa Lebow, 252–70. Chichester: Wiley Blackwell, 2015.

Ong, Aihwa. *Flexible Citizenship: The Cultural Logics of Transnationality*. Durham, NC: Duke University Press, 1999.

Papadopoulos, Dimitris, Niamh Stephenson, and Vassilis Tsianos. *Escape Routes: Control and Subversion in the 21st Century*. London: Pluto Press, 2008.

Paper Dolls. Directed by Tomer Heymann. Strand Releasing, 2006.

Parreñas, Rhacel Salazar. *Illicit Flirtations: Labor, Migration, and Sex Trafficking in Tokyo*. Stanford: Stanford University Press, 2011.

Pennell, C. R. *Morocco: From Empire to Independence*. Oxford: Oneworld, 2003.

Phelan, Peggy. *Unmarked: The Politics of Performance*. New York: Routledge, 1993.

Phuket Plastic Surgery Institute. "Gender Change." N.d. Accessed May 6, 2008. https://www.phuketpsi.com/gender-change.html.

Piepmeier, Alison. *Girl Zines: Making Media, Doing Feminism*. New York: New York University Press, 2009.

Plemons, Eric. "Anatomical Authorities: On the Epistemological Exclusion of Trans-Surgical Patients." *Medical Anthropology: Studies in Cross-Cultural Health and Illness* 34, no. 5 (2015): 425–41.

Plemons, Eric. "Description of Sex Difference as Prescription for Sex Change: On the Origins of Facial Feminization Surgery." *Social Studies of Science* 44, no. 5 (2014): 657–79.

Plummer, Ken. *Telling Sexual Stories: Power, Change and Social Worlds*. London: Routledge, 1995.

Poletti, Anna. *Intimate Ephemera: Reading Young Lives in Australian Zine Culture*. Melbourne: Melbourne University Press, 2008.

Potential, Boots. "Monster Trans." In *From the Inside Out: Radical Gender Transformation, FTM and Beyond*, edited by Morty Diamond, 32–40. San Francisco: Manic D Press, 2004.

Povinelli, Elizabeth A. *The Cunning of Recognition: Indigenous Alterities and the Making of Australian Multiculturalism*. Durham, NC: Duke University Press, 2002.

Povinelli, Elizabeth A. *Economies of Abandonment: Social Belonging and Endurance in Late Liberalism*. Durham, NC: Duke University Press, 2011.

Power, Samantha. "US Leadership to Advance Equality for LGBT People Abroad." White House memorandum, December 13, 2012. https://www.whitehouse.gov /blog/2012/12/13/us-leadership-advance-equality-lgbt-people-abroad.

Pozner, Jennifer. "Gender Immigrant: Interview with Jennifer Finney Boylan." *Alternet*, May 13, 2004. http://www.alternet.org/story/18671.

Pratt, Mary Louise. *Imperial Eyes: Travel Writing and Transculturation*. New York: Routledge, 1992.

Prodigal Sons. Directed by Kimberly Reed. Big Sky Film Productions, 2008.

Prosser, Jay. "Exceptional Locations: Transsexual Travelogues." In *Reclaiming Gender: Transsexual Grammars at the Fin de Siècle*, edited by Kate More and Stephen Whittle, 83–114. London: Cassell, 1999.

Prosser, Jay. "No Place Like Home: The Transgendered Narrative of Leslie Feinberg's Stone Butch Blues." *Modern Fiction Studies* 41, nos. 3–4 (1995): 483–514.

Prosser, Jay. "A Palinode on Photography and the Transsexual Real." *a/b: Auto/ Biography Studies* 14, no. 1 (1999): 71–92.

Prosser, Jay. *Second Skins: The Body Narratives of Transsexuality*. New York: Columbia University Press, 1998.

Puar, Jasbir K. "Bodies with New Organs: Becoming Trans, Becoming Disabled." *Social Text* 33, no. 3 (2015): 45–73.

Puar, Jasbir K. "Circuits of Queer Mobility: Tourism, Travel, and Globalization." *GLQ: A Journal of Lesbian and Gay Studies* 8, nos. 1–2 (2002): 101–37.

Puar, Jasbir K. *Terrorist Assemblages: Homonationalism in Queer Times*. Durham, NC: Duke University Press, 2007.

Race, Kane. "Recreational States: Drugs and the Sovereignty of Consumption." *Culture Machine* 7 (2005). http://www.culturemachine.net/index.php/cm /article/viewArticle/28/35.

Raimondo, Meredith. "The Queer Intimacy of Global Vision: Documentary Practice and the AIDS Pandemic." *Environment and Planning D: Society and Space* 28, no. 1 (2010): 112–27.

Rajan, Kaushik Sunder. *Biocapital: The Constitution of Postgenomic Life*. Durham, NC: Duke University Press, 2006.

Rancière, Jacques. "Discovering New Worlds: Politics of Travel and Metaphors of Space." In *Travellers' Tales: Narratives of Home and Displacement*, edited by George Robertson, Melinda Mash, Lisa Tickner, Jon Bird, Barry Curtis, and Tim Putnam, 36–60. London: Routledge, 1994.

Ravine, Jai Arun. *The Romance of Siam: A Pocket Guide*. Oakland, CA: Timeless, Infinite Light, 2016.

Ravine, Jai Arun. "Toms and Zees: Locating FTM in Thailand." *TSQ: Transgender Studies Quarterly* 1, no. 3 (2014): 387–401.

Raymond, Janice G. *The Transsexual Empire: The Making of the She-Male*. Boston: Beacon Press, 1979.

Read, Jason. *The Micro-Politics of Capital: Marx and the Prehistory of the Present*. Albany: State University of New York Press, 2003.

Rebecca. "Rebecca's Life on Mars." *AOL Hometown*. N.d. Accessed July 12, 2007. Site removed December 2008.

Reddy, Chandan. *Freedom with Violence: Race, Sexuality, and the US State*. Durham, NC: Duke University Press, 2011.

Rees, Mark. *Dear Sir or Madam: The Autobiography of a Female-to-Male Transsexual*. London: Cassell, 1996.

Rees-Roberts, Nick. "Down and Out: Immigrant Poverty and Queer Sexuality in Sébastien Lifshitz's *Wild Side* (2004)." *Studies in French Cinema* 7, no. 2 (2007): 143–55.

Regales, Jackie. "My Identity Is Fluid as Fuck: Transgender Zine Writers Constructing Themselves." In *Queer Youth Cultures*, edited by Susan Driver, 87–104. Albany: State University of New York Press, 2008.

Richards, Renée, with John Ames. *Second Serve: The Renée Richards Story*. New York: Stein and Day, 1983.

Rifkin, Mark. *When Did Indians Become Straight? Kinship, the History of Sexuality, and Native Sovereignty*. New York: Oxford University Press, 2011.

Roberts, Dorothy. *Fatal Invention: How Science, Politics, and Big Business Re-create Race in the Twenty-First Century*. New York: New Press, 2011.

Robertson, George, Melinda Mash, Lisa Tickner, Jon Bird, Barry Curtis, and Tim Putnum, eds. *Travelers' Tales: Narratives of Home and Displacement*. London: Routledge, 1994.

Roen, Katrina. "Transgender Theory and Embodiment: The Risk of Racial Marginalisation." *Journal of Gender Studies* 10, no. 3 (2001): 253–63.

Rohy, Valerie. *Anachronism and Its Others: Sexuality, Race, Temporality*. Albany: State University of New York Press, 2009.

Rosaldo, Renato. *Culture and Truth: The Remaking of Social Analysis*. Boston: Beacon Press, 1993.

Rosenberg, Jordy. "The Molecularization of Sexuality: On Some Primitivisms of the Present." *Theory and Event* 17, no. 2 (2014). https://muse.jhu.edu/article/546470.

Rubin, Gayle. "The Traffic in Women: Notes on the 'Political Economy' of Sex." In *Toward an Anthropology of Women*, edited by Rayna R. Reiter, 157–210. New York: Monthly Review Press, 1975.

Said, Edward W. *Orientalism*. New York: Vintage, 1979.

Salah, Trish. "'Time Isn't after Us': Some Tiresian Durations." *Somatechnics* 7, no. 1 (2017): 16–33.

Salamon, Gayle. *Assuming a Body: Transgender and Rhetorics of Materiality*. New York: Columbia University Press, 2010.

Sanders, Douglas. "The Rainbow Lobby: The Sexual Diversity Network and the Military-Installed Government in Thailand." Paper presented at the 10th International Thai Studies Conference, Bangkok, Thailand, January 2008.

Sarnsmak, Pongphon. "New Sex Change Regulations from Nov. 29." *The Nation*, September 12, 2009. http://www.nationmultimedia.com/2009/09/12/national /national_30112040.php.

Schick, Irvin C. *The Erotic Margin: Sexuality and Spatiality in Alteritist Discourse.* New York: Verso, 1999.

Schulman, Sarah. "A Documentary Guide to Brand Israel and the Art of Pinkwashing." *Mondoweiss.com*, November 30, 2011. http://mondoweiss.net/2011/11/a -documentary-guide-to-brand-israel-and-the-art-of-pinkwashing.

Scott, Joan W. "The Evidence of Experience." *Critical Inquiry* 17, no. 4 (1991): 773–97.

Serano, Julia. *Whipping Girl: A Transsexual Woman on Sexism and the Scapegoating of Femininity.* Berkeley, CA: Seal Press, 2007.

Sexton, Jared. "People-of-Color-Blindness: Notes on the Afterlife of Slavery." *Social Text* 28, no. 2 (2010): 31–56.

Shakhsari, Sima. "Killing Me Softly with Your Rights: The Politics of Rightful Killing." In *Queer Necropolitics*, edited by Jin Haritaworn, Adi Kuntsman, and Silvia Posocco, 93–110. Oxford: Routledge, 2014.

Sharma, K. K. *Tourism and Development.* New Delhi: Sarup and Sons, 2006.

Shim, Janet K. *Heart-Sick: The Politics of Risk, Inequality, and Heart Disease.* New York: New York University Press, 2014.

Simpson, Mark. *Trafficking Subjects: The Politics of Mobility in Nineteenth-Century America.* Minneapolis: University of Minnesota Press, 2005.

Sinnott, Megan. *Toms and Dees: Transgender Identity and Female Same-Sex Relationships in Thailand.* Honolulu: University of Hawai'i Press, 2004.

Sinnott, Vikki. "Best Practice Models for the Assessment, Treatment and Care of Transgender People and People with Transsexualism: A Discussion Paper for Victoria (Australia)." Victorian Department of Human Services Discussion Paper. June 2005. http://www.glhv.org.au/sites/www.glhv.org.au/files/DHS _discussion_paper_trans.pdf.

Snorton, C. Riley. *Black on Both Sides: A Racial History of Trans Identity.* Minneapolis: University of Minnesota Press, 2017.

Snorton, C. Riley, and Jin Haritaworn. "Trans Necropolitics: A Transnational Reflection on Violence, Death, and the Trans of Color Afterlife." In *The Transgender Studies Reader 2*, edited by Susan Stryker and Aren Z. Aizura, 66–76. New York: Routledge, 2006.

Spade, Dean. "Mutilating Gender." In *The Transgender Studies Reader*, edited by Susan Stryker and Stephen Whittle, 315–32. New York: Routledge, 2006.

Spade, Dean. *Normal Life: Administrative Violence, Critical Trans Politics, and the Limits of the Law.* New York: South End Press, 20011.

Spade, Dean. "Under the Cover of Gay Rights." NYU *Review of Law and Social Change* 37, no. 79 (2013): 79–100.

Spivak, Gayatri Chakravorty. "Can the Subaltern Speak?" In *Marxism and the Interpretation of Culture*, edited by Cary Nelson and Lawrence Grossberg, 271–313. Urbana: University of Illinois Press, 1988.

Spivak, Gayatri Chakravorty. "Poststructuralism, Marginality, Postcolonialism and Value." In *Contemporary Postcolonial Theory: A Reader*, edited by Padmini Mongia, 198–122. London: E. Arnold, 1997.

Spivak, Gayatri Chakravorty. "Scattered Speculations on the Question of Value." In *In Other Worlds: Essays in Cultural Politics*, 154–75. New York: Methuen, 1987.

Stanley, Eric A. "Introduction: Fugitive Flesh. Gender Self-Determination, Queer Abolition and Trans Resistance." In *Captive Genders: Trans Embodiment and the Prison Industrial Complex*, edited by Eric A. Stanley and Nat Smith, 7–20. Oakland, CA: AK Press, 2015.

Starr, Paul. *The Social Transformation of American Medicine: The Rise of a Sovereign Profession and the Making of a Vast Industry*. New York: Basic Books, 1982.

Stone, Sandy. "The Empire Strikes Back: A Posttranssexual Manifesto." In *Body Guards: The Cultural Politics of Gender Ambiguity*, edited by Julia Epstein and Kristina Straub, 280–304. New York: Routledge, 1991.

Straayer, Chris. "Transgender Mirrors: Queering Sexual Difference." In *Between the Sheets, in the Streets: Queer, Lesbian, Gay Documentary*, edited by Chris Holmlund and Cynthia Fuchs, 207–23. Minneapolis: University of Minnesota Press, 1997.

Stryker, Susan. "Call for Papers, Transsomatechnics Conference." Unpublished, 2007.

Stryker, Susan. "Christine Jorgensen's Atom Bomb: Transsexuality and the Emergence of Postmodernity." In *Playing Dolly: Technocultural Formations, Fantasies, and Fictions of Assisted Reproduction*, edited by E. Ann Kaplan and Susan Squier, 157–71. New Brunswick, NJ: Rutgers University Press, 1999.

Stryker, Susan. "My Words to Victor Frankenstein above the Village of Chamounix: Performing Transgender Rage." *GLQ: A Journal of Lesbian and Gay Studies* 1, no. 3 (1994): 237–54.

Stryker, Susan. *Transgender History*. Berkeley, CA: Seal Press, 2008.

Stryker, Susan. "Transgender History, Homonormativity, and Disciplinarity." *Radical History Review* 2008, no. 100 (2008): 145–57.

Stryker, Susan. "*We Who Are Sexy*: Christine Jorgensen's Transsexual Whiteness in the Postcolonial Philippines." *Social Semiotics* 19, no. 1 (2009): 79–91.

Sukontapatipark, Nantiya. "Relationship between Modern Medical Technology and Gender Identity in Thailand: Passing from 'Male Body' to 'Female Body.'" MA thesis, Mahidol University, Bangkok, 2005.

Sullivan, Louis. *From Female to Male: The Life of Jack Bee Garland*. Boston: Alyson, 1990.

Sullivan, Nikki. *A Critical Introduction to Queer Theory*. New York: New York University Press, 2003.

"SRS, Procedures." *The Suporn Clinic*. 2006. http://www.supornclinic.com.

Swarr, Amanda Lock. *Sex in Transition: Remaking Gender and Race in South Africa*. Albany: State University of New York Press, 2012.

Szasz, Thomas. "Male and Female Created He Them." In *The Therapeutic State: Psychiatry in the Mirror of Current Events*, 327–29. Buffalo, NY: Prometheus, 1984.

Szasz, Thomas. *Sex by Prescription: The Startling Truth about Today's Sex Therapy.* Syracuse, NY: Syracuse University Press, 1990.

Tadiar, Neferti Xina M. *Fantasy-Production: Sexual Economies and Other Philippine Consequences for the New World Order.* Hong Kong: Hong Kong University Press, 2004.

Tan, Michael. "From Bakla to Gay: Shifting Gender Identities and Sexual Behaviors in the Philippines." In *Conceiving Sexuality: Approaches to Sex Research in a Postmodern World,* edited by Richard G. Parker and John H. Gagnon, 85–96. New York: Routledge, 1995.

Taste This Collective. *Boys Like Her: Transfictions.* Vancouver: Press Ghang, 1998.

Thacker, Eugene. *Biomedia.* Minneapolis: University of Minnesota Press, 2004.

Thai Medical Council. "Regarding Guidelines for Persons Manifesting Confusion concerning Their Sexual Identity or Desiring Treatment by Undergoing a Sex Change Operation." *Thai Law Forum,* November 17, 2009. http://www.thailawforum.com/Guidelines-sex-change-operations.html.

Thompson, Raymond, with Kitty Sewall. *What Took You So Long? A Girl's Journey into Manhood.* London: Penguin, 1995.

Tocqueville, Alexis de. *Democracy in America.* Edited by Olivier Zunz. Translated by Arthur Goldhammer. New York: Library of America, 2004.

Tolbert, T. C., and Trace Peterson, eds. *Troubling the Line: Trans and Genderqueer Poetry and Poetics.* New York: Nightboat Books, 2013.

Tongson, Karen. *Relocations: Queer Suburban Imaginaries.* New York: New York University Press, 2011.

Tourism Authority of Thailand e-magazine. "Health Tourism—The Rising Star: Strategies for Success." TATNews.org. N.d. Accessed June 14, 2007. http://web.archive.org/web/20070110061510/http://www.tatnews.org/emagazine/1983.asp.

Towle, Evan B., and Lynn M. Morgan. "Romancing the Transgender Native: Rethinking the Use of the 'Third Gender' Concept." *GLQ: A Journal of Lesbian and Gay Studies* 8, no. 4 (2002): 469–97.

Transamerica. Directed by Duncan Tucker. Belladonna Productions, 2005.

Transsexual and Transgender Road Map. Last modified June 2, 2015. Accessed June 13, 2017. http://www.tsroadmap.com.

Trinh T. Minh-ha. "The Totalizing Quest of Meaning." In *Theorizing Documentary,* edited by Michael Renov, 12–36. New York: Routledge, 2012.

Tuck, Eve, and K. Wayne Yang. "Decolonization Is Not a Metaphor." *Decolonization: Indigeneity, Education and Society* 1, no. 1 (2012): 1–40.

Turner, Louis, and John Ash. *The Golden Hordes: International Tourism and the Pleasure Periphery.* New York: St. Martin's Press, 1976.

University College London. "Transgender Issues: Guidance Notes on Inclusive and Supportive Practice." In *Human Resources and Policy Procedure Manual. UCL Online,* September 2010. http://www.ucl.ac.uk/hr/docs/transguidance.php.

Valentine, David. *Imagining Transgender: An Ethnography of a Category*. Durham, NC: Duke University Press, 2007.

Valerio, Max Wolf. *The Testosterone Files: My Hormonal and Social Transformation from Female to Male*. Emeryville, CA: Seal Press, 2006.

Van Esterik, Penny. *Materializing Thailand*. Oxford: Berg, 2000.

Van Esterik, Penny. "The Politics of Beauty in Thailand." In *Beauty Queens on the Global Stage: Gender, Contests and Power*, edited by Colleen Ballerino Cohen, Richard Wilk, and Beverly Stoeltje, 203–16. New York: Routledge, 1996

Virno, Paolo. *A Grammar of the Multitude: For an Analysis of Contemporary Forms of Life*. Los Angeles: Semiotext(e), 2004.

Virno, Paolo. *Il ricordo del presente: Saggio sul tempo storico*. Torino, Italy: Bollati Boringhieri, 1999.

Virno, Paolo. "Notes on the General Intellect." Translated by Cesare Casarino. In *Marxism beyond Marxism*, edited by Saree Makdisi, Cesare Casarino, and Rebecca E. Karl, 265–73. New York: Routledge, 1996.

Virno, Paolo, and Michael Hardt, eds. *Radical Thought in Italy: A Potential Politics*. Minneapolis: University of Minnesota Press, 1996.

Walker, David, and Agnieszka Sobocinska. "Introduction: Australia's Asia." In *Australia's Asia: From Yellow Peril to Asian Century*, edited by David Walker and Agnieszka Sobocinska, 1–23. Crawley, Australia: UWA, 2012.

Wallerstein, Immanuel. "The Ideological Tensions of Capitalism: Universalism versus Racism and Sexism." In *Race, Nation, Class: Ambiguous Identities*, edited by Étienne Balibar and Immanuel Wallerstein, 29–36. New York: Verso, 1991.

Walworth, Janis. "Managing Transsexual Transition in the Workplace." *Center for Gender Sanity*. August 2003. http://www.gendersanity.com/shrm.html.

Ward, Jane. "Gender Labor: Transmen, Femmes, and Collective Work of Transgression." *Sexualities* 13, no. 2 (2010): 236–54.

Weston, Kath. "Get Thee to a Big City: Sexual Imaginary and the Great Gay Migration." *GLQ: A Journal of Lesbian and Gay Studies* 2, no. 3 (1995): 253–77.

Whittaker, Andrea. "Pleasure and Pain: Medical Travel in Asia." *Global Public Health: An International Journal for Research, Policy and Practice* 3, no. 3 (2008): 271–90.

Wilchins, Riki. *Read My Lips: Sexual Subversion and the End of Gender*. Milford, CT: Firebrand Books, 1997.

Wilson, Ara. *The Intimate Economies of Bangkok: Tomboys, Tycoons, and Avon Ladies in the Global City*. Berkeley: University of California Press, 2004.

Wilson, Ara. "Medical Tourism in Thailand." In *Asian Biotech: Ethics and Communities of Fate*, edited by Aihwa Ong and Nancy N. Chen, 118–43. Durham, NC: Duke University Press, 2010.

Wolanen, Michael K. *Writing Tangier in the Postcolonial Transition: Space and Power in Expatriate and North African Literature*. Burlington, VT: Ashgate, 2011.

Women and Equality Unit. *Gender Reassignment: A Guide for Employers*. London: Women and Equality Unit, 2005. http://www.scotland.gov.uk/Resource/Doc /924/0018960.pdf.

INDEX

9/11, 99
1990s Asian economic crisis, 25, 186

ability, 10, 144, 153, 175
academia, 11, 15, 56, 83–84, 183, 213
Aden: *Fat Sexy Gender*, 160–62, 166–69, 172–73
The Advocate, 36
affect, 17, 38, 55, 66, 83–84, 139, 159, 163, 169, 208, 210; affective labor, 20, 112, 127, 174–75, 179, 188, 194–200, 202–4, 211, 214, 216, 219, 224n52; anger, 117, 162, 169; femininity and, 76, 112, 127, 174–75, 179, 188, 193–200, 224n52; frustration, 160–62; grief, 84–85, 87; happiness, 108, 110, 124, 202; humor, 9, 119; irony, 9, 218; melancholia, 86–89, 231n81; racialized, 87, 99, 175, 179, 188, 193–200, 204, 224n52
affect theory, 208, 210–11
Affordable Care Act, 171
Africa, 51, 70, 73–78, 120, 138, 230n48, 237n33. *See also individual countries*
The Aggressives, 107
Ahmed, Sara, 175–76, 178
AIDS. *See* HIV/AIDS
Algeria, 59
Alliez, Eric, 168
Althusser, Louis, 224n51
Altman, Dennis, 22
American Psychological Association, 29
American Weekly, 44–45, 47
America Online, 192
Ames, Jonathan, 64
Amichai, Yehuda: "Songs for a Woman," 119
Amin, Kadji, 2

analogy, 97, 175, 216; limitations of, 19, 82, 89–92. *See also* metaphor
Ang, Ien, 87
Anh, 177–78
anthropology, 15–17, 125, 147, 215, 223n38
antidiscrimination legislation, 10
ANZPATH, 171
Aoi, 194
Aotearoa, 205. *See also* New Zealand
apartheid, 150–51
April Ashley's Odyssey, 32, 40, 60, 73
Arab News Agency, 71, 74
Arabs, 72, 99, 120, 123
Argentina, 125
Armstrong, Johnny: *Linda/Les and Annie*, 103
Ashanti people, 77
Ashley, April, 59, 63; *April Ashley's Odyssey*, 32, 40, 60, 73
Asia, 25, 51, 117–18, 152, 154, 181, 184–86, 188, 193, 212, 237n26, 239n5, 241n47; Asia Pacific region, 138, 199, 205; South, 78; Southeast, 121, 139, 148, 155, 179, 205, 217; West, 74–75, 230n48. *See also individual countries*
Asia-Pacific Transgender Network, 205
asylum, 100–101. *See also* refugees
Australia, 107, 120, 158, 162, 176, 189–90, 199, 205, 222n12, 237n39, 238n42; gender reassignment in, 5–6, 15, 24, 137–38, 140, 148–49, 151–54, 159–60, 165, 167, 172–73, 178, 191, 198, 222n11; Melbourne, 4, 7, 111, 155–56, 160, 164, 172–73; South Australia, 222n10; Sydney, 83, 159, 176
Australian Good Tranny Guide, 222n12

Huggan, Graham, 74
human bisexuality (theory), 43
Hygeia Beauty, 190
hysterectomy, 13

"ideal" transsexual subject, 31, 34–35, 198
imaginary, 12, 19, 32, 81, 88–91, 97–99,
    103, 112, 116, 120, 166, 168, 218; colonial
    imaginaries, 40, 102; gender reassignment
    imaginaries, 2–4, 8, 15, 18, 41–42, 50, 60,
    80, 151, 199
I'm Fine, 217–19
imperialism, 3, 9, 20, 22, 32, 57, 67, 89, 95,
    105, 116, 182, 200, 207, 210, 214; British,
    69–80, 230n48; European, 40, 223n19;
    imperial eyes, 18, 61; Israeli, 99, 113; neo-
    imperialism, 232n7; US, 99. *See also* colo-
    nialism; neocolonialism; postcolonialism
India, 212, 230n48, 233n25; Mumbai, 208,
    210, 212
indigeneity, 22, 182, 187
Indigenous peoples, 120, 152, 213, 237n33.
    See also Ashanti people; Native Americans
Industrial Revolution, 57
informed consent, 5, 153, 221n7
Insects in the Backyard, 217–18
interdisciplinarity, 15, 169, 213
intersexuality, 153. *See also* hermaphrodites
Iran, 237n30; Shiraz, 148; Tehran, 148–49
Iraq, 149
Ireland, 85–86, 88–89
Irving, Dan, 48
Islam, 77, 237n30. *See also* Muslims
Islamophobia, 99, 237n36
Israel, 96, 99, 101, 116, 119–20, 122, 232n2,
    234n56; Brand Israel, 105–6, 113; Eilat, 114;
    invasion of Egypt, 78; Israeli colonialism/
    occupation of Palestine, 99, 106, 120,
    234n56; Occupied Territories, 234n56; Tel
    Aviv, 93–95, 112–13, 117–18; B'nai B'rak,
    115–16. *See also* pinkwashing
Issy, 124, 126–29
Italy: Venice, 82
It Gets Better, 217

Jackson, Peter, 181–82, 189
Jacobson, Matthew Frye, 88–89, 231n78
James, Andrea: *TS Roadmap*, 1–2

Jan, 95, 112, 115, 122, 234n50
Japan, 117, 138, 176, 184, 241n46
Jen, 109–10
Jenner, Caitlyn, 89
Johns Hopkins University, 146, 236n17
Jorgensen, Christine, 23, 30–31, 33–36,
    42–43, 47–55, 57, 64, 102, 226n17, 227n45,
    227n59; *A Personal Autobiography*, 44–46,
    60, 62–63. *See also The Christine Jorgensen
    Story*
joyas, 57
Judaism, 88, 111, 117; Ashkenazi Jews, 94;
    Hasidic (Orthodox) Jews, 94, 113, 115;
    Mizrahi Jews, 120; Russian Jews, 120
Juggling Gender, 103

Kabbani, Rana, 75–76
Kaiser Permanente, 239n59
Käng, Dredge, 182, 205
Kaplan, Caren, 17, 22, 69, 97–98, 135
Karen, 155–56, 158–60, 164, 166, 178, 191
kathoeys, 176, 180–85, 187, 189–90, 193–96,
    198, 204–5, 215, 218–19, 237n26, 239n4
Keating, Paul, 154
Keegan, Cáel, 209
Kennedy, Trudy, 156
Kenya: Nairobi, 208, 210
Khomeini, Ayatollah, 149
Kinglake, Alexander: *Eothen*, 75
Korea, 138, 210, 241n46; Seoul, 208
Koubkov, Zdenek, 51–52
Krafft-Ebing, Richard von: *Psychopathia
    Sexualis*, 62
Kulick, Don, 125
Kuntsman, Adi, 98

labor, 34, 50, 90, 144, 186, 222n54, 241n48;
    archaeological, 15; affective, 20, 112, 127,
    174–75, 179, 188, 194–200, 202–4, 211, 214,
    216, 219, 224n52; colonial, 51; ethniciza-
    tion of, 100, 130–32, 195–96; immaterial,
    20, 55, 224n52, 225n55; immigrant, 68,
    94, 100–101, 107, 111–13, 116, 122, 125–27,
    130–32, 154, 232n2, 237n33; multiplica-
    tion of, 233n28; real subsumption of, 19,
    224n52; translation, 16
ladyboys, 176–77, 215–16, 239n4
LA Times, 113

North America, 3, 11, 31, 35, 41, 43, 50–52, 58, 60, 70, 80, 89, 96, 138, 140–41, 147, 149, 151, 170, 184–85, 189, 212. *See also individual countries*

Northwestern University, 146

Norway, 88

novels, 3, 75, 81, 90, 190–91, 231n81

Nyong'o, Tavia, 234n38

Oceania, 51

Ochoa, Marcia, 140, 147

Ohio, 108

Oishi, Eve, 233n35

Olympics, 52

Ong, Aihwa, 188

online journals, 3, 15, 160

oophorectomy, 13

Orange Is the New Black, 208

orchiectomy, 13, 148, 185, 204

orientalism, 18, 23, 34, 40, 51, 60–61, 69, 72–75, 91, 117, 187, 192–93, 212, 215–16, 219, 229n5, 241n46; self-orientalization, 179, 188–89, 204, 241n47. *See also* exoticism

OUTLAW, 103

overseas contract workers (OCWs), 94–95, 111–22, 232n1

Pacific Islands, 154

Palestine, 74, 232n2; Israeli occupation of, 99, 106, 120, 234n56; Occupied Territories, 234n56

Pandemic, 105

Paper Dolls, 93–96, 99, 101, 106–7, 111–24, 127, 131–32, 216, 232nn1–2, 234n51, 234n56, 234nn50–51. *See also Bubot Niyar (Paper Dolls)*

Paris Is Burning, 95–96, 103–4, 107, 232n4, 232n6, 233n35

passing, 87, 103, 110–11, 213–14, 219; limits of, 12, 167, 209; material stakes of, 68; privileging of, 2, 6, 145

Peddle, Daniel: *The Aggressives*, 107

Pennsylvania, 96, 98, **109**–10; Philadelphia, 83; Pittsburgh, 108

performativity, 34, 38, 40, 53, 95, 103, 196, 223n27

phalloplasty, 13, 137, 139, 199

phet-thi-sam, 239n4

Philby, Kim, 78

Philippines, 94, 101, 114, 116, 232n1, 234n51; Manila, 117, 121–22

photography, 15, 44–45, 47, 82, 106, 120, 122, 129, 156, 159–60, 163, 177, 179, 190, 192, 194, 217, 238n49

Phuket Plastic Surgery Center, 189–90, 235n1

phu-ying kam phet, 205

piecing, 209–10, 213–14, 219, 242n3

pinkwashing, 99, 106, 113

Piyawate Hospital, 165, 175, 186

Plemons, Eric, 169–71

Plummer, Ken, 65

Poland, 88

Portugal, 126

Posocco, Silvia, 98

postcolonialism, 22, 51, 59–60, 136, 223n19, 232n7. *See also* neocolonialism

post-Fordism, 19, 55, 124, 165, 197, 224n52. *See also* neoliberalism

postmodernity, 23, 35, 52–54, 56, 139, 228n73

poststructuralism, 20, 59

Pratt, Mary Louise, 18, 61, 78

Preecha Aesthetic Institute (PAI), 175, 235n1

Preecha Tiewtranon, 165, 175, 177–78, 182, 184, 188, 235n1

Prince, Virginia, 11

prisons, 128; abolition, 10; prison-industrial complex, 90

privatization, 145–47, 153, 169, 171, 205, 221n7. *See also* neoliberalism

Prodigal Sons, 107

Prosser, Jay, 18–19, 32, 45, 61, 64–66, 74; *Second Skins*, 33–34, 65–66

protest psychosis, 162

provincializing, 8–9, 31, 35, 51–52, 56, 58, 102, 136, 141, 150

psychiatry, 181; antipsychiatry movement, 55, 146, 224n54; constructions of trans-sexuality, 5, 11, 125, 160, 222n11, 222n16; role in trans body modification, 4, 14, 24, 32, 63, 72, 83–84, 138, 140, 146, 148–51, 155–58, 162, 166–68, 182–83, 185–86, 238n46. *See also* standard transsexual narrative

psychology, 6, 29, 33, 43, 66–67, 77, 83, 138, 148, 181, 191

Puar, Jasbir, 18, 99, 180, 209, 242n3

punk, 201